No. 1746
$17.95

GOING ON-LINE
WITH YOUR MICRO

BY LOU HAAS

 TAB BOOKS Inc.
BLUE RIDGE SUMMIT, PA. 17214

FIRST EDITION

FIRST PRINTING

Copyright © 1984 by TAB BOOKS Inc.
Printed in the United States of America

Library of Congress Cataloging in Publication Data

Haas, Lou.
Going on-line with your micro.
Includes index.
1. Data transmission systems—Directories.
I. Title.
TK5105.H33   1984   384.3   83-25829
ISBN 0-8306-0746-3
ISBN 0-8306-1746-9 (pbk.)

Contents

Preface

Anyone who is interested in telecommunications today and who wants to use a home computer in telecommunications faces a great dilemma. When you go into your friendly neighborhood computer store, the ex-stereo salesman is interested in meeting his quota, and you can't blame him. He tries to load you up with the goodies. When you go to your mass-merchandiser, the kid behind the counter does not know what he is talking about. And when you look to a big computer company to help you, say Big Blue, they come out with a box that they call home computer that is worse than the one they call Personal Computer or PC. What is even worse, by the time you have any ability to do tele-communications, you will have to spend a lot of money. To configure a PCjr to talk to another computer means that you have to buy an optional modem, a device that allows you to hook up your computer to the telephone. And that's not all, you need software too. How much for all that? Too much.

Are there cheaper and better ways? Yes on both parts. You can go and buy a computer with a real keyboard, not a "chiclet" one; you can buy a computer that has all the software that you need bundled in the purchase price; you can get software that is in the public domain and a set of instructions on how to use it by reading on. Once you know how to go on-line with your computer, this book will be your constant companion. It will guide your elec-tronic travels.

Furthermore, a good assessment will be made of what home computers can do for you and what their limitations are. The CP/M operating system, the dominant piece of software in the 8-bit world of computers is at the heart of many discussions. It is a proven piece of software around which thousands of other programs have gathered. Many of these are in the public domain.

Detailed instructions are given to show you how to dial up other computers and how to obtain software and even information on jobs. The more successful information utilities are also identified. Some manufacturers offer you free trial sessions with these data banks.

While this book will not serve to give you your first lesson on computing, it will not talk down at you. Its purpose is to help you go on-line at the price you can afford as quickly as possible. Once you begin, the telephone line is the only limit.

Acknowledgments

First and most I must thank my friend John P. Hely IV for the generous submission of more material than I could possibly use in this book.

Many thanks for the courtesy of providing requested material to Diane Ottinger of Commodore, Richard Moore of Miller Communications, Ken Price from Compaq Computer Corporation, Evie Turner of Novation Inc., Andrew Fluegelman of The Headlands Press, Jeffrey Swartz of CompuPro, Rocky Awalt of Molecular Computer, Geoffrey Soule of KAYPRO, Ed Juge and his buyers W. Walters and David Fraser from Radio Shack, David Leonnig from Texas Instruments, A. J. Sekel from ATARI, and Rose Stevenson from the U.S. Postal Service.

The following trademarks are acknowledged. IBM: International Business Machines Corporation. CP/M, MP/P, C-Basic: Digital Research, Inc. Microsoft Basic, MS/DOS: Microsoft Corporation. Smartmodem, Micromodem, Smartcom: Hayes Microcomputer Products, Inc. Apple Computer: Apple Computer, Inc. Tymnet, Inc.: Tymeshare Company. Sprint: Southern Pacific Communications Company. TRS-80: Radio Shack, a division of Tandy Corp. Heath: Heath Company. Zenith: Zenith Radio Corporation. E-COM: U.S. Postal Service. Dow Jones: Dow Jones & Company. The Source: The Source Telecomputing, subs. of Readers Digest Assoc. Inc. CompuServe: CompuServe, Inc., an H& R Block company. CAT, CCITT CAT, D-CAT, 212-AUTO-CAT, SMART-CAT, APPLE-CAT: Novation, Inc. Z-80: Zilog, Inc. Wordstar: MicroPro International. KAYPRO II, KAYPRO 4, KAYPRO 10: KAYPRO Corporation. 8080, 8086: Intel Corp.

Introduction

One night, after spending a delightful session poking around different computers in my local calling area, I decided to look for a book that would explain all the gobbledygook to me. Much to my surprise, there wasn't one. After thoroughly looking at all the different computers that I was able to access, I learned that the only way to find what was of interest to me was to keep on poking around, which I did. I made notes and concluded that telecommunications are really a tremendous asset for anyone. For a nominal outlay you are able to get the hardware that will allow you to do telecommunications. That in turn will let you utilize your home computer better than ever. Tremendous changes are taking place in the home computing world.

Slick ad agencies and their megabuck sponsors are at work. If you turn on your television, you see all these fancy ads trying to get you to be one of their happy customers. No matter what the ads say, for the purpose of this book a home computer is a home computer. Whether you call it a personal computer or PC for short, or any other small computer by any other name, when I say home computer I mean a computer or an intelligent terminal that you can hook up to the telephone in your home

and use for one express purpose: telecommunications. The names, kneetops, portables, transportables, desktops, personals, pocket computers, and whatever there is, are as manifold as the companies that make those products.

The purpose of this book is to get you started in the right direction and to provide you with some fundamental tools that will allow you to look at the programs you need to get on-line to other computers. Software selections made in this book rely a lot on existing home computer technology and versions of the CP/M operating system by Digital Research or DRI. The reason for this is plain: much of the pioneering in the field of home computing and telecommunications for home computers started in the days when home computing was done by hobbyists. Due to the lack of adequate software, hobbyists wrote much of their own software. When they found each other in the same no-adequate-software boat, they started exchanging access to their program libraries. Before too long, a trickle of software for telecommunications was available—all at no cost, and all in the public domain. The hardware in the meantime is not only much better; it is also a lot cheaper.

This evolution goes back quite a number of years, and the programs described have improved as drasticly as the hardware. They have been polished to a high gloss by the continuous process of program innovations and improvements. Much of the material you will be exposed to is such public domain software and supporting documentation. The inclusion of as much meaningful and reliable data as possible was limited only by time. *Going On-Line with Your Micro* gives you a nice start in expanding your computing horizons and makes a fine gift for a loved one. There are many excellent products in existence today that could not be covered. My apologies to those that didn't respond to my requests for information; my heartfelt thanks to those of you who did. Better luck next time!

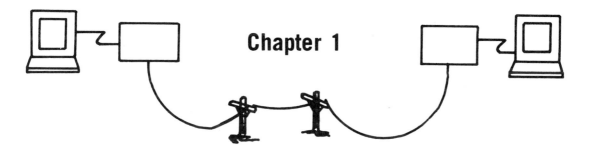

Chapter 1

Telecommunications

A BRIEF HISTORY

Back in the 1950's a group of engineers at a company then called UNIVAC started to experiment with the idea of transmitting data from one computer to another computer by using the telephone wires. John P. Hely, IV was one of that group. At a recent retirement dinner in his honor, he could not help but reminisce about the good old days. It is a surprise to most people to find out that it was not a communications giant like Ma Bell but a company that had nothing to do with telephones other than using them for voice communications that started the ball rolling.

Jack continued, saying, "Just peek over the shoulder of Charlotte Lowrie, who, in the house-paper of Sperry Univac (now just called Sperry Computer Corporation) chronicled the story at length." Her article, *The first modem - they said it couldn't be done*, starts with a quiz, which lets you guess who invented the first data set or modem, the device that hooks your home computer to the telephone and lets you talk to other computers. Was it AT&T, IBM, Mortimer Modem, Sperry Univac, or Western Union? If your answer was Sperry Univac, you were a winner. Sperry Univac? Yes it is a little known but true fact that the high technology of telecommunications had its humble beginnings in a former glider factory in Sperry's St. Paul facilities. These humble beginnings were a far cry from the slick black boxes in use today!

John P. Hely, IV, was none other than one of our communications pioneers in the early 1950's. It was he, along with a group of other researchers and developers, who gave us the capabilities we take so much for granted. The project got started, when UNIVAC I, a computer designed by J. Presper Eckert and John Mauchly was sold to James H. Rand of the Remington Rand Corporation. It quickly became apparent that the UNIVAC was a good number cruncher. It could spew out tons of data faster than the old punched cards could be read, but to be a viable entity in business computing, it needed jazzing up. And jazzed up it was: newer versions were equipped with faster and larger memory, magnetic tape for data storage of data and multiprogramming—all taken for granted today—but then years ahead of their time. However, telecommunications capabilities were still lacking.

Communications between UNIVAC computers were then only possible using either punched cards or magnetic tape, methods which are indirect or off-line and are cumbersome and inefficient. In the back of the minds of Hely and his associates existed the *transceiver*: a combination of magnetic tape transmitter/receiver, telephone wires, and a means or a protocol of letting two such transceivers talk to each other to transmit data. However, pumping data through telephone wires posed a problem, the telephone company said it couldn't be done. The wrong assumption was that computers work on direct current which could not flow through telephone lines. The solution was to reduce direct current to digits and tones. Once this great transformation was reality—binary zeroes and ones converted to tones—the tones could travel as far as the human voice. On one end magnetic tape was read, the binary was converted to tones, and the modulated result was transmitted. After traveling across telephone wires to the destination, a demodulator on the other end converted the tones back to digits. These digits were then written onto a magnetic tape. Voila! UNIVAC talks to UNIVAC, and business data processing can now begin in earnest.

Sperry Univac decided to concentrate on *mainframes*, the big computers of the day, and turned over the manufacture of modems to both Bell Labs (the research arm of AT&T) and Western Union. After these two companies delivered prototypes of their modems to Sperry for checkout, Sperry spurned competition between the two by quoting that each company was working under tight deadlines. After Western Union's project scientist died, that company withdrew from joint development work, and Bell and Sperry continued the project until working prototypes satisfied both sides of acceptable solutions.

Having turned over a future billion dollar business to others for reasons of convenience, it is sad to chronicle that the transceiver project was then turned over to a company called Collins Radio. And the saddest part of this whole story is that on April 1, 1983 the once so proud name of UNIVAC was taken out of circulation.

This story reminds me of the fellow who went out to trade his Hudson for a Packard, and then the Packard for a Studebaker, and then the Studebaker for a DeSoto. . . .A prudent observer could have guessed what had happened. Whoever went to UNIVAC facilities located at the Remington Rand building on lower Park Avenue in the early 60's saw only incandescent lightbulbs all over the place while all the other office buildings that make up that magnificent skyline were drenched by lights of fluorescense! A similar anecdote goes like this: Jack was riding past the old IBM office in Boston, when a fellow passenger remarked, "Isn't that the place where they make all those UNIVAC's?"

When I told Jack that I was writing this book, I also asked him to provide me with some material that I could use. He flooded my den with enough goodies to pen another one. However, he couldn't talk me out of sharing the following with you. Thanks for the info Jack. I wish you a happy and enjoyable retirement.

COMMUNICATION'S HISTORY ACCORDING TO JACK HELY

1558 Electrical communications is proposed by Porta.

1774 LeSage demonstrates electrical communication.

1816 Ronalds proposes single line communication.

1844 First electrical telegraph line is opened from Baltimore to Washington by F. B. Morse.

1849 A "Printing Telegraph Machine" transmits text between Philadelphia and New York City.

1873 E. Remington & Sons completes the first typewriter.

1874 A five-unit signaling code, named after Emile Jean Baudot, is developed, which includes both figures and letters. Contrary to the majority of publications on the subject, the Baudot code was not the USA five level standard. Instead, a US Signal Corps officer, Lieutenant Donald Murray, developed the five level code used in American Telegraphy and similar services.

1876 The telephone is invented by Alexander Graham Bell.

1877 The nation is being served by 7,500 Western Union Telegraph offices.

1900 The nation's homes are now being served by 1,300,000 telephones.

1908 Asynchronous start-stop transmission is developed by Howard Krum.

1915 Telephone signals are amplified by the introduction of telephone repeater units.

1919 The first automatic dialing system is put in operation.

1921 The predecessor company of the Teletype Corporation, the Morkrum Kleinschmidt Corporation develops paper-tape and page printers operating at 240 characters a minute.

1925 Morkrum develops a teleprinter which types on narrow gummed paper.

1928 Teletype comes out with perforated tape, which allows Automatic Send and Receive (ASR) transmissions as opposed to Keyboard Send and Receive (KSR).

1930 Morkrum Kleinschmitt Corporation bought by AT&T and made Western Electric Division subsidiary called Teletype.

1931 Bell introduces TWX service.

1932 to 1942 Carrier Communications become widespread. Private teletypewriter networks become popular.

1943 Western Union and the Postal Telegraph merge.

1952 Teleregister, predecessor to Bunker Ramo, delivers the world's first airline reservation system, a seat-availability inventory, using electrical relays.

1955 UNIVAC Data Communications projects are underway to develop a MODEM and magnetic-tape to magnetic-tape transmission. AT&T and Western Union use the UNIVAC MODEM as the basis for their own developments.

1957 AT&T experiments at Bell Labs indicate that bit rates in excess of 750 bit per second are practicable.

1959 UNIVAC announces specifications for the first real-time system, the 490, for Commercial Data Processing that allows the simultaneous input and output of messages over many different lines. By then the UNIVAC 'FILE' computer had already been used for communications in Airline Reservation Systems and Air Traffic Control for several years.

1960 The prototype UNIVAC 490 is completed and undergoing tests.

1962 AT&T commences dial-up TWX service. UNIVAC demonstrates Satellite Communications via Telstar.

1963 UNIVAC delivers its Standard Communications System with a capacity of 32 communication lines. GE delivers DATANET 30.

1966 UNIVAC completes delivery of the NASA communications network computers, which carry satellite control information around the world.

1968 Jim Babcock, of Allen-Babcock Computing in Los Angeles, shows his company's timesharing services, live, via satellite telecommunications, to the Alfred B. Nobel Prize laureates in Stockholm, using his companies computers located in Century City (sorry for sneaking this one in on you Jack, but I conceptualized the actual program used for an earlier demonstration of Jim Babcock's then new and outstanding offering).

1969 Anderson-Jacobson deliver a MODEM equipped with acoustic coupler.

1970 The Micro-Computer is born. The first microcomputer on a chip at Intel, the 4004, goes into production.

MODEMS

The need for two computers to talk to each other lead to the development of a transmission device that read information on one end from a magnetic tape, transmitted the information over telephone wires from the sending to the receiving computer, and then wrote it to another magnetic tape. A magnetic tape of those days was not oxide coated cellophane but a metallic band, a reel weighing in at over forty pounds! What made all the transfer of data possible was a device known today as a modem. The word modem is a combination of both MODulator and DEModulator. Figure 1-1 illustrates the process.

Bits, Bytes, And Baud

Data stored in your computer consists of bits and bytes. A *bit* is the smallest representation of the electronic states one or zero, and all information used in computers and telecommunications today consists of bits. In order to make those little rascals more manageable, they get organized into what is called a *byte*. A byte (don't you love that word - it was coined by the same people that gave us disk)

consists of eight bits and could look like this: 01010011 . For easier reading, it is usually broken up into two groups, so that the more common representation will look like this: 0101 0011.

Now if I had to define the word byte, I would say that a byte can represent all letters from A through Z and from a through z, all numerals from 0 through 9, the special characters \ ! " # $ % & ' ( ) * = – ' @ ~ ^ < > ? + { } [ ] < > ? , . /, and finally, in binary representation, any number from zero (0000 0000) to 65,536 (1111 1111). Powerful stuff!

Dr. Baudot, a leading advocate of early telecommunications technology, gave us the 5 bit Baudot code. He was responsible for our naming the measure bits per second *baud*. All modem speeds are measured in baud, and a common speed for modems is 300 baud, which means 300 bits per second get processed.

Data Transmission

To transmit digital data, a conversion or modulation of a given digit to a tone of a unique frequency takes place. The noise you get when you punch numbers on your pushbutton telephone rep-

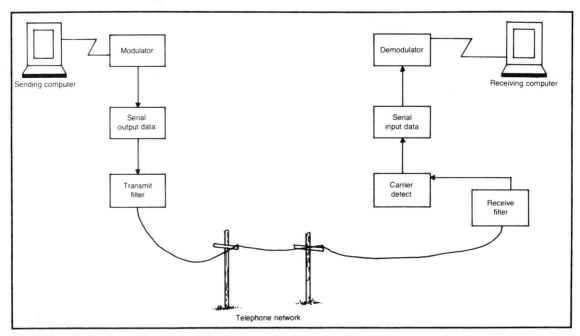

Fig. 1-1. The telecommunications environment.

4

resents modulated data. At the other end, this tone then gets reconverted, or demodulated, into digital data. Also, to send and to receive data a modem must be on either end.

Modems come in different shapes and work at different speeds. Some modems, especially the newer ones, are very small, consist of built-in components, and are integrated in higher priced equipment. They are also directly coupled to the telephone line with a modular telephone jack. Older modems were the size of a shoe box and used the acoustic method of coupling where the headset of the telephone was inserted into cushioned modem components to couple both the mouthpiece and the receiver. The speed of transmission for a modem is expressed in baud.

MINIMUM CONFIGURATION

Unfortunately, you can not communicate using a modem at any speed without the use of a terminal. A terminal can be defined as an input/output or I/O device. Most terminals have a keyboard and the ability to display input and output. Many use a television like cathode ray tube, or CRT, as their display device and are often housed in the same cabinet. Others, especially later models, have a detachable or stand alone keyboard. Others use a printer or a regular tv set as their display device.

The difference between a regular tv set and a terminal CRT is usually the ability of the terminal to display more columns per horizontal line. Fancy computer terminals have monitors that can display graphics in color and are quite expensive. So, our home computer has to have a terminal and a modem to be used for telecommunications.

A modem and terminal form a minimum configuration to communicate with others. However, many times there is a need to store the information received, a computer program for example. Such storage requires a mass storage device. A mass storage device can be a cassette tape or a floppy disc with disc being the preferred and, unfortunately, the more expensive device. The use of disc or tape allows us also to reduce our telephone line charges, especially when calling long distance.

However, if your main purpose of communica-

tions is to just look at information, not storing it, you can get away with a minimum terminal configuration at surprisingly low cost. Radio Shack sells a minimum configuration Information Terminal for less than two hundred dollars that includes a keyboard with built-in modem and built-in communications software. All you have to do is to hook up your tv set and your telephone, using a modular telephone jack. Presto, you are in business.

For investors requiring access to a financial data base, this is a terrific way to go—two way communications at a very reasonable cost. If plain vanilla is not your taste, the same store will sell you a Micro Executive Workstation, a fancy notebook size portable computer with built-in modem, a nice display, and all the software needed for less than eight hundred dollars. It runs on batteries, retains information in memory for thirty days, hooks up to a cassette recorder, and can be used in conjunction with a printer. This is by no means the top of the line, but it is a sure indication of a whole new generation of computing and communications capabilities coming our way. And as with the camera and stereo industry offerings, the next model will always have more features at the same or an even lower price. At this pace, the day can not be far away when the pocket computer—not a fancy adding machine, but a full powered machine—can not be far off.

Figure 1-2 summarizes the primary ingredients in any telecommunications system. The next two sections detail the hardware and software more fully.

HARDWARE

Telecommunications hardware comes in a variety of sizes, shapes and prices. As mentioned for $200 or less you can acquire a complete terminal, and by adding a telephone and a tv set you can communicate. The idea of a keyboard having other components besides the keyboard itself is not new. Quite a few home computers use the same setup called a console. Here is where it becomes necessary to take a little time to examine the hardware that makes telecommunications possible: There

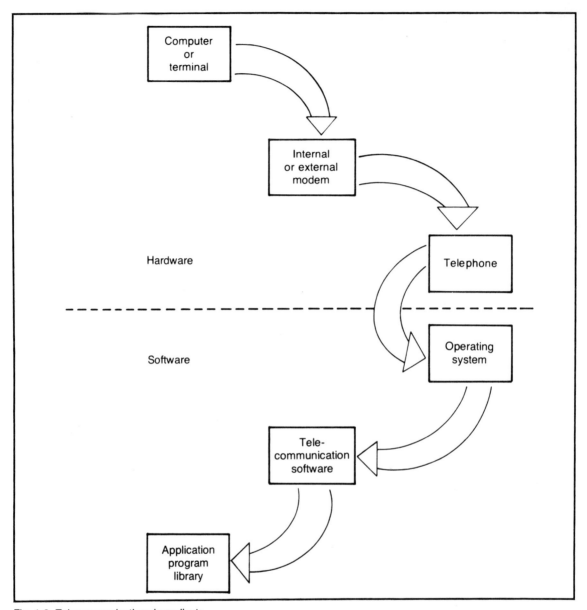

Fig. 1-2. Telecommunications ingredients.

are a variety of systems, and, while concentrating on home computers, I do not want to glance over our bigger and older brothers too lightly.

Old mechanical klonkers called teletypewriters, or Telex machines, predated our current crop of goodies by a score of years. They are slowly going the way of the stand-up desk, the old plug-in switchboard and the chalk toteboard. Manufacturing economies as well as the outrageously high cost of maintaining older gear make it economical for us to discard gear today as opposed to having it repaired. In the old days, the saying in the communications circles was that the teletype was not goldplated, but the maintenance contract was!

Modems

I have already introduced the workings of a modem, but what you have to remember is that new computers already have many components conveniently packaged or integrated. The MC-10 Information Terminal sold by Radio Shack not only has the modem but also the control programs integrated into the console of the keyboard. Many home computers manufacturers make the modem an attachment that plugs into a slot on the computer console. Older modems are not coupled directly by using a modular phone jack. Instead, they come with plastic or rubber cups that acoustically couple the telephone speaker and receiver to the terminal or computer.

Terminals

Terminals consist of component parts or an integrated unit: many home computers use a TV set as part of their input/output capability, and other terminals have built-in screens or CRT's. Some use typewriter-like impact printers; the quiet variety uses sensitized paper and burns away a layer of protective covering. The newest and more expensive terminals use liquid crystal displays (LCD) that look much like the display on a digital wrist watch. Among the advantages of LCD displays are their low power consumption, which makes them excellent candidates for battery powered portables.

Computers

The computer primarily consists of a central processing unit, or CPU, and a memory. The capacity of a memory is expressed in K bytes, which means one thousand bytes. Most home computers have a minimum capacity of 4 K, which translates into 4,000 bytes of memory. Other components are a power supply, connectors for terminals, secondary storage devices such as disc drives or cassette tapes, connectors for line power and for a modem, joy sticks, game paddles, modems, printers, and other accessories. The way they are packaged can be confusing. Many units combine terminal, CPU, memory, disc drives, power supply and modem into one convenient package, while others separate components to a point where the resulting mess of cables is not only unsightly but can create a real traffic hazard!

Those of you using a home computer on a heavy duty basis will do much better using an integrated unit. Also important is the noise level many units generate. While you are not at all aware of the noise some computers and their accessories create when you're looking at them in the showroom of your favorite computer store, the quiet sessions in your cozy den will soon reveal the noise of those wind makers, the fans. If possible, try before you buy.

SOFTWARE

Telecommunications could not exist without *software*—computer instructions gathered into a program or a series of programs that execute and connect the computer to the outside world. Basic ingredients for most computers consist of a steering program, called the *executive* or *operating system*. This operating system is the traffic cop; he makes sure that the different operations and processes don't get in each others way. The operating system also executes the communications software.

When you lift your telephone to dial a number, you establish a connection to talk to another party. Using our computer for telecommunications, you just substitute the computer for the telephone. Traffic has to be in an ordered fashion and proceeds something like this: you start up your computer and get your communications software resident in memory. Then you or your computer dials the number of the computer you wish to call. If the other number is not busy and the other computer is in the receive mode, (meaning the communications software on the other computer is ready-to-receive), and if our equipment is compatible, you can establish a connection.

Many factors in both software programming and hardware incompatibility can cause a lot of heartache. I often thought that I was finally all set up, when, much to my deep disappointment, I discovered that nothing was happening at all. This is especially true when hardware and software of different manufacturers is used or when software that has not been fine-tuned to the system is used.

If you are of an experimental nature and have the time, by all means, take your sweet old time putting things together. On the other hand, if time is of the essence, only a completely set-up system will do, and the price will be in strict relationship to the quality and performance capabilities of the selected components. The recommendation here is to have everything set up and tested right at the place of purchase.

On the other hand, I must point out an unbelievable bargain. In one of their regular sales catalogs, they are not only offering the integrated Information Terminal mentioned earlier for less than $100, but they are also throwing in one hour of connect time on a couple of Network Data Services for free! This is the way to go if you are interested in the lowest price of getting going. It's also a cheap way to find out if all this computer stuff is really for you.

On the other hand, a list of all possible combinations of software and all the hardware needed to make the software hum would fill too many pages to possibly be of value to anyone. So when I make my recommendations, I will try to be objective and give you a pretty good idea of what your dollars can buy.

HOW DO YOU START?

While much has been said about computers for your home and office in the newspapers and news magazines, two observations can be made: one, there is quite a difference in the perception of the needs of the average household, and two, telecomunications are rarely mentioned, if at all. The same holds very much true for many of the tv ads and some of the so called computer shows on tv. This points to the arcade game mentality that brought us paddles and joysticks and great boredom.

Many attempts by game makers to break out of their arcade mold have not done to well for many of them. Many owners of their machines buy add-in boards that allow a given computer to run software for another one. For instance, there are CP/M boards for both Commodore 64 and ATARI computers. But by the time you add up the total cost,

you could have gotten similar capabilities by buying the correct kind of gear in the first place. On the other hand, if you have a game console and you can update it to a home computer, you do not have to let go of an old friend.

New products are announced all the time. IBM now has it's Peanut or PC Junior, and Coleco has announced a new computer, the ADAM. For around $700 you get a home computer with a letter quality printer, and the machine can be equipped for telecommunications, I am sure. The reason that the ADAM is so attractive is that CP/M can be run on it, and the basic machine comes equipped with 80 K bytes of memory, quite a difference when compared to other offerings. You can buy a basic machine for $200 and end up paying another $200 to add 16 K of memory.

ATARI has also announced new models, and the company claims CP/M compatibility across the line of seven different computers and built-in modems on two top-of-line models, the ATARI 1400XL and the 1450XLD. A letter quality printer for $349.95, the ATARI 1027, is also part of their offering. So ATARI and Coleco are companies that have recognized the benefit of all the CP/M software. Before too long, other manufacturers are likely to jump on to the CP/M compatible software band-wagon. Such a move will bring us home computers that can use a tremendous software base.

KAYPRO computers have that capability. Although they are a higher priced product, their sales are rapidly rising. They should be looked upon as quality products that take advantage of the many communications routines available and running under this popular operating system. The list of CP/M computers is not complete here, but a summary can be found in Appendix A.

The final hurdle then is software. What is an easy and comfortable way to really get going using all this hardware you read about? Two popular choices can be made. First, you can start programming from scratch using a computer language such as BASIC. Many excellent texts exist for the beginner and many computer makers have come out with BASIC courses that lead all the way up to and include advanced business routines and graphics.

Many texts are accompanied by discs or tapes, that contain learn-while-you-do programs. This software teaches BASIC asking you to write routines that will be progressively more complex to teach you all the syntax. Once you are bored with BASIC, graduation to higher level languages and assembly programming is the way to go. Should all that bore you, you then must take the second choice, which leaves you to get your software ready-made. Here is where this book becomes handy. I show you not only what programs you need but also how to get them either free from or manufacturers of hardware and software.

Available Languages

It is hard to make recommendations, but I know of no problem in home computing that you can not solve using BASIC or one of it's many dialects. Then there is a whole slew of other popular languages. Pascal, the language C, Ada, and Modula 2 are all fairly new and all rather complex to learn. So it may not be easy to make a quick choice at a local computer store. In the business world about 90 percent of all programs used there are written in Cobol. Yes, Cobol? It is a language that is quite a number of years old, but it has all the facilities needed to define data in great detail and then to process it efficiently. It is taught today, and many job ads for the Data Processing field call for Cobol programmers. Should you try? Certainly! Versions of NEVADA Cobol are being sold for less than $50. A company called Ellis Computing sells BASIC, Fortran and others at the same terrific price. They include a big manual, and for such small investment you can afford to experiment.

When does Cobol not fill the bill? When Engineering calculations, scientific programming or other mathematical processing has to be done, a more suitable language such as Fortran, Algol, or PL/1 should be considered.

Software Packages

Store or mailorder bought, ready-made software is available in abundance, or you can acquire a system that comes bundled. The total offering includes all hardware and software for one price. I have packages, such as editors and word processors, that have been prepared to do one job

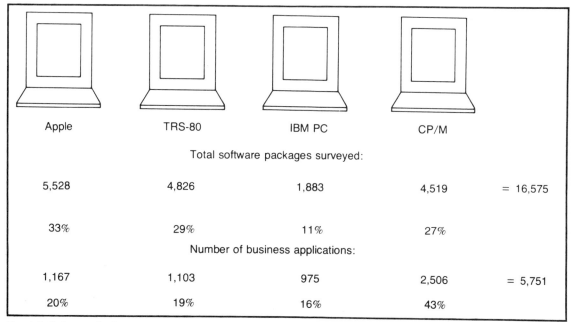

Apple	TRS-80	IBM PC	CP/M	
Total software packages surveyed:				
5,528	4,826	1,883	4,519	= 16,575
33%	29%	11%	27%	
Number of business applications:				
1,167	1,103	975	2,506	= 5,751
20%	19%	16%	43%	

Fig. 1-3. Software distribution by popular make.

only. For a CP/M or PC system, Wordstar must be given serious consideration. It is clearly among the best. Other software packages, too numerous to mention here, are address, accounting, payroll, sales analysis, inventory and other business oriented subjects. And don't let me forget all those spreadsheets. Software packages that try to solve many different problems are known as report generators and data base systems. They go to market under many different names and may be of help if you do not have much time to do your own customized programming.

Figure 1-3 surveys several home computers and the CP/M operating system. Note the software distribution between them and the number of business applications.

Other Sources of Software

Two other sources bear looking into: first the rental libraries, and second, software in the public domain. Rental libraries allow you access to expensive software packages, so that you can make up your own mind by trying them out before you go out and spend your hard earned cash. The second, software in the *public domain*, is a bargain at any price. By public domain, I mean software available by telecommunications links between computers. This includes a large number of computer bulletin boards and club computers as well as services like CompuServe.

A Suggested Software Library

What should be in your home computer software library? A good editor, a good word processor, a good BASIC, and a good telecommunications package. In a CP/M environment, a good editor for program development is VEDIT. A second choice is the editor of Digital Research that is part of CP/M to begin with. In word processors, Wordstar is among the best. Basic offers excellent choices. For CP/M there is C-80 from Digital Research, which comes in a version that executes your code with the aid of a runtime interpreter. You first put your source code together with an editor, compile your program and then run the resulting file. Another version can be compiled and executed like

an ordinary BASIC. Counterparts from Microsoft are MBASIC, their interpretive BASIC and Bascom, the compiled version. The advantage of MBASIC is that it has been installed on many different makes of computers and this offers a nice degree of portability; you can take it with you! Public domain software has many excellent languages available.

Two BASICS mentioned here are on the extreme end of the performance spectrum: LLL BASIC, on one of the early CP/M users group discs, is a full blown implementation of a BASIC compiler and interpreter for the 8080/Z80 chips. On the other end, there is Tiny BASIC, first published in a computer hobby magazine and then implemented in various versions by the user community. As the name implies, it is small but a good learning tool, easy to use, and a spectacular piece of software. Another BASIC implementation in the public domain that should not be overlooked is E-BASIC, the predecessor of C-BASIC, now called C-80. While it lacks many of the features that have gone into later implementations, it is very powerful.

THE FUTURE

If you own a home computer and a telecommunications link, the world is yours! You can do much of your own computing where and when you so desire, and access to data banks, computing services, and other home computer users is at your disposal.

One step further down the road will be the ability to hook up terminals and peripherals regardless of make, speed or capacity on the same circuit, locally or remote. Such hookups are called networking and there is a lot of talk about Local Area Networks or LANs. It is far cheaper to hook up a single workstation to a bus like the one made by Molecular Computer, interconnecting all terminals, discs, and printers, than it is to buy a single LAN connection. Another reason is that those universal networks do nothing to preserve a given vendors existing customer base and thus the proprietary interests of a given manufacturer.

Further down the road will be an acceleration

of the trend of cutting out whole layers of clerical and other human interfaces, that you have to deal with at the current time. Let us quickly look at three samples. Banks are replacing tellers with automated window machines, airlines allow you to make your own travel reservations (and thus saving the Travel Agent's commission), and many banks already allow their customers to make automatic transfers of monthly payments. Once you are able to hook into all these reservation banks, it will be a lot more fun to select the flights, hotels, tours, and what have you, that really suit your needs at home in armchair comfort instead of having to rush downtown at a most inconvenient time, to find no parking, and, after you finally do, to discover the place is closed.

Other innovations of doing business are going to come in ticket sales, the electronic stock market, and the computerized swap meet. There is already on-line shopping available on CompuServe and the Source, and here on the West Coast you can avail yourself of job-offerings and buying services that are all accessible using telecommunications and available when you want to use them, 24 hours a day, seven days a week.

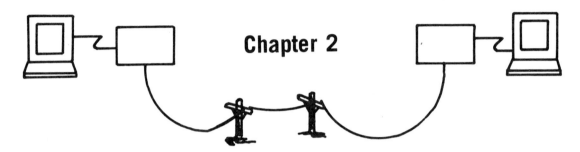

Chapter 2

Telecommunications Ingredients

HARDWARE

The problem of selecting a suitable home computer set up for telecommunications can be broken into two distinct parts:

- ☐ Starting from scratch.
- ☐ Updating existing equipment.

But before I examine these categories, let me cover an often greater criteria: cost.

Cost

If money is no object, consider yourself an exception! For the rest of us, let us settle on high priced, regular priced, and low priced capabilities and zero in on some of the choices that are available in each category. Then I will return to the other two categories.

High Priced Systems. What makes the micros of Bourroughs, Hewlett-Packard, Digital Equipment Corporation, Data General, NCR, Sperry and Xerox so expensive? These established computer companies are not set up to sell and respond to the true needs of this new home market.

The reason they are selling, or better put, trying to sell micros is certainly not by design, but by default. As the capabilities of microcomputers grow, you will see the rate of new acquisitions for what we call minicomputers today go by the wayside.

As we see the era of the super micros beginning, a severe erosion of the domain of our big mainframe computers is bound to follow. I am not predicting their total demise, but I am forecasting a shift away from the big boxes because of the rapid advances in the processing and throughput capabilities of the new super micros. Based on rapid advances being made bringing us reasonably priced *Local Area Networks*, this trend will not only continue, but will definitely accelerate, LNAs will allow us to connect different makes of terminals, computers and peripherals to distribute data processing using different solutions: solutions other than just using mainframes and minicomputers.

To participate in these coming changes economically, these companies have to change their product lines completely. They have done so, or are trying to catch up, but they are still using their established methods of engineering, manufacturing, marketing and pricing. This, of course, leaves them out of the competition with the offerings from leaders of this new home computer market. Yet, by size alone, they are always a force to be reckoned with.

It is interesting to observe the inroads that have been made by Home Computers in the world of big business. After the Apple first came out, many home computerists broke out of the corporate straightjacket of: you can not have this job done a) this year, b) your way, c) for less than umpteen thousand dollars! Many users have been able to convince their management of the usefulness of having their own computers, and small businessmen were also the first to recognize the savings of doing a lot of jobs in-house as opposed to having them done outside. In addition, many have found home computers and telecommunications the answer to solve problems and to explore new vistas in the armchair at home.

Another category that has to be looked at is portables. With the PR departments coming up with buzz words faster than we can assimilate them, the ones that define portability have been used to excess: totables, desktops, kneetops, transportables. Heck, any computer I ever saw was transportable. It was just a question of how small you hacksawed the pieces! Anyhow, the high end of the new portable generation is definitely in the high priced category. Just as their names span the alphabet from Atache to Zorba, they range in price from under $1,000 to ten times that. Their weight goes anywhere from 4 to 40, and the ones on the high end set usually market trends that will be followed to a degree by many others. First of all there is the snob appeal of "I've got the Cadillac of the line," and then there is the real utility of having a small, effective instrument that can perform the same duties as a much larger machine. In the high priced category of portables is a computer called Compass made by GRID. It has a large display using an electroluminescent flat panel as opposed to a liquid crystal display (LCD). This flat panel allows excellent graphics resolution in addition to giving access to 25 lines times 80 characters, the desirable 2,000

character screen. Another high priced offering is the Gavilan.

Medium Priced Systems. The IBM PC will have a lion's share of the medium sized offerings, and if the PC look-alike market continues to develop, good news is in the making. Offshore manufacturing of IBM look-alikes will bring their prices down. They will be substantially less than offerings from IBM, because you do not pay for that fancy logo. It is hoped that they will also have a better keyboard than the one they put on the PC, especially if you are used to the comforts of, ironically, another IBM keyboard, the Selectric.

Similar offerings in Apple look-alikes has eroded the big profit margins that Apple once enjoyed: if you can purchase quality boards and accessories for Apples at a fraction of the Apple price, why shouldn't you. So a dream system—the best of all worlds—would be a PC look-alike without that awful keyboard. Then an Apple board, to use the cream of all that existing software for stocks, commodities, and those beautiful color graphics. And finally, a CP/M board to use the thousands of programs written for this great operating system. And with the prices of disc coming down, a fine system can be put together in that medium price category.

Talking about irony; here I am talking about spending money to get a 16-bit computer and suggesting buying 8-bit boards so that you can run all this good 8-bit software. For those of you more comfortable with a ready made product, look at Apple, Eagle, Franklin, IBM PC, KAYPRO, Radio Shack TRS-80 Model IV, Zenith/Heath and many other fine makes running as either 8-bit or 16-bit computers. Some makes even combine 8-bit and 16-bit capabilities in the same computer just like the dream machine mentioned before. This approach gives the best of both 8-bit and 16-bit worlds.

Low Priced Systems. These offerings abound, and many of these fine computers have excellent telecommunications capabilities. When Sinclair (later Timex) first broke through the $100 barrier, everybody could really afford to get their hands on one of those things, although their ultimate utility could be classified as only marginal at best. Now we have more than one offering in the below $100 category, although price alone can be very misleading. If you avail yourself of a VIC-20, one of Commodore's offerings under $100, you still need a data recorder or a disc drive, a printer, and a modem. Before you are done you have spent quite a bit more. And this is only the hardware. Try to look for software and you will quickly find another problem; the best computer will be of little value unless it has at least an operating system, an editor or a word processor for program and document creation, some communications capability, and a data file manipulator (often called a data base system). Where do you get all that? Not an easy task, especially in the store where you buy the box.

This problem is one of the reasons that bundled software helps sell computers; for one set price, they give their owners good home computing capabilities. Fortunately for everyone, the capabilities of low priced computers are rapidly improving. New models, like the Timex Sinclair 2068, have a large amount of built-in memory. The days, when you buy a computer with 4,000 bytes of memory and then pay more for an additional 16,000 byte memory upgrade than you did for the box you attach it to, are rapidly coming to an end. The 2068 has 68,000 bytes of built-in memory, uses the popular Z80 microprocessor, and is priced below $200.

Other offerings in the low priced category are from ATARI, Coleco, Commodore, Mattel, Texas Instruments, and Radio Shack. If a kneetop is your hearts desire, watch the offering of Radio Shack's TRS-80 Model 100. It has telecommunications, *BASIC*, a wordprocessor, and other programs built into ROM. It is battery powered and has an outstanding keyboard. The price is a little on the high side, and the display and the memory will undoubtedly be enlarged. This is the trend-setter for a whole new class of fine machines, so be on the lookout for them.

Recommendations

Obtain any of the high priced systems in my list if you can get it free! If you buy Hewlett-Packard you get a Cadillac, and the service will certainly be excellent if you can afford it.

The IBM PC or a PC look-alike, preferably with hard disc and the Apple and CP/M cards, is a best bet for a medium priced system.

Any low priced system that is CP/M capable gives you the unsurmountable advantage of all that available software, and there is always more on the way!

Starting From Scratch

Definitions and price categories established, I can now concentrate on the easiest choice: starting from scratch. If you are not absolutely sure about computing and the use of telecommunications, go out and blow $100 or so on a TRS-80 COCO console at one of their upcoming sales. They'll even give you one hour each on the Dow Jones and CompuServe data-networks. Access to these networks is covered in detail in Chapter 8, Information Services. It pays to do a little homework before trying. By reading up on what they have to offer and how to avail yourself of these offerings you can save additional time by retrieving data while you are on-line as opposed to learning by doing.

At any rate, should this all get you into the "YES I WANT TO" category, look favorably upon a bundled system, especially if you do not want to tinker with a Heath kit and put everything under the sun together yourself. By *bundled*, I mean a package that contains everything you need to get going. For instance, one of the excellent KAYPRO systems gives you all you need in hardware and software to go on-line in style, and you will do quite well in telecommunications. A sampling of the documentation that accompanies a KAYPRO II computer shows they have done a commendable job of giving you enough of the kind of information to get you started in the right direction. To boot, you followed the recommendation made to get an all CP/M system. KAYPRO is already one of the leading CP/M computers. You can start exchanging all kinds of data the minute you set up shop. CP/M is not the only kind of software that is plentiful. An acquaintance of mine volunteered for the job as chairman of documentation for his local chapter of the Apple Corps, one of the many groups for Apple (or look alike) users. Guess what happened? Well, before I tell you, you should know that this chapter is in a large and prosperous area and is probably one of the larger ones in the country. A whole van-load of documentation, cassettes and discs was dumped on his front lawn! True story.

Updating Existing Equipment

Let me explain my recommendations about adding telecommunications capabilities to existing gear. You can buy a modem on a board and stick it into one of the expansion slots in back of your IBM PC, Apple, Commodore, Timex, or TRS-80 or you can buy an external modem. By attaching one plug of the modem cord to our computer and the other end to a modular phone jack, you are ready to begin.

Some computers have the ability to accommodate an older type modem by attaching it to a serial port. By older type, I mean the one with rubber cups for the telephone handset. Those are called acoustically coupled modems as opposed to the newer direct coupled models.

Your computer literature and your local computer store can guide you through what's available in both hardware and software to give you the telecommunications capabilities that you want. My recommendations are based on products that have been in use for a while. This approach assures that a given combination of computer, modem, and software will achieve desired results.

SOFTWARE

Ward Christensen is credited with giving telecommunications and the home computer a protocol that allows efficient and low cost communications. This protocol, called XMODEM, consists of three programs, called MODEM, XMODEM, and BYE, which all run under the CP/M operating system.

The intent of this section is to acquaint the reader with telecommunications software for the home computer. To show users a true picture of software used in telecommunications, different program environments are addressed. Many programs used in home computing perform the same function in telecommunications on the Apple, on the ATARI, on CP/M systems, on the IBM PC-XT, and on the many PC compatibles. A user has the difficult choice of what to buy, where to buy and at what cost. Here is good news: all the programs described in this chapter are **free**. They exist as public domain software and can be freely obtained on the many bulletin boards described and listed in Chapter 4. So all you need is some reasonably priced hardware. Keep looking for a good buy right now.

The Osborne portable computers, which started a new era in portable computing when they first came out a couple of years ago, quickly dominated that new market. But the competition took notice and zeroed in on Ozzy's shortcomings. Overnight KAYPRO, Compaq, Atrona, Zorba, and a host of other makes arrived on the scene. Where is Ozzy now? The Osbornes filled a need, and found a nice niche in the worlds of home computing, CP/M and telecommunications. If you can find a place that will support (repair if needed!) an Ozzy for you, it may be a good buy in a low priced starter system. Otherwise look to the fine machines made by KAYPRO and bundled with a lot of useful software as a good buy in a portable computer. If portable is too heavy, try a kneetop. Kneetops are the smallest computers equipped with modems for telecommunications and offerings from many manufacturers are available.

The first set of software for telecommunications acquaints us with the XMODEM protocol and the programs MODEM, XMODEM and BYE, all running under the CP/M family of operating systems and originally written for the Intel 8080 chip and later updated for others, such as the Z-80 and the many PC's. These programs have been extensively modified over the years, and MODEM has had its modest beginnings in the year 1977. Many different variations have made it one of the premier software products for the home computing environment. The many enhancements and modifications this program has received to date have been carefully documented.

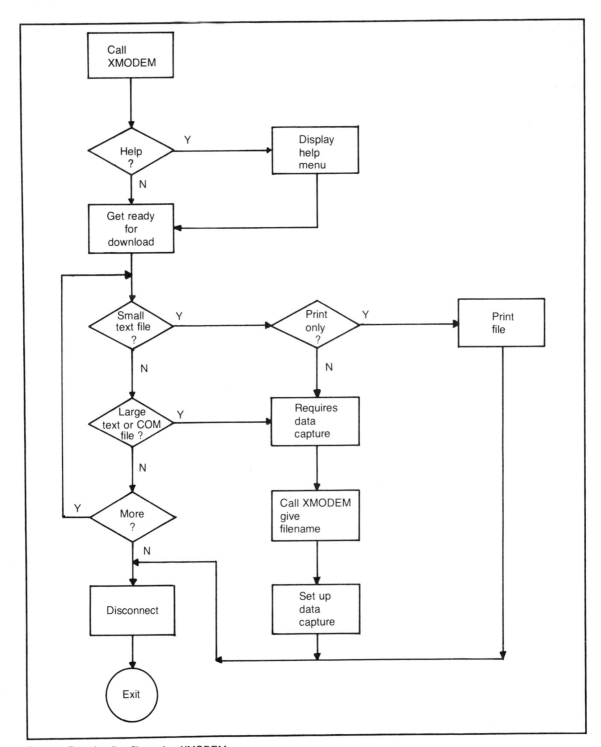

Fig. 2-1. Downloading files using XMODEM.

MODEM 707

MDM707 is a late version of the original MODEM program. It enables a computer to communicate with another computer. This is normally done by using standard telephone lines but with special audio tones sending serial data. Two common speeds are used depending on the facilities available: 300 Baud or 1200 Baud.

The modem itself is a hardware utility, usually costing from $100 to $250 for a typical 300 baud device and from $600 to $850 for a system offering 1200 baud as well as 300 baud. Some of these (such as the PMMI S-100 modem board) plug directly into the computer itself, while others are totally independent of the computer and use an interconnect cable (usually a RS-232 type) to control the external modem. A Bell 212A is an excellent example of this type modem. MDM 707 allows each computer involved to directly control its own modem. For short distances, no modems are required as the computer can provide the necessary digital voltages to support direct wired communications from one computer to the other. This discussion is centered around systems intended for use over distances ranging from several miles to literally around the world.

Features

A program to communicate with another computer can range from very simple to very complex. MDM707 is one of the more complex such programs available today. It started in 1977 as a relatively simple program. At that time, it was intended to be used primarily as a means of exchanging programs with other people in other cities. Since that time a number of other features have been added, including improved methods of program transfer. Figure 2-1 and Fig. 2-2 illustrate the XMODEM file transfer process. A partial list of features offered by this particular program include:

☐ Ability to talk with another computer via keyboard at each end. (Called the "terminal mode".)

☐ Ability to operate a remote mainframe computer such as TYM-SHARE, or special data

bank systems now commonplace. This includes bulletin board systems for receiving, sending or just reading messages or other types of information.

☐ Ability to upload (send) or download (receive) programs from other computers whether TYM-SHARE data banks, remote hobby systems or just another individual in another location.

☐ Ability to copy incoming information on a printer. If the printer is too slow to copy the data directly, the extra characters back into a large storage buffer.

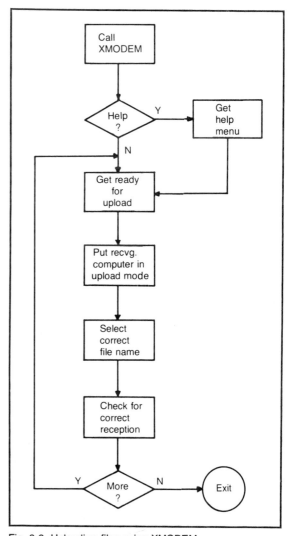

Fig. 2-2. Uploading files using XMODEM.

17

☐ Ability to copy incoming data into memory for automatic transfer to a disk file.

☐ Accommodates any computer clock speed up to 25.5 MHz. in 0.1 MHz. increments for uniform results.

☐ This particular program has additional features of special interest to the S-100 type computers using the PMMI modem board. Those features basically include automatic dialing and redialing (if requested) until the other computer is finally able to answer.

a) Automatic selection of a particular phone number from a library of names and numbers.

b) Entry of a hand-typed number. Although it might be as simple to dial the number as hand-type it, that number can then be automatically redialed indefinitely.

Using The Program

For now, I shall assume the program is ready to use on your equipment. (Normally the user must make some modest changes to the program before it can be used. This includes changing the port numbers and some other personal options. These will be covered later in the section that describes how to adapt it to your equipment.) Asking for MDM707 brings up this display:

MDM706 - 04/11/83
Version for S-100 PMMI modem starting at
    port: COH
B> COMMAND (H for Help): x

The cursor stops at point x waiting for some sort of command. Typing an H followed immediately by a RETURN, shows the first page of a 4-page help guide. If you do not have a PMMI modem, you would have seen this:

MDM707 - 04/11/83
Version for Non-PMMI modem
B> COMMAND (H for Help): x

In this case, only a 3-page help guide is used, since the 4th page is used to assist those with the PMMI modem. It tells them a little about selecting the number to dial, or auto-redial, how to change from originate to answer mode, how to change baud rates, how to disconnect, etc. Several commands are similar to those already used for CP/M, such as ERA, DIR and the ability to change disk drives and user areas. This adds tremendous flexibility while remaining in the modem command mode. To change disk drives, just say:

B> COMMAND (H for Help): A: <RET>

and you are in the same user area on the A: drive. You can also say:

A> COMMAND (H for Help): A: 12 <RET>

to change user areas. When finished (using this example), say:

A12> COMMAND (H for Help): CPM
    <RET>

and you will go back to CP/M with the original driver and user area. Although you can get the following information from the help guide in MDM707, showing it here will allow me to discuss the various features in somewhat better detail.

The Help Guide

There are basically three types of commands that may be used with this program:

☐ Single-letter commands shown on page one (see Fig. 2-3).

☐ Three-letter commands shown on page 2 (see Fig. 2-4).

☐ Control-<char.> commands shown on page 3.

Page four is only used if a PMMI MODEM is connected to the system.

Page 1. An explanation for each command in Fig. 2-3 follows:

?—shows current parameters. As these are closely tied in with some of the other options, we shall show a typical example later in this discussion.

```
        ? - Display current settings
        H - Display this information
        E - Terminal mode with echo
        L - Terminal mode with local echo
        T - Terminal mode
For copying text to disc use T (or E or L) FILENAME.TYP
Start or Stop toggles described on subsequent screen.

        R - Receive CP/M file using Christensen Protocol
        S - Send CP/M file using Christensen Protocol
Command: R (or S) FILENAME.TYP
        R and S can use the following subcommands:
        B - Bulk transfer using wildcards (e.g., *.*)
        Q - Quiet mode (no messages to console)
        T - Return to terminal mode after transfer
        V - View bytes transferred on console

Note: The single letter commands may also be used on the
        command line when the program is initially executed.
```

Fig. 2-3. Single-letter commands on page one of the help guide.

```
       CPM - Exit from this program to CP/M
        DIR - List directory and space free (may specify drive)
       ERA - Erase file (may specify drive)
       LOG - Change default drive/user no. (specific drive/user)
              and reset disks. e.g.,LOG A0: or LOG B: (user #
              unchanged)
       SPD - Set speed of file output in terminal mode
        TIM - Select Baud rate for "time-to-send" message
       TCC - Toggle CRC/Checksum mode on receive
       TBR - Toggle backspace to rubout conversion
       TLC - Toggle 1) local command immediate
                    2) local command after CTL-^
       TLF - Toggle send linefeed after carriage return in T mode
       TXO - Toggle XOFF testing in terminal mode file output
       CAL - Dial number
       DSC - Disconnect
       BYE - Disconnect and reboot

       The following are terminal text buffer commands:

       DEL - Delete memory buffer and file
       NOL - Return to terminal mode - no loss of data in buffer
       WRT - Write memory buffer to disk file
```

Fig. 2-4. Three-letter commands on page two of the help guide.

H—shows the help guide, a page at a time. You may abort after any completed page with a control-C.

E—terminal mode with echo. When talking with another terminal also using MDM707 (or a comparable program), one of you must send an *echo-back* so you can both see what the other person is typing. This is needed for full-duplex operation. Usually the person originating the call will type E instead of T. However either may do this. If both computers use the echo mode, the program usually starts typing a string of feedback characters since both computers are resending the same character over and over. You can stop this by just returning to command mode (type control-E) and then retyping T rather than E.

L—terminal mode with local echo. Shows what you are typing but does not send an echo of the other person's typing back to him. Can be used at both ends, in place of one person using E. Both E and L are useful at times for some types of modems that do not use full duplex, or for some main frame units that run half duplex. The combination of T, E and L gives an excellent choice to use on various systems. Normally the T mode is sufficient except when talking with another person and then the E mode at one end or L mode at both ends will provide normal results.

T—if typed as the first (primary) option, puts the program directly into terminal mode, allowing it to send from the keyboard to the other computer, and to copy anything coming from the other computer with the exception of file transfers (use R to receive those).

R—used only for receiving files from the other computer. These are usually sent in binary form with either checksum verification or more commonly, CRC (Cyclic Redundancy Checking). If ready to receive another file, you have several choices, depending on the program used by the other computer. After notifying him you are ready (or will be very shortly), you can type:

B>   COMMAND (H for Help): R HEL-LO.DOC <RET>

and when he starts to send you will receive the program which then goes directly to the disk when finished, or every 16 K if longer than 16 K total. You could also have said:

B>   COMMAND (H for Help): RT HEL-LO.DOC <RET>

and when the transfer was completed, it will automatically return you to the terminal mode. This is useful when tranferring programs to/from other systems, as it automatically places you in a "ready to go again" situation when the transfer is finished. Another R option would be:

B> COMMAND (H for Help): RB <RET>

This is called the *batch mode* and is an extremely useful way to receive programs automatically, from another computer using a similar program. He will use the batch mode for sending the programs and that automatically provides the file names at the receiving end. In this manner, large numbers of programs can be transferred completely automatically, including full disks. (Assuming you care to pay the toll calls for the time it will take!)

The ideal way to receive batch mode would be:

B> COMMAND (H for Help): RBT <RET>

since you may not know in advance how many programs he will be sending. When the transfer is complete, you are automatically in the T mode and he can start typing to you, immediately, with any comments relative to the progress of the transfer, etc.

S—Send programs. Similar to R but sends instead of receives. If the other system is ready to receive, you can type:

B>   COMMAND (H for Help): S HEL-LO.DOC <RET>

It will tell you how many records are involved and how many minutes and seconds it will take to send the program. If the other system is ready to receive, it starts the transfer, showing how many records have been sent. If any errors occur during transmission, it shows what they are and counts them. It will resend any records not correctly received at the other computer. If too many consecutive errors occur (usually set at 10), the program is halted and questions the operator if it should be tried again or abort. You can also use the batch mode for sending:

B> COMMAND (H for Help): SB HELLO.∗

will send all files starting with HELLO, or can send just one file, or can send several nonrelated files in this manner:

Page 2. An explanation for each three letter command in Fig. 2-4 follows:

CPM—This returns you to the CP/M program and exits MDM707. CAUTION: It does not disconnect the modem from the phone line.

DIR—Enables the user to see the library of any disk without needing to return to CP/M first. Can be adjusted when installing the program to show 3, 4, 5, etc. columns depending on the number of columns your console has available. Normally set to 5 for 80-column consoles. Shows the disk spacing remaining on the logged-in default drive. (You must log in any drive you wish to write on, or see the correct free disk space remaining.) See the LOG feature below.

ERA—Enables the user to erase any files from any disk without the need to return to CP/M first. Wild cards (∗ and ?) available.

LOG—When a new disk is inserted, you can see the directory and read files from it but cannot write to it without getting a BDOS ERR. This command allows you to log in a new disk so you can immediately write on it without first returning to CP/M for a warm boot. You can select drive and user number. (This also enables DIR to show the correct free disk space remaining.)
You can say:

LOG <RET> for same drive, user area, new
    disk
LOG A
LOG A:
LOG A14 (user areas are 0-15)
LOG A11:

SPD—Sets the delay between characters and/or delay lines in the T mode when using control-T to upload a pre-typed file. Since most bulletin boards and TYM-SHARE systems normally use line editors that require a delay after they have received a line, you can add delay between characters (in increments of 10 ms.) and/or enter delay between lines (in increments of 100 ms.). This is a preset for most systems at 50 and 500 ms. They can be changed at any time. Current values can be checked by using the ? command.

TIM—This option lets you set the file transfer time from 110 baud to 9600 baud. You can preset it (when installing the program) to the value normally used, but at times it is nice to be able to conveniently change the time shown to a different rate. Some initialization routines (discussed in the install section) can make this change automatically. This command does not show if using the PMMI board as the speed is automatically changed to agree with the current baud rate selection.

TCC—Most modem programs originally used simple checksum verification of received sectors. Most now use Cyclic Redundancy Checking which finds certain transmission errors the simple checksum system might overlook. This toggle allows the user to select checksum for those systems known to not offer CRC. When set normally to CRC, the program automatically switches to checksum after trying several times to use CRC.
TBR — Some systems use the rubout key for backspace. This toggle allows you to readily adapt to those systems. Rarely used.

TLC—Nearly all computers use control-characters to do various tasks such as move the cursor around, clear the screen, reboot the system, etc. You might want to send a control -E character to the local computer and not have it go to the remote system at the same time. Say a moment later you would like to send a control -E only to the remote computer. You would do this:

control -E   (goes to local computer
                         only)
control - control -E   (goes to the remote
                         computer only)

All other control-characters would operate in a

similar manner. This gives extra flexibility in using this program for special systems like TYM-SHAR, etc.

If using control-^is awkward, you can pick a different character when installing the program initially.

TLF—If talking to another individual, he will not automatically echo a line feed character. It is a nuisance typing control-J to turn up a new line, so activating this toggle will follow all locally typed CR with a LF if in T, E, or L mode. Very useful when chatting via the keyboard to another individual.

TXO—Used when uploading pre-typed text files to other systems such as TYM-SHAR or bulletin boards, etc. Most of those have line editors that take a moment to move the line you just finished from their edit buffer into memory. The XOFF character halts your system from sending until it is ready for a new line. Used only in the terminal mode.

CAL—PMMI command, shows the phone library for auto-dialing. If not using a PMMI, this and the following two commands will not be shown, instead NUM is shown. If typed, the telephone library is displayed. This is useful even for non-PMMI users, as will store useful phone numbers for manual dialing.

DSC—PMMI command, disconnects the modem from the phone line whenever selected. (Hangs up the phone, so as to speak.)

BYE—PMMI command, disconnects the modem from the phone line, aborts MDM707 and reboots back to normal CP/M. This enables fully automatic systems to bring up other programs when file transfers are completed. (Warm reboots unless CLDBOOT at 0122H has been given the cold boot address which some may prefer for programs off a cold reboot.)

NUM—Not shown if using PMMI. This shows the non-PMMI people the phone library numbers, if desired, for manual dialing.

DEL—If copying incoming information into memory, and you decide you do not want to bother saving it to disk after all, this closes then deletes the disk file you had opened.

NOL—When copying into memory (T mode)

for saving to disk, and you return to the command mode, you can easily lose the saved data unless you either use this "no loss of data" command before you return to T (normally resets all pointers to zero otherwise) or save it to disk with the WRT command.

WRT—saves what you have been copying to the disk file already opened for that purpose. When returning from the T mode to command mode, a warning is shown that you may lose what has been saved unless you use WRT (write to disk).

Page 3. An explanation for each control-<CHAR> command follows:

CTL-E—returns to command modem from T, L, E modes.

CTL-D—PMMI command disconnects the modem from the phone line.

CTL-@—Sends a break character to the other computer. Used in some TYM-SHAR systems, etc.

CTL-B—PMMI command, changes the baud rate from 110-710, in addition changes the file transfer time accordingly.

CTL-P—Toggles the printer on-off. Very, very useful feature. Similar to normal control -P but in this case if the modem is running faster than normal printer speed, the characters merely back into a special buffer while the printer tries to catch up. Most dot matrix printers are considerably faster than most telephone modems, however. Can be toggled at any time you are in the T, L or E modes. Often used to copy things from bulletin boards, etc. that are not worth permanently saving on disk.

CTL-Y—Used only in terminal mode. If a file was opened prior to going to "T" (terminal) mode, nothing will be saved until control-Y is typed. This places a : (colon) at the start of each new line, indicating the memory is hot and is now copying for saving to a file. You can toggle this off by using control -R.

CTL-R—Stops the copy into memory, shuts off the : (colon) at start of each line. These two commands (control -Y to start, and the control -R to stop) control what is being saved. When returning to command (via control -E), you will then be warned to save the information to disk via the WRT command or it will likely be lost. (These commands, CTL-P, CTL-Y, and CTL-R give MDM707 tremendous versatility. You can copy incoming data either to disk or to printer.)

Page 4. The special PMMI subcommands are shown in Fig. 2-5. When first using MDM707 with the PMMI board, you must tell the modem whether you need originate or answer tones. O and A are used for this purpose. This also puts the modem on-line, since up to now the actual audio tones have not been sent from the modem to the phone line. This enables it to dial prior to putting the tones on the line. In addition to telling the PMMI modem if it should use originate or answer tones, you need to tell it what baud rate to use. A typical command (once connection is made to another modem) would be:

B> COMMAND (H for Help): TO.300 <RET>

This puts the tones on the phone line for originate and at the same time sets the PMMI board for 300 baud. Another typical response might be:

B> COMMAND (H for Help): RABT.600 <RET>

This places the answer tones on the phone line, sets the program for receiving batch mode at 600 baud and returns to terminal mode when the transfer is completed.

Other optional PMMI commands seem self-explanatory, such as disconnect, etc.

PMMI Features

There are several very useful and versatile features offered exclusively for the PMMI users. These are centered around the ability to switch from originate to answer tones, change baud rates from 110, 300, 450, 600 or even 710 and also auto-dial. There are several ways to auto-dial.

☐ from the command line.
☐ from the phone number library line.

In addition, you can auto-redial from either of these lines. Once the number has auto-dialed and there is no answer, it will ask you if you want it to continuously auto-redial until it does receive an answer (or you decide to abort). When the library is shown (type CAL <RET> on the command line) you then normally just type the alphabetic character

---

Modem control:

    A - Send or receive on Answer tone
    O - Send or receive on Originate tone
    D - Disconnect option
    X - Disconnect, then reboot to CP/M

Parity options:

    1 - Set and check for odd parity
    0 - Set and check for even parity

Both ends must be capable of these options which are available only in R and S modes. The parity checking will be part of the file transfer protocol.

Speed Options:

After entering your primary and secondary options, you can set the modem speed by placing a "." after the options followed by the speed e.g., 300, 1200.

    Example: SBOT.600 will set the modem
        to run at 600 baud.

Fig. 2-5. Special PMMI page of the help guide.

at the start of that line. It will then show the number being dialed. You can also do this from the main command line if you know in advance what alphabetic chair. is associated with that particular number:

B> COMMAND (H for Help): CAL P <RET>

This calls up the P line in the library and dials that number, and then, if busy, asks if you want it to continue redialing. This works on either normal numbers or on ringback numbers. You can also use:

B> COMMAND (H for Help):
CAL 213 555 1212 <RET>

and it will dial the number specified. You can then do either of these on the library command line, as well. This gives a versatility.

Cascading Commands

Several commands may be used on the same line. Ones normally used are: A, B, D, E, L, O, Q, R, S, T, V, X (and baud rate if PMMI). A typical PMMI selection might be RABQ.300.

The commands have already been listed previously, but I will show them here in alphabetical sequence:

A- answer tones for PMMI S-100 modem, puts tones on-line.

B- batch mode (must be used at both ends if used at all).

D- disconnect when done, for PMMI S-100 modem.

E- echo mode for conversing with a system not offering echo.

L- local echo shows what you are sending if no remote echo.

O- originate tones for PMMI S-100 modem, puts tones on-line.

Q- quiet mode, suppresses messages on local console.

R- receive file transfers with CRC or checksum protocol.

S- send file transfers, also shows transfer time.

T- terminal mode—operates computer at other end like a remote terminal. Also stands for text mode. When in T mode you can copy incoming to printer or to disk, and send pretyped ASCII text files via CTL-T.

V- visual -- lets you see incoming ASCII files while being sent to the disk system.

X- disconnect when done, reboot CP/M. (Cold reboot if user has set CLDBOOT, otherwise warm reboot.)

Note: The baud rate is only used for the PMMI S-100 modem.

Typical Parameters Shown by The ? Command

By this time, most of these parameters are self-explanatory. They primarily show how the options and toggles have been set. The user can check on any of the major parameters at any time by:

☐ Typing control -E to return to command mode and

☐ Typing ? to see the list of current parameters.

For example typing ? produces the following results:

B> COMMAND (H for Help): ? <RET>

CRC mode set.
Printer is off.
Rate for the S modem time-to-send message is set to 300 baud.
Backspace is backspace.
Linefeed NOT sent after <CR> in terminal mode.
Use CTL-^ to send local command to remote.
Terminal modem file buffer is inactive.
Unused portion of buffer is 34048 bytes.
XOFF testing NOT used in terminal mode file output.
XON NOT automatically tested after <CR> in terminal mode file output.
Char. delay (terminal file mode) is: 50 ms. per character.
Line delay (terminal file mode) is: 500 ms. per character.

Installing The Program

Although this is obviously the very first thing that needs to be done, it was saved until last for several reasons. The most important of these was the need to first explain what some of the options will do when selected. By this time the user should have a fairly good idea what options would work best for him. When looking at the beginning of the program where these are selected, it should now be rather easy to pick the ones that are most useful.

There are various ways to change the program to suit a specific user. These are discussed to a modest extent in the information file called MDM707.INF. Essentially you are given several methods. You can edit MDM707.ASM with your selections, then assemble it. You can use the object code program MDM707.COM and in conjunction with a printout of MDM707.SET (a text file showing what the various bytes represent in the front part of the program) readily change the toggle options and the port numbers, etc. Or you can use DDT together with MDM707.COM and one of the overlay programs, the most versatile being MDM707.ASM. This is essentially the complete front end of MDM707.ASM, and changing those equates, etc., is identical to assembling the main program. Thus, various methods are available, one of which should provide the easiest method for your system.

Note: Although designed with special emphasis on the auto-dialing and redialing capability of the PMMI S-100 modem, the other features work equally well on non-PMMI modems.

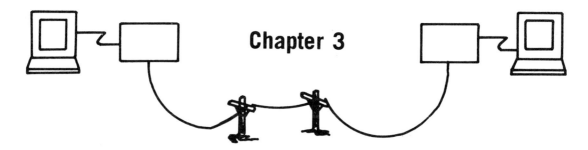

XMODEM Protocol

In exploring telecommunications it is important that you know about existing communications protocols that give us the ability to transfer messages and files between computers. The protocol used for quite a number of years by home computing enthusiasts is the XMODEM protocol, which originated simultaneously with the computer hobby movement. Consisting of a series of communications programs written in machine language, these programs and their derivatives have been in constant use for quite a while. Many different versions of these programs exist today. They have been implemented on many different home computers for the use by many different modems. The importance of the fact can not be overlooked; by constant use many of the flaws or bugs inherent in programs of that complexity have been found. So many improvements have been made, that a log of all of them fills many pages.

To get an idea of what it took to get the XMODEM series of programs to the fine state they are in today, in the last chapter, I gave you a users manual and summary of the basic workings of the MODEM/XMODEM series of programs as well as a detailed description of the MODEM/XMODEM protocol used worldwide.

In Appendix A, you are provided with references for both hardware and software that you must acquire so that you are properly equipped for telecommunications on many home computers. And in the following chapter, I take you along as I make contact with another home computer.

ACCESS PROTOCOLS

Here is what happens: after I initiate a call to another computer, I enter into a phase called *handshaking*, the subprogram used to contact the computer and the modem on the other end. Once I have successfully established the desired contact, a particular access protocol that my computer uses together with the appropriate communications software start to send and receive information. Data between two computers using the XMODEM protocol is sent in 128 byte blocks, numbered, and appended by a checksum at the end of each block.

A *checksum* is a control count of all characters contained in a block of data before the block gets transmitted. The receiving computer repeats the same calculation and then the two compare results. If all went well, one computer sends the other an *ACK*nowledge, the signal that all went well. If noise on the line or some other reason caused an interruption in the transmission, a NAK, or Negative AcKnowledgement will be used to arrange for retransmission of the garbled block. After all is well, the sending computer transmits an *EOT*, End Of Transmission, and the receiving one sends one more *ACK*.

This all goes on without much interference by the operators on either end. I have described data transmission using the protocol XMODEM in a very condensed fashion.

When using the XMODEM protocol you are dealing with two distinct program entities. The MODEM part is the one that has to reside in the calling computer, the one that originates communications. The second part of the XMODEM protocol is the software program BYE that has to reside in the answering computer, the one that receives communications. BYE, when invoked, puts the receiving computer in a wait state—waiting for the ring of the calling computer. Upon detection of the ring, request for communications, BYE detects a carrier signal and starts handshaking and sign-on procedures.

PASSWORDS AND USER LOGS

To protect the receiving computer from unauthorized access, passwords can be issued and only the user of a correct password can access the computer. Password security can be split, in other words access to a computer can be granted to everybody, but certain files can be put under password protection. This feature is used on most bulletin boards to protect private messages and to put the ability to erase messages under the control of the originator. In order to protect the receiving computers files from execution by anyone calling in, the receiving computer can arrange that all access to programs and any execution of them is also protected. This can be by password or by limiting public access to files and disc drives that are either write-protected or contain no code that can be executed.

In order to keep track of users, the BYE program contains elaborate user logs. These logs can contain information that can be selected by option. Some of the information can contain caller number, caller ID, time of sign-on, time of sign-off, and type of files accessed. Many bulletin boards are limiting their access time to one hour, and announce to the calling computer the time left in minutes.

Now, if you are interested in running a bulletin board yourself, take a look in the next chapter and see what category you would like to operate. Many boards follow the line of make, ABBS stands for Apple Bulletin Board System. Many bulletin boards use as part of their log-on a preamble identifying the type of system you have dialed into, and some have detailed files identifying the equipment used on their particular system. Observe an actual sign-on in the next chapter.

The beauty about all this telecommunications jazz is, that it has a lot in common with the old teletype operator, who could not only talk to his buddies, but he also got a lot of technical skinny over the grapevine. The similarities are also reminiscent of the ham operators.

CP/M BULLETIN BOARD COMMANDS

Before you go charging off to the next bulletin board it may behoove you to take a look at some of the commands that you may encounter. The bulletin board usually has a help facility, and many operators have set up extensive help files. Because you may want to run a bulletin board yourself, I have included detailed instructions in how to construct and use HELP files and HELP facilities, in other parts of the book, so look them up in the index, if you need to know how they operate.

Control Commands

The combination of the control key on your terminal and a letter is shown as follows: ^ S means push down first the CONTROL KEY, hold it down, and then push the letter S. It does not matter if you use a capital or lowercase s. I want to explain the meaning of the different control key/letter combinations that you will need.

^S - stops your text from scrolling on your screen, any key will continue scrolling.

^K - abandons the text you were scrolling.

^C - interrupts and abandons the process you are currently performing and returns you to the system's operating system showing you the drive user partition in use as part of the prompt, A1> means that you are logged into disc drive A using the partition 1.

^H - backspace, moves your cursor to the left.

^U - deletes the current line, line cursor is on.

^X - same as ^U.

^J - line feed.

^M - RETURN or ENTER, depending on your terminal.

^M^J - carriage return - line feed, the end of a line the carriage of course is a throwback to the typewriter.

So just remember that CONTROL S is written as ^S, and it does not matter if you use an uppercase S or a lowercase s.

Other Commands

A lot of commands in use with CP/M are three letter abbreviations of their long versions. In order to be a good navigator, I am going to equip you with a tolerable minumum of those, so that you can get around any bulletin board like a pro.

DIR - stands for DIRECTORY and will list for you all files on the currently logged disc drive. You will have to change drive and user to look at different drives/user areas. To get to a different user issue USER followed by a number from 0 to 15, you guessed it, there are up to 16 of them under CP/M.

BBS - will enter the bulletin board/message system.

BYE - will terminate your session, usually will request comments by you.

XMODEM - used to upload/download files. XMODEM is the program that receives and transmits files on the bulletin board that you are calling

up. BYE is the program that recognizes the calling computer, that uses one of the versions of the program MODEM to make the call.

HELP - HELP ? will list available subjects for self-instruction - invokes a program that has subprograms on different subjects.

TEACH - see HELP. HELP BASIC or TEACH BASIC will invoke the HELP file BASIC (if available).

TYPE - lists the contents of a file on your terminal, certain types of files can not be printed.

WHATSNEW - displays files recently added or deleted on a particular disc drive.

CHAT - allows you to talk to the systems operator, the guy that runs the bulletin board. The sysop is summoned to his computer to talk to you. Don't be surprised if he is not answering; he may be busy having some conversation.

FILE TRANSFER

The normal mode of file transfer is by the use of two complementary programs: XMODEM (on the system being called), and MODEM (on the calling system). The program XMODEM will communicate with the program MODEM on the calling system to transfer a specified file either to or from the system that is being called. To use XMODEM, enter XMODEM S FFFFFFFF.TTT to send from the computer that is being called or use XMODEM R FFFFFFFF.TTT to receive a file. Note that FFFFFFFF.TTT stands for an eight character filename.three character file type/ extension. Also, you can not receive a file with the extension .COM. All files with the extension .COM should be renamed to an .OBJ extension/type before and after transmission.

The reason a computer that you call does not leave any .COM types around is that you can not start execution of files without that extension. There are of course exceptions, such as TYPE, and of course, DIR. A sysop can use other means to hide files from you by setting given files a distinction of SYSTEM files. A system file under CP/M will not show in a DIRECTORY and can not be shown on the screen, as it will not respond to the TYPE command. Let me give you a crash course on CP/M file conventions right here.

FILE NAMING CONVENTIONS

File handling in many operating systems today follows conventions that have been used for quite a number of years by DEC, the Digital Equipment Corporation, and by CP/M. A file is named fffffff.ttt where fffffff is from one to eight characters and is referred to as the *file name*, and ttt is from zero to three characters and is known as the *file type* or interchangeably the *file extension*. Here is a little guided tour through the mumbo-jumbo of file types/extensions and what everybody thinks they mean.

Program Source Files

```
ASM — RMAC Assembler source
BAS  — BASIC source
C    — C language source
COB — COBOL source
FOR  — FORTRAN source
MAC — MAC Assembler source
PAS  — PASCAL source
PLI   — PL/I source
PLT  — PILOT source
```

Text Files And Machine Object Code Files

```
$$$  — or TMP temporary files used in editing
ASC  — ASCII text file
BAK  — Backup file — previous version of a
         Word* file
CRF  — CROSS-REFERENCE file
COM — CP/M command object code program file
DOC  — Document file
HEX  — HEXADECIMAL interim object code
         program file
PRN  — Printer listing file
REL   — Relocateable object file for Linking
SYM  — SYMBOL table fileTABLE
TXT   — Text file (usually for/from word
         processor)
```

Q Files

If you come across files which have the letter Q in the middle of the type/extension, you are dealing with a file that has been *squeezed* — a compressed format which is not readable until it has been *unsqueezed*. This technique can save a lot of file space and transmission time when sending or receiving files while Ma Bells long distance ticker is humming. This was especially true when software was in high demand and everybody wanted a new release of some goodies. The programs used to squeeze and to unsqueeze are called SQUEEZE. COM and UNSQEZ.COM, and can be found on many bulletin boards.

Help Files

To look at desired HELP files take a quick on-line lesson and enter HELP followed by the subject. Here are some quick samples.

The DIR command is many an operating system's way to search disc directories. It will list for you the files it finds and their sizes in K bytes (1,000 bytes = 1 K bytes), as well as the selected disc drive and the selected user. DIR may be followed by a wildcard * as a substitute for a filename or file extension or a wildcard ? as substitution for any given character.

DIR has its shortcomings in that it will only search one disc at a given command. Substitute FILEFIND for a global search. DIR just by itself assumes that you want a list of all the files on the current disc. DIR B: will list all the files on the B: disc. DIR *.BAS will list all files whose type is .BAS, DIR *.ASM means all .ASM files, and so on. These may be combined, as in DIR B:*.ASM to list all ASM files on the B: disc. If you desire to search for a file, but you only know the first few letters of its name, or if you group files by their names, then you can use DIR to find all files whose names begin in a specified pattern, but whose ending may be anything. The wildcard search may be used separately to the file title as well as the type. Examples:

DIR CPM*.* DIR CPM.C* DIR B: STAR*.BAS

In the next chapter, you are going to put all this to good use!

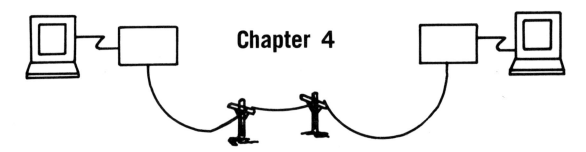

Chapter 4

Where to Go On-Line

The intent of this chapter is to acquaint the reader with computer bulletin boards. By going on-line with bulletin boards, you have access to a huge deposit of public domain software. And even more important all of this software is mostly free. The listings in this chapter will give you lots of places to look for the software you want.

COMPUTER BULLETIN BOARDS

One of the most delightful adventures is to take your computer and to hook it up to a computer bulletin board. These have been around for a while, with CACHE, the Chicago Area Computer Hobbyist's Exchange, being in business for quite a while. From my list of bulletin boards in the United States and Canada, select one that is near your home and after you have done that, I will dem-

onstrate in the next chapter an actual sign-on and a session, step by step. My list of boards carries the following anotations:

*24—denotes 24-hour operation
#1—denotes original system of that type
-rb—denotes call, let ring once and call back
-so—sexually oriented messages
-rl—religious orientation
-!—new system or new number to existing system
$—supports VADIC 1200 baud operation
&—supports 212A 1200 baud operation
%—supports BAUDOT operation

```
ABBS ABACUS II, Toledo, OH......................(419) 865 1594

ABBS ABSS, Dallas, TX..........................(214) 661 2969*24

ABBS AGS, Atlanta, GA..........................(404) 733 3461*24
```

```
ABBS AIMS, Oak Brook IL.....................(312) 789 0499*24

ABBS Akron Digital Group, Akron, OH.........(216) 745 7855*24

ABBS Apple Cider, Las Vegas, NV.............(702) 454 3417

ABBS Apple Crate I, Seattle, WA.............(206) 935 9119

ABBS Apple Crate II, Seattle, WA............(206) 244 5438

ABBS Apple Group N.J., Piscataway, NJ.......(201) 968 1074

ABBS Apple-Med, Iowa City, IA...............(319) 353 6528

ABBS Apple-Mate, New York, NY...............(201) 864 5345

ABBS Baileys Computer Store, Augusta, GA....(404) 790 8614

ABBS Baton Rouge, LA........................(504) 291 1360

ABBS Byte Shop, Ft. Lauderdale, FL..........(305) 486 2983

ABBS Byte Shop, Miami, FL...................(305) 261 3639

ABBS Calvary Mission Church, Minneapolis, MN.!(612) 471 0252

ABBS CCNJ, Pompton Plains, NJ...............(201) 835 7228

ABBS Century Next Computers, St. Louis, MO...(314) 442 6502

ABBS Charlotte, NC..........................!(704) 364 5254

ABBS Cleveland, OH..........................(216) 779 1338

ABBS CODE, Glen Ellyn IL....................(312) 537 7063*24

ABBS Colortron Computer, WI.................(414) 637 9990*24

ABBS Compumart, Ottawa, Ontario, Canada.....(613) 725 2243

ABBS Computerland, Fremont, CA..............(415) 794 9314

ABBS Computer Corner, Amarillo, TX..........(806) 355 5610

ABBS Computer Conspiracy, Santa Monica, CA...(213) 829 1140

ABBS Computer Crossroads, Columbia, MD......(301) 730 0922
```

```
ABBS Computer Lab, Memphis, TN.................(901) 761 4743

ABBS Computer Room, Kalamazoo, MI.............(616) 382 0101

ABBS Computer Store, Toledo, OH..............(419) 531 3845

ABBS Dallas Info Board.......................(214) 248 4539

ABBS Denver, CO..............................(303) 759 2625

ABBS Detroit, MI.............................(313) 477 4471

ABBS Downers Grove, IL.......................(312) 964 7768

ABBS Electro-Mart, Spokane, WA...............(509) 534 2419*24

ABBS Fort Walton Beach, Destin, FL...........(904) 243 1257

ABBS Gamemaster, Chicago, IL.................(312) 475 4884*24

ABBS Hayward, CA.............................(415) 881 5662

ABBS Illini Microcomputer, Naperville, IL....(312) 420 7995

ABBS Ketchikan, AK...........................(907) 225 6789

ABBS Louisville, KY..........................(502) 245 7811*24

ABBS Madam Bokeatha Society, Houston, TX.....(713) 455 9502

ABBS Memphis, TN.............................(901) 725 5691

ABBS Michigan Apple-Fone, Southfield, MI.....(313) 357 1422

ABBS Newport Beach, CA.....................!(714) 645 5256*24

ABBS Oak Brook Computer, Oak Brook, IL.......(312) 941 9009

ABBS Omaha, NE...............................(402) 339 7809

ABBS PCnet, San Francisco, CA................(415) 863 4703*24

ABBS Pacific Palasades, Los Angeles, CA......(213) 459 6400

ABBS Peoria, IL..............................(309) 692 6502

ABBS Phoenix, AZ.............................(602) 898 0891
```

```
ABBS Pirates Cove, Long Island, NY...........(516) 698 4008

ABBS Rogers Park, Chicago, IL................(312) 973 2227

ABBS Saddlebrook, NJ.........................(201) 843 4563

ABBS San Antonio, TX.........................(512) 737 0214*24

ABBS Software Sorcery, Herndon, VA..........!(703) 471 0610

ABBS South of Market, San Francisco, CA......(415) 469 8111-so

ABBS Spokane, WA.............................(509) 456 8900

ABBS St. Louis, MO...........................(314) 838 7784*24

ABBS Teledunjon I, Dallas, TX................(817) 469 1626

ABBS Teledunjon II, Dallas, TX...............(214) 530 0858

ABBS Teledunjon III, Dallas, TX..............(214) 960 7654

ABBS The Moon, Dallas, TX....................(214) 931 3437*24

ABBS Turnersville, NJ........................(609) 228 1149

ABBS Vancouver, B.C..........................(604) 437 7001

ABBS Vermont, Essex Junction, VT.............(802) 879 4981*24

ABBS VIBBS, Nashua, NH.......................(603) 888 6648

ABBS West Palm Beach, FL.....................(305) 848 3802

ABBS Rob Roy Computer, Yakima, WA............(509) 575 7704

ABBS Youngs Elect Svc., College Station, TX..(713) 693 3462*24

ABBS #X, Atlanta, GA.........................(404) 256 1549

A-C-C-E-S-S Annapolis, MD....................(301) 267 7666*24

A-C-C-E-S-S Olympia, WA......................(206) 866 9043*24

A-C-C-E-S-S Phoenix, AZ..................#1 (602) 996 9709*24

A-C-C-E-S-S Phoenix, AZ..................&(602) 957 4428*24
```

```
A-C-C-E-S-S Phoenix, AZ........................(602) 274 5964

A-C-C-E-S-S Scotsdale, AZ....................(602) 998 9411*24

A-C-C-E-S-S Wyckoff, NJ......................(201) 891 7441*24

AMIS A.R.C.A.D.E. Sterling Heights, MI.......(313) 978 8087*24

AMIS Chicago, IL.............................(312) 789 3610*24

AMIS APOGEE Miami, FL........................(305) 238-1231-rb

AMIS GRAFEX Cupertino, CA....................(408) 253 5216

AMIS G.R.A.S.S. Grand Rapids, MI.............(616) 241 1971*24

AMIS IBBBS San Jose, CA......................(408) 298 6930

AMIS M.A.C.E. Detroit, MI................#1 (313) 868 2064*24

AMIS Magic Lantern, Madison, WI..............(608) 251 8538

AMIS Starbase 12 Philadelphia, PA............(617) 876 4885

AMIS T.A.B.B.S. Sunnyvale, CA................(408) 942 6975

ARMUDIC Washington, DC...................#1 (202) 276 8342

ARMUDIC Computer Age, Baltimore, MD..........(301) 587 2132

BBS Annandale, VA............................(703) 978 9754

BBS B.R., Los Angeles, CA....................(213) 394 5950*24

BBS Computer Applications Co., Poland, OH....(216) 757 3711

BBS Electronic Exchange, Chicago, IL.........(312) 541 6470*24

BBS Homestead, FL............................(305) 246 1111

BBS IBM PC Billings, MT......................(406) 656 9624

BBS IBM PCUG Annandale, VA...................(703) 560 0979

BBS Living Videotext, Menlo Park, CA.........(415) 327 8876*24

BBS Pensacola, FL............................(904) 477 8783
```

```
BBS SUE Milwaukee, WI.........................(414) 483 4578

BBS-80 Cincinnati, OH.........................(513) 244 2983

BBS-80 DALTRUG, Dallas, TX....................(214) 235 8784*24

BULLET-80 Akron, OH...........................(216) 645 0827*24

BULLET-80 Boston, MA.......................&(617) 266 7789*24

BULLET-80 Chesterland, OH.....................(216) 729 2769

BULLET-80 Clarks Summit, PA...................(717) 586 2112

BULLET-80 Danbury, CT.......................#1(203) 744 4644

BULLET-80 Fayetteville, GA....................(404) 461 9686

BULLET-80 Hawkins, TX.........................(214) 769 3036

BULLET-80 Houston, TX.........................(713) 331 2599

BULLET-80 Ironton, OH.........................(614) 532 6920

BULLET-80 Lancaster, CA.......................(805) 947 9925

BULLET-80 Langhorne, PA.......................(215) 364 2180

BULLET-80 Littlefield, TX.....................(806) 385 6843

BULLET-80 Mt. Clemens, MI.....................(313) 465 9531

BULLET-80 Orange County, Anaheim, CA.........(714) 952 2110

BULLET-80 Poughkeepsie, NY....................(914) 278 2375-so

BULLET-80 Redwood City, CA....................(415) 367 1339*24

BULLET-80 Riverside, CA.......................(714) 359 3189

BULLET-80 San Jose, CA........................(408) 241 0769

BULLET-80 Seymour, CT.........................(203) 888 7952

BULLET-80 Springfield, IL.....................(217) 529 1113

BULLET-80 Tulsa, OK...........................(918) 749 0059*24
```

```
BULLET-80 Tyler, TX.............................(214) 595 4217

CBBS Atlanta, GA................................(404) 394 4220*24

CBBS Baton Rouge, LA............................(504) 273 3116*24

CBBS Bloomington, IN............................(812) 334 2522

CBBS Boston, MA.................................(617) 646 3610*24

CBBS Cedar Rapids, IA...........................(319) 364 0811

CBBS Chicago, IL.........................#1 (312) 545 8086*24

CBBS Corpus Christi, TX.........................(512) 855 1512

CBBS CPEUG/ICST Gaithersburg, MD............(301) 948 5717

CBBS Lambda, Berkeley, CA.......................(415) 658 2919-so

CBBS Lawrence General Hospital, Boston, MA...(617) 683 2119

CBBS LICA LIMBS, Long Island, NY.............(516) 561 6590*24

CBBS London, England.(European standard)..(044) 1 399 2136

CBBS Long Island, NY............................(516) 334 3134*24

CBBS MAUDE Milwaukee, WI........................(414) 241 8364*24

CBBS NW, Portland, OR...........................(503) 646 5510*24

CBBS PACC, Pittsburgh, PA.......................(412) 822 7176*24

CBBS Prince George, B.C., Canada.............(604) 562 9515

CBBS Proxima, Berkeley, CA......................(415) 357 1130

CBBS RAMS, Rochester, NY........................(716) 244 9531

CBBS Richfield, MN..............................(612) 869 5780

CBBS TSG, Tucson, AZ............................(602) 746 3956*24

CBBS Vancouver, BC, Canada......................(604) 687 2640*24

CBBS Waco, TX...................................(817) 776 1375
```

```
COMM-80 OCTUG.....................................(714) 530 8226

COMM-80 Orange County, Fullerton, CA..........(714) 530 8226

COMM-80 Queens, NY..............................(212) 897 3392*24

CONNECTION-80 Centereach, NY..................(516) 588 5836

CONNECTION-80 Denver, CO......................(303) 690 4566*24

CONNECTION-80 Escondido, CA...................!(714) 746 6265

CONNECTION-80 Fremont, CA.....................(415) 651 4147*24

CONNECTION-80 Gaithersburg, MD...............(301) 840 8588*24

CONNECTION-80 Great Neck, NY.................(516) 482 8491*24

CONNECTION-80 Lansing, MI....................(517) 339 3367

CONNECTION-80 Little Rock, AS................(501) 372 0576

CONNECTION-80 Manhattan, NY..................(212) 991 1664

CONNECTION-80 Orlando, FL....................(305) 644 8327*24

CONNECTION-80 PAUG, Portland, OR.............(503) 281 7653

CONNECTION-80 Peterborough, NH...............(603) 924 7920

CONNECTION-80 Tulsa, OK......................(918) 747 1310*24

CONNECTION-80 W. Mich. Micro Group, MI.......(616) 457 1840*24

CONNECTION-80 Winter Garden, FL..............(305) 877 2829*24

CONNECTION-80 Woodhaven, NY..................(212) 441 3755*24

CONNECTION-80 Tampa, FL......................(813) 977 0989

CONFERENCE-TREE #2, San Francisco, CA........(415) 928 0641

CONFERENCE-TREE #3, Hayward, CA..............(415) 538 3580

CONFERENCE-TREE #4, Santa Monica, CA.........(213) 394 1505

CONFERENCE-TREE Anchorage, AK................(907) 344 5251
```

```
CONFERENCE-TREE Flagship, Denville, NJ.......(201) 627 5151*24

CONFERENCE-TREE Kelp Bed, Los Angeles, CA....(213) 372 4800

CONFERENCE-TREE Minneapolis, MN..............(612) 227 0307

CONFERENCE-TREE ?, New Jersey................(201) 627 5151

CONFERENCE-TREE Victoria, TX.................(512) 578 5833

DIAL-YOUR-MATCH #1...........................(213) 842 3322-so

DIAL-YOUR-MATCH #3...........................(912) 233 0863-so

DIAL-YOUR-MATCH #4...........................(213) 704 9819-so

DIAL-YOUR-MATCH #7...........................(212) 456 2528-so

DIAL-YOUR-MATCH #9...........................(213) 345 1047-so

DIAL-YOUR-MATCH #11.........................!(714) 242 1882

FORUM-80 Albany, NY..........................(518) 785 8478

FORUM-80 Augusta, GA.........................(803) 279 5392

FORUM-80 Charleston, SC......................(803) 552 1612*24

FORUM-80 Cleveland, OH.....................&(216) 486 4176

FORUM-80 #1, Denver, CO......................(303) 341 0636*24

FORUM-80 #2, Denver, CO......................(303) 399 8858*24

FORUM-80 El Paso, TX.........................(915) 755 1000*24

FORUM-80 Ft. Lauderdale, FL..................(305) 772 4444*24

FORUM-80 Hull, England..................(011) 44 482 859169

FORUM-80 Kansas City, MO.................#1 &(816) 861 7040*24

FORUM-80 Kansas City, MO.....................&(816) 931 9316

FORUM-80 Las Vegas, NV.......................(702) 362 3609*24

FORUM-80 Linden, NJ..........................(201) 486 2956*24
```

```
FORUM-80 Medford, OR............................(503) 535 6883*24

FORUM-80 Medical, Memphis, TN..................(901) 276 8196*24

FORUM-80 Monmouth, NJ..........................(201) 528 6623*24

FORUM-80 Montgomery, AL........................(205) 272 5069

FORUM-80 Nashua, NH............................(603) 882 5041

FORUM-80 Orange County, Anaheim, CA..........(714) 545 9549

FORUM-80 Pontiac, MI...........................(313) 335 8456

FORUM-80 Prince William County, VA...........(703) 670 5881*24

FORUM-80 San Antonio, TX.......................(512) 340 6720

FORUM-80 Seattle, WA...........................(206) 723 3282

FORUM-80 Sierra Vista, AZ......................(602) 458 3850*24

FORUM-80 Shreveport, LA........................(318) 631 7107*24

FORUM-80 Westford, MA..........................(617) 692 3973

FORUM-80 Wichita, KA.........................&(316) 682 2113*24

FORUM-80 Wichita Falls, TX.....................(817) 855 3916

HBBS Denver, CO................................(303) 343 8401*24

HBBS El Paso, TX...............................(915) 592 1910

HBBS Oklahoma City, OK.........................(405) 848 9329*24

HBBS San Fernando Valley.......................(213) 366 4837

MCMS C.A.M.S. Chicago, IL..................#1 (312) 927 1020*24

MCMS J.A.M.S. Lockport, IL.....................(815) 838 1020*24

MCMS L.A.M.S. Round Lake, IL...................(312) 740 9128

MCMS Message-82, Chicago, IL...................(312) 622 4442*24

MCMS Metro West Database, Chicago, IL........(312) 260 0640*24
```

```
MCMS NC Software, Minneapolis, MN.............(612) 533 1957*24

MCMS WACO Hot Line, Schaumburg, IL..<pvt>....(312) 351 4374*24

MICRO-COM Computer City, Weston, CT..........(203) 227 1829

MOUSE-NET Nashua, NH.........................(603) 673 9476*24

MOUSE-NET Orlando, FL........................(305) 277 0473*24

MSG-80 Everett, WA...........................(206) 334 7394

NESSY Chicago, IL.........................#1 (312) 773 3308

NESSY Terry and Gwen's, Palatine, IL.........(312) 289 6393

NET-WORKS Apple Grove, Dallas, TX............(214) 644 5197

NET-WORKS Apple Shack, Dallas, TX............(214) 644 4781*24

NET-WORKS Armadillo, Grand Fork, ND..........(701) 746 4959

NET-WORKS Aurora, CO.........................(303) 343 8401*24

NET-WORKS Big Apple, Miami, FL...............(305) 948 8000

NET-WORKS C.A.M.S., Decatur, IL..............(217) 429 5541

NET-WORKS CLAH, Arlington Heights, IL........(312) 255 6489

NET-WORKS Coin Games, Los Angeles, CA........(213) 336 5535

NET-WORKS COMM Center NW3NAGAD, Laurel, MD...(301) 953 1110

NET-WORKS Computer City, Providence, RI......(401) 331 8450*24

NET-WORKS Computer Emporium, Des Moines, IA..(515) 279 8863

NET-WORKS Computer Emporium, San Jose, CA....(408) 227 0227

NET-WORKS Computer Pro, Ft. Worth, TX........(817) 732 1787

NET-WORKS Computer Station, St. Louis, MO....(314) 432 7120

NET-WORKS Computer World, Los Angeles, CA....(213) 859 0894*24

NET-WORKS Crescent City, Baton Rouge, LA.....(504) 454 6688
```

```
NET-WORKS Dallas, TX............................(214) 361 1386*24

NET-WORKS Dayton, OH............................(513) 223 3672

NET-WORKS Eclectic Computer Sys., Dallas, TX.(214) 239 5842

NET-WORKS Encino, CA............................(213) 345 3670

NET-WORKS Granite City, IL.....................(618) 877 2904

NET-WORKS Greenfield, IN.......................(317) 326 3833*24

NET-WORKS Hacker-net, Dallas, TX..............(214) 824 7160

NET-WORKS Hawaii...............................(808) 521 7312

NET-WORKS Info-Net, Costa Mesa, CA...........(714) 545 7359

NET-WORKS MAGIE, Galesburg, IL...............(309) 342 7178

NET-WORKS Magnetic Fantasies, Los Angeles, CA(213) 388 5198

NET-WORKS Montreal, Canada.....................(514) 937 2188*24

NET-WORKS Pirate's Harbor, Boston, MA.........(617) 738 5051

NET-WORKS Pirate's Inn.........................(213) 454 3075

NET-WORKS Pirate's Nest, Weston, CT...........(203) 227 1829

NET-WORKS Pirate's Ship, Chicago, IL.........(312) 935 2933*24

NET-WORKS Portsmouth, NH.......................(603) 436 3461

NET-WORKS Softworx, West Los Angeles, CA.....(213) 473 2754

NET-WORKS Sparklin' City, Corpus Christi, TX.(512) 882 6569

NET-WORKS St. Louis, MO........................(314) 781 1308

NET-WORKS Warlock's Castle St. Louis, MO.....(618) 345 6638

NET-WORKS Winesap, Dallas, TX.................(214) 824 7455

ONLINE CDC, San Diego, CA....................!(714) 452 6012

ONLINE Houston, TX.............................(713) 528 7025*24
```

```
ONLINE Dickinsons Movie Guide, Mission, KS...(913) 432 5544

ONLINE Indianapolis, IN.<ID#=GUES, pswd=pass>(317) 787 9881*24

ONLINE ON-LINE Computer Center, KC, MO.......(913) 341 7987

ONLINE Saba, San Diego, CA...................!(714) 291 5229

ONLINE Santee, CA....<ID#=GUEST, pswd=PASS>..(714) 561 7271*24

PASBBS Bellflower, CA........................(213) 531 1057

PASBBS Torrance, CA..........................#1 (213) 516 7089*24

PBBS Co-operative Comp Svc, Palatine, IL.....(312) 359 9450*24

PET BBS S.E.W.P.U.G., Racine, WI.............(414) 554 9520*24

PET BBS Commodore Comm., Lake St. Louis, MO.!(314) 625 4576*24

PMS - **IF**, Anaheim, CA....................(714) 772 8868*24

PMS - Anchorage, AK..........................(907) 344 8558

PMS - Apple Bits, Kansas City, MO............(913) 341 3502*24

PMS - Apple Guild, Weymouth, MA..............(617) 767 1303*24

PMS - Arlington Heights, IL..................(312) 870 7176*24

PMS - Baltimore, MD..........................(301) 764 1995*24

PMS - Campbell, CA...........................(408) 370 0873*24

PMS - Century 23, Las Vegas, NV..............!(702) 878 9106*24

PMS - Chicago, IL............................(312) 373 8057*24

PMS - Cincinnati, OH.........................(513) 671 2753

PMS - Computer City, Danvers, MA.............(617) 774 7516

PMS - Ellicott City, MD......................(301) 465 3176

PMS - Escondido, CA..........................(714) 746 0667

PMS - Ft. Smith Computer Club, Ft. Smith, AK!(501) 646 0197
```

```
PMS - Gulfcoast, Freeport, TX.................(713) 233 7943*24

PMS - Indianapolis, IN........................(317) 787 5486*24

PMS - Lakeside, CA. (type PMS to activate)...(714) 561 7271*24

PMS - Los Angeles, CA.........................(213) 334 7614*24

PMS - Massillon, OH...........................(216) 832 8392*24

PMS - McGraw-Hill Books, New York, NY.........(212) 997 2488

PMS - Mesa Systems, San Diego, CA............!(714) 271 8613

PMS - Minneapolis, MN.........................(612) 929 6699*24

PMS - Mission Valley, CA......................(714) 295 8280

PMS - I.A.C., Lake Forest, IL.................(312) 295 6926*24

PMS - O.A.C., Woodland Hills, CA..............(213) 346 1849*24

PMS - Pikesville, MD..........................(301) 653 3413

PMS - Pleasanton, CA..........................(415) 462 7419*24

PMS - Portola Valley, CA......................(415) 851 3453*24

PMS - RAUG, Akron, OH.........................(216) 867 7463*24

PMS - Richland, WA............................(509) 943 6502*24

PMS - Rutgers Univ. Microlab, Piscataway, NJ.(201) 932 3887

PMS - San Diego, CA...........................(714) 582 9557*24

PMS - Santa Clara, CA.........................(408) 554 9036

PMS - Santa Cruz, Aptos, CA...................(408) 688 9629*24

PMS - Santee, CA...........................#1 (714) 561 7277*24

PMS - Shrewsbury, NJ..........................(201) 747 6768

PMS - Software Unltd, Kenmore, WA.............(206) 486 2368*24

PMS - Your Computer Connection, KS Cty, MO...(913) 381 1021
```

```
PSBBS Baltimore, MD.............................(301) 994 0399*24

PSBBS Washington, DC............................(202) 337 4694*24

RATS Systems...........................#1 (201) 887 8874

RATS Pequannock, NJ.............................(201) 696 8647

RATS Little Falls, NJ..........................(201) 785 3565

RATS Homewood, IL..............................(312) 957 3924

RATS Wenonah, NJ...............................(609) 468 5293

RATS Wenonah, NJ #2............................(609) 468 3844

RBBS Big Top, Milwaukee, WI....................(414) 259 9475

RCP/M AABB New York, NY........................(212) 787 5520

RCP/M AIMS Hinsdale, IL.......................!(312) 789 0499

RCP/M Arlington, VA...........................!(703) 536 3769

RCP/M CBBS ANAHUG, Anaheim, CA.................(714) 774 7860

RCP/M CBBS CF/M Net Simi Valley, CA..........(805) 527 9321

RCP/M CBBS Columbus, OH........................(614) 272 2227*24

RCP/M CBBS Frog Hollow, Vancouver, BC, CN...!(604) 873 4007*24

RCP/M CBBS HUG, Chicago, IL...................(312) 671 4992*24

RCP/M CBBS Pasadena, CA.......................(213) 799 1632*24

RCP/M CBBS RLP, MacLean, VA..................!(703) 524 2549*24

RCP/M CBBS Sacramento, CA....................!(916) 483 8718*24

RCP/M CBBS Vancouver, BC, Canada.............(604) 687 2640*24

RCP/M Chuck Forsberg, OR.....................!(503) 621 3193

RCP/M Collossal Oxgate, ?? ..................!(408) 263 2588

RCP/M CUG-NOTE, Denver, CO...................!(303) 781 4937*24
```

```
RCP/M CUG-NODE, PA State College.............!(814) 238 4857*24
RCP/M Detroit, MI...............................(313) 584 1044-rb
RCP/M Geneseo, IL.............................!(309) 944 5455
RCP/M HAPN Hamilton, Ontario, CN.............!(416) 335 6620*24
RCP/M IBM-PC, Niles, IL......................&!(312) 647 7636*24
RCP/M Logan Square, Chicago, IL...............(312) 252 2136
RCP/M MCBBS Keith Petersen, Royal Oak, MI....(313) 759 6569-rb
RCP/M MCBBS Ken Stritzel, Flanders, NJ.......!(201) 584 9227*24
RCP/M MCBBS Superbrain, Lexington, MA......$&(617) 862 0781*24
RCP/M MCBBS TCBBS Dearborn, MI................(313) 846 6127*24
RCP/M Mississauga, Toronto, Ontario, CN....$&(416) 826 5394*24
RCP/M Mississauga HUG, Toronto, Ontario, CN$&(416) 826 5394*24
RCP/M NEI, Chicago, IL........................(312) 949 6189
RCP/M Palatine, IL...........................&(312) 359 2553*24
RCP/M Piconet Oxgate, ?? .....................(415) 965 4097*24
RCP/M RBBS Allentown, PA......................(215) 398 3937*24
RCP/M RBBS ANAHUG, Anaheim, CA................(714) 774 7860*24
RCP/M RBBS Arvada Elect., Colorado Springs,CO(303) 634 1158*24
RCP/M RBBS Boulder, CO........................(303) 499 9169
RCP/M RBBS Bethesda, MD......................!(301) 229 3196
RCP/M RBBS Comp. Tech. Assoc., El Paso, TX..!(915) 533 2202*24
RCP/M RBBS Computerized Services, Tampa, FL..(813) 839 6746
RCP/M RBBS Computron, Edmonton, Alberta, Can.(403) 482 6854*24
RCP/M RBBS Cranford, NJ.......................(201) 272 1874
```

```
RCP/M RBBS DataTech, San Carlos, CA..........(415) 595 0541

RCP/M RBBS Edmonton, Alberta, Canada.........(403) 454 6093*24

RCP/M RBBS El Paso, TX.......................(915) 598 1668

RCP/M RBBS Fort Mill, SC.....................(803) 548 0900*24

RCP/M RBBS GFRN Dta Exch., Garden Grove, CA$&(714) 534 1547*24

RCP/M RBBS GFRN Dta Exch., Palos Verdes, CA$&(213) 541 2503*24

RCP/M RBBS Grafton, VA.....................!(804) 898 7493

RCP/M RBBS Huntsville, AL....................(205) 895 6749-rb

RCP/M RBBS Hyde Park, IL.....................(312) 955 4493

RCP/M RBBS Laurel, MD......................!(301) 953 3753*24

RCP/M RBBS Larkspur, CA......................(415) 461 7726*24

RCP/M RBBS Long Island, NY...................(516) 698 8619-rb

RCP/M RBBS Marin County, CA................!(415) 383 0473*24

RCP/M RBBS MUG, Mission, KS.................&(913) 362 9583*24

RCP/M RBBS Napa Valley, CA...................(707) 253 1523

RCP/M RBBS New York, NY......................(516) 791 1767

RCP/M RBBS Ocean, NJ.......................&(201) 775 8705

RCP/M RBBS San Jose Oxgate, San Jose, CA....!(408) 287 5901*24

RCP/M RBBS Surrey, Vancouver, BC, CN........!(604) 5842643*24

RCP/M RBBS Pontiac, MI.....................!(313) 338 85-5

RCP/M RBBS Paul Bogdanovich, NJ............!(201) 747 7301

RCP/M RBBS Rochester, NY.....................(716) 223 1100*24

RCP/M RBBS Rutgers, New Brunswick, NJ........(201) 932 3879*24

RCP/M RBBS San Diego, CA..................$&!(714) 273 4354*24
```

```
RCP/M RBBS Sofwaire Store, Los Angeles, CA...(213) 479 3189*24F

RCP/M RBBS Software Tools, Austrailia......... (02) 997 1836

RCP/M RBBS South Florida.......................(305) 255 6027

RCP/M RBBS Southfield, MI......................(313) 559 5326*24

RCP/M RBBS Thousand Oaks, CA...................(805) 496 9522*24

RCP/M RBBS Westland, MI........................(313) 729 1905-rb

RCP/M RBBS Woodstock, NY......................!(914) 679 8734

RCP/M RBBS Yelm, WA............................(206) 458 3086-rb

RCP/M Silicon Valley, CA.....................!(408) 246 5014*24

RCP/M SJBBS Bearsville, NY.....................(914) 679 6559-rb

RCP/M SJBBS Johnson City, NY...................(607) 797 6416

RCP/M TRS-80 Chicago, IL.......................(312) 949 6189

RCP/M Terry O'Brien, Vancouver, BC, Canada...(604) 584 2543

Remote Northstar Atlanta, GA..............#1 (404) 926 4318*24

Remote Northstar Denver, CO...................(303) 444 7231

Remote Northstar Largo, FL....................(813) 535 9341*24

Remote Northstar NASA, Greenbelt, MD.........(301) 344 9156

Remote Northstar Santa Barbara, CA...........(805) 682 7876

Remote Northstar Santa Barbara, CA...........(805) 964 4115

Remote Northstar Virginia Beach, VA..........(804) 340 5246

ST80-CC Lance Micklus, Inc., Burlington, VT#1(802) 862 7023*24

ST80-PBB Monroe Camera Shop, Monroe, NY......(914) 782 7605

TCBBS B.A.M.S. New York, NY...................(212) 362 1040*24

TCBBS Leigh's Computer World, NY.............(212) 879 7698
```

```
TCBBS W.E.B.B. New York, NY...................#1(212) 799 4649

TRADE-80 Ft. Lauderdale, FL................#1 (305) 525 1192

TRADE-80 Omaha, NE.............................(402) 292 6184

TRADE-80 Erie, PA..............................(814) 898 2952*24

Adventure BBS..................................(516) 621 9296

Alpha, Tampa, FL..<acct#=ABCD00, pwd=TRYIT>..(813) 251 4095*24

Apollo's Chariot, Apollo, FL..................(813) 645 3669

ARBB Seattle, WA...............................(206) 546 6239

Aunt Dru'S X Rated, North Whales, PA..........(215) 855 3809

Aviators Bulletin Board, Sacramento, CA.......(916) 393 4459

Bathroom Wall BBS, San Antonio, TX...........!(512) 655 8143

Baton Rouge Data System, Baton Rouge, LA.....(504) 926 0181

Boston Information Exchange, Boston, MA......&(617) 423 6985*24

Bronx BBS, NY..................................(212) 933 9459

BR's BBS Santa Monica, CA.....................(213) 394 5950

Bradley Computer BBS .........................(813) 734 7103

BSBB Tampa, FL................................(813) 885 6187

Capital City BBS, Albany, NY..................(518) 346 3596*24

Carrier 2 Alexandria, VA......................(703) 823 5210

C-HUG Bulletin Board, Fairfax, VA............(703) 360 3812*24

Compusystems, Columbia, SC....................(803) 771 0922

Computer Arts Message System, Newhall, CA....(805) 255 6445

Computer Conspiracy...........................(213) 829 1140

Corsair, Goldcoast, FL........................(305) 968 8653
```

```
CoxCo, Arvada, CO..............................(303) 423 5001*24

Databoard BBS, Atherton, CA...................!(415) 367 7638*24

Datamate, Canoga Park, CA....................#1 (213) 998 7992-so

Dimension-80 Orange, CA.........................(714) 974 9788

Dragon's Game System........(pass=DRAGON)...(213) 428 5206

Electric Line Connection, Sherman Oaks, CA...(213) 789 9512

Experimental-80 Kansas City, MO..............(913) 676 3613

FBBS Skokie, IL...............................#1 (312) 677 8514

Greene Machine, WPB, FL.......................(305) 965 4388-so

Hermes-80 Allentown, PA......................(215) 434 3998

HEX Silver Spring,MD..........................%(301) 593 7033*24

HMS Horny MessageSystem, Oakland, CA........(415) 845 2079-so

IAC Message Base, Menlo Park, CA.............(415) 367 1339*24

INFO-NET Foster City, CA.....................(415) 349 3126

INFOEX-80 West Palm Beach, FL................(305) 683 6044*24

JCTS Redmond, WA.............................(206) 883 0403*24

Kinky Kumputer, San Francisco, CA...........(415) 647 9524-so

Kluge Computer Whittier, CA..................$&(213) 947 8128*24

L.A. Interchange, Los Angeles, CA...........(213) 631 3186*24

Lehigh Press BB, PA..........................#1 (215) 435 3388

Long Beach Community Computer...............(213) 591 7239*24

Mail Board-82 Seattle, WA....................(206) 527 0897*24

Market 80, Kansas City, MO...................(816) 931 9316

MARS/RP Rogers Park, IL......................(312) 743 8176*24
```

```
Micro-80 West Palm Beach, FL..................(305) 686 3695

Micro Informer.................................(813) 884 1506

Midwest, St. Louis, MO.........................(314) 227 4312-so

Mini-Bin Seattle, WA...........................(206) 762 5141*24

NBBS Norfolk, VA..............................!(804) 444 3392

New England Comp. Soc., Maynard, MA...........(617) 897 0346

New Jersey TELECOM.........................#1 (201) 635 0705*24

NMS Natick, MA................................(617) 653 4282*24

North  Largo, FL..............................(813) 535 9341*24

North Orange County Computer Club.............(714) 633 5240

Novation CO., Los Angeles, CA....<pass=CAT>..(213) 881 6880

Nybbles-80 Elmsford, NY.......................(914) 592 5385

OARCS Portland, Oregon........................(503) 641 2798

Oracle North Hollywood, CA....................(213) 980 6743-so

ORACLE Classified System, Austin, TX..........(512) 346 4495

Orange County Data Exchange, Garden Grove, CA(714) 537 7913

Personal Message System-80, Deerfield Bch, FL(305) 427 6300*24

PHOTO-80, Haledon, NJ.........................(201) 790 6795

Potomac Micro Magic Inc., Falls Church, VA...(703) 379 0303*24

Remote Apple Jackson, MS......................(601) 992 1918*24

SATUG BBS, San Antonio, TX...................!(512) 494 0285

Scanboard-80, Atlanta, GA.....................(404) 457 8384

Seacomm-80 Seattle, WA........................(206) 763 8879*24

SIGNON Reno, NV...................<pswd=FREE>..(702) 826 7234
```

```
SISTER Staten Island, NY..............................(212) 442 3874*24

SLAMS St. Louis, MO...................................(314) 839 4307

SMBBS New York, NY....................................(212) 884 5408

Sunrise Omega-80, Oakland, CA.....................(415) 452 0350

Talk-80 ROBB, Portsmouth, VA.....................(804) 484 9636

TCUG BBS, Washington, DC..........................(703) 451 8475*24

Telcom 7 New Fairfield, CT.......................(203) 746 5763*24

Telemessage-80, Atlanta, GA.....................(404) 962 0616

Westside Download, Detroit, MI.................(313) 533 0254

Wild goose board, ?  .........................(813) 988 7400

XBBS Hamilton, OH................................(513) 863 7681*24

ZBBS Minneapolis, MN............................(612) 426 9028
```

Enough? The next thing you must learn is the sign of a popular bulletin board — the busy signal! If you are fortunate and own one of the more expensive modems with auto-dial, you can set up your computer to redial until the number is available and then be summoned to the console. The other alternative is for you to keep trying to look for a number that is available. Having choosen a board, we now come to the moment of truth: let us begin!

OTHER SOURCES OF SOFTWARE

Here are more bulletin boards that you can use as sources and contacts to obtain all that free software. A summary of many operating CP/M

software exchange bulletin boards using the MODEM/XMODEM protocol for the exchange of public domain software follows.

Unless otherwise indicated all systems are up 24 hours a day seven days a week with no callback. Hours are listed after the sysop's name, all times listed are local time. Callback systems are indicated with a cb. Alternate Long Distance Services are shown after the phone number: I=ITT, M=MCI, S=Sprint, W=Western Union. Baud rates are shown after sysop's name or hours: 1=110, 3=300, 4=450, 6=600, 7=710, B=Bell 212A 1200, V=Vadic 1200. Disc Capacity, DSK, is the total disk space shown after baud rates: K=Kilobytes, M=Megabytes.

```
NORTHEAST
Connecticut

Rainbow DBBS RCP/M................... (203) 865-1794 IMSW

Jim Ryan; (3B;5M); Osborne Kaypro Compaq IBM;

16 Bit Software (New Haven)
```

Maine

Programmer's Anonymous RCP/M .... (207) 839-2337 W
Ralph Trynor; (3B;180K); Osborne Software; (Gorham)

Milford RCPM/CBBS .... (617) 478-4164 W
Howard Moulton Jr.; (3B;180K); system is Osborne 1

Milford S-100 User's System .... (617) 478-6062 W
Howard Moulton Jr.; (no answer when in use); (3B;1.1M);
access password = PDBIN (must be upper case only);
IMSAI S-100 w/Z80

Bellingham RBBS .... (617) 966-0416 W
Jim Devoid; (no answer when in use); (3;180K);
Heath H8 system

Massachusetts
SuperBrain RCPM .... (617) 862-0781 IMSW
Paul Kelly; M-F 7P-7A wknd 24 hrs; (3BV;300K); Superbrain
CP/M programs; (Lexington)

New Hampshire
Nashua NH RCP/M &C-80 BBS........... (603) 888-4488 MS
Steve Peterfreund; (1,3,4,B;1.9M); DEC Communications Ham C;
(So. New Hampshire)

New York
Manhattan RCP/M RBBS .... (212) 255-7240 IMSW

Dwight Ernest; (3B;550K); Ham Radio Typesetting UNIX; (NYC)

C U R A RCP/M .... (212) 625-5931 MSW
Brian Callahan; (3;10M); Kaypro Osborne Zram Softbox;
(Fort Greene Brooklyn)

Mid-Suffolk RCP/M and Data Exchange (516) 751-5639 MSW
Al Klein; M-F 5P-9A 5P Fri-9A Mon; (3;400K); (Long Island)

LION RCP/M (Long Island Osborne Network) (516) 472-3111 IMSW
Lenny Jacobs; (up Mon. and Tues. nights ONLY; 9P Mon-7A Tues
and 8P Fri-8A Sat); (3;180K); (Long Island)

Johnson City NY SJBBS .... (607) 797-6416 W
Charles; Eves etc.; (3;2M); (Upstate NY)

Rochester RBBS .... (716) 425-1785 IMSW
Arnie McGall; (3BV;2.4M); (Upstate NY)

Brewster RBBS .... cb (914) 279-5693 W
Paul Bosshold Carl Erhorn; M-F 9P-8A wknd 24 hrs;
(1-7;500K); (Downstate NY)

Bearsville Town SJBBS .... (914) 679-6559 W
Hank Szyszka; (1-7;4M); (Upstate NY)

Woodstock RCP/M RBBS .... (914) 679-8734 W
John Doak; (134B;2.8M); (answers after 3rd ring)

Ham radio software. CPMUG RCPM library available.

Ontario Canada

Toronto Ontario RCP/M System THREE . (416) 231-1262 M
Jud Newell; (3B;16M); available as free system until
membership filled; Kaypro II w/ Xebec Hard Disk.

Rhode Island
Providence RCP/M .... cb (401) 751-5025 MSW
Mark Rippe; 10A Sat-10P Sun; (3;1.2M)

EAST CENTRAL
Maryland

BHEC RBBS/RCPM .... (301) 661-2175 IMSW
Walt Jung,Charlie Schnepf,Harry Barley; (3;10M); (Baltimore)

Microcomp. Electr. Info. Exchange... (301) 948-5718 MSW
John Junod Lynne Rosenthal; (3;64K); (Gaithersburg)

Laurel MD. RCPM/RBBS .... (301) 953-3753 SW
Wayne Hammerly; (3 B;64M); Note numbers 953-3753,3754
are 300 baud, 953-3755 is 1200 baud; (Washington DC area)

New Jersey

CP/M-Net (tm) East (The Second!) ... (201) 249-0691 IMSW
(Sysop anonymous); (3B;20M); (Piscataway NJ)

RIBBS of Cranford New Jersey ...... (201) 272-1874 MSW
Bruce Ratoff; (1-7 B on request;3M); bulletin board of
SIG/M (Special Interest Group/Microcomputers ACGNJ)

KUGNJ1 RBBS Atlantic Highlands NJ . (201) 291-8319 MSW
George Frankle; (3B;400K (10M soon)); RBBS of Kaypro User
Group of New Jersey; (Password= KUGNJ1)

Flanders NJ RCPM .... (201) 584-9227 W
Ken Stritzel; (3B 1-7 on request;26M)

The C-Line .... (201) 625-1797 SW
David Fiedler; M-F 8P-9A
wknd 24 hrs; (1-7;2M); UNIX/UNIX-like systems
C software; (Northwest NJ)

Paul Bogdanovich's RBBS .... (201) 747-7301 SW
Paul Bogdanovich; M-F 6P-11P wknd 8A-11P; (1-7;1M)

Pennsylvania

Allentown RBBS/RCPM System .... (215) 398-3937 IMSW
Bill Earnest; (1-7BV;10M); bulletin board of the Lehigh
Valley Computer Club

State College PA. CUG-NODE .... (814) 238-4857 W
Joe Shannon; (3;3M)

Virginia

Arlington RCPM/DBBS of Virginia .... (703) 536-3769 IMSW
Eliot Ramey; M-F 10P-3P wknd random; (1-7;800K); (DC area)

OxGate-007 Grafton VA .... (804) 898-7493 SW
Dave Holmes; (3;200K); CP/M TRS-80 & Apple software;
(Tidewater)

MIDWEST
Illinois
Logan Square RCPM .... (312) 252-2136 IMSW
Earl Bockenfeld; (1-7;1M); Special interest databases. Daily
change on B; (Chicago)

IBM-PC BBS .... (312) 259-8086 IMSW
Gene Plantz; M-F 6P-7A wknd 24 hrs; (3BV;200K); (Chicago area)

Chicago C-NODE .... (312) 352-5681 MSW
? Sysop; M-F 5P-7A wknd 24 hrs; (1-7;20M); system organized
in 'Rooms' use HELP after login.

Palatine RCPM .... (312) 359-8080 IMSW
Tim Cannon; (3B;4.8M); Disks on B C & D are changed daily;
(Chicago area)

AIMS Hinsdale Ill . ... (312) 789-0499 IMSW
Mark Pulver; (1-7;10M); (Chicago area)

NEI RCPM System .... (312) 949-6189 IMSW
Chuck Witbeck; M-F 6P-1A wknd 12P-1A; (1-7;2M);
communications programs; (Chicago area)

Kansas
Wichita RBBS/RCPM .... (316) 682-9093 SW
George Winters; (8P Fri-11P Sun); (3B;300K); member of FOG
OPEK (Osborne Portable Enthusiasts of Kansas) chapter.

Mission KA RCPM .... (913) 362-9583 SW
Dave Kobets; (3B;2M)

AlphaNet RCP/M RBBS .... (913) 843-4259 MW
Larry Miller; 6P-9A daily; (3;700K); B drive changes daily;
(Lawrence)

Michigan
Schooner Cove (Ypsilanti) RCP/M .... (313) 483-0070 SW
Michael Wesley; (3;644K); B: changed daily, sysop will
mount any disk on request. (Ann Arbor-Detroit area)

MINICBBS/Sorcerer's Apprentice Group (313) 535-9186 IMSW
Bob Hageman; (1-7;500K); Sorcerer software and hardware;
(Detroit area)

Southfield MI RBBS/RCPM .... (313) 559-5326 IMSW
Howard Booker; (3;2.7M); BDS C programs doc. files.

Royal Oak CP/M .... cb (313) 759-6569 IMSW

Keith Petersen; (1-7 B on request;10M); (Detroit area)

Technical CBBS .... (313) 846-6127 IMSW

Dave Hardy; (1-7;3M); RCPM sysops desiring access to

passworded RCPM Clearing House system should leave msg on

TCBBS; (Detroit)

Missouri

OxGate-009 St. Louis BBS/RCPM ...... (314) 227-3258 MSW

Don Brown; M-F 7P-9A (sometimes 24 hrs); (3B;2M)

Ohio

West Carrolton RCP/M .... (513) 435-5201 SW

Rich Malafa Bob Drake; (1-7;11M); (Dayton)

Cincinnatti RBBS .... (513) 489-0149 SW

Henry Deutsch; 6P-6A daily; (1-7;1.8M)

Columbus CBBS .... (614) 272-CBBS IMSW

John Walpole; (1-7;300K); BDS-C programs

Pickerington RBBS .... (614) 837-3269 SW

Greg Bridgewater; (3;1M); Running TRS-80 with Omikron

Wisconsin

Beer City BBS .... (414) 355-8839 IMSW

Jim Miller Mike Wesolowski and Tim Winslow; (1-7;5M 16M);

Running on three seperate systems. Call system for individual board times. Heath Osborne TRS80 Software; (Milwaukee)

Fort Fone File Folder .... (414) 563-9932 W
Al Jewer Shawn Everson Ron Fowler; (1-7;20M); (Ft. Atkinson)

SOUTH

Alabama
NACS/UAH RBBS/RCPM .... cb (205) 895-6749 W
Don Wilkes; (1-7;700K); (Huntsville)

Florida
Orlando RCPM/RBBS .... (305) 671-2330 IMSW
Larry Snyder; (3B;3.3M); communications dBase Heath PDS; (Winter Park FL)

Tampa RCP/M .... (813) 831-7276 IMSW
Charlie Hoffman; (3B;2.4M); CP/M programs. Interest in 'C'; RCP/M for the Tampa Bay CP/M User's Group

Tampa Bay Bandit Board RCP/M .... (813) 937-3608 IMW
Steve Sanders; (3;200k); Special interest in Kaypro ZCPR2; RCP/M for the Tampa Bay Kaypro User's Group

Georgia
Atlanta RCP/M....................... (404) 627-7127 IMSW
Jim Altman; (3;1.8M); Interest in 'C'

Louisiana

REDSTICK RCPM ....temporarily out of service IMSW
Back up soon with new SYSOP (Ken Shutt), Phone number, and
hours. Old USER Nos still valid for signon. (Baton Rouge)

Tennesee

Winchester TN RCP/M................ (615) 967-6889
Dudley Fort; 5P-8A; (3;200K); Dedicated to beginning
programmers and physicians. (Winchester)

WEST

CALIFORNIA

Northern California

OxGate-005 Fresno Mico Fone......... (209) 227-2083 IMSW
Bob Robesky; M-F 7P-7A wknd 24 hrs; (3BV;22M); Standard
and new CP/M 80/86 MP/M 8-16, 'C', dBASE II, etc.

Oxgate-002 RCP/M Milpitas........... (408) 263-2588 IMSW
Mel Cruts; (1 3;12M); (south SF bay area)

PicoNet #4 Wizard's Keep RBBS-RCP/M (408) 281-7059 IMSW
Rick Hobbs; (3;20M); Will answer technical questions on
Osborne 1; (San Jose)

OxGate-008 Monte Sereno Ca .... (408) 354-5934 IMSW
Chuck Metz & Paul Traina; (1-7;20M) (San Jose Area)

60

OxGate-012 San Jose Ca .... (408) 378-7474 IMSW
Waybe Masters; (1-7;2M)

OxGate-dBASE II RCP/M Campbell Ca .. (408) 378-8733 IMSW
Roger D. Brown; (3B;4M); dBASE II is available on this
system to demonstrate software from independent software
developers. System will soon be converting from OxGate
to a BBS written in dBASE II. (San Jose area)

Skyhouse Systems .... (408) 578-6185 IMSW
Kirk De Haan; (3B;10M); We Skydive!; (San Jose)

RCP/M Sunnyvale .... (408) 730-8733 IMSW
Eric Sarti; 3:30P-10P daily; (3;256K); Apple][CP/M based;
(south SF bay area)

Silicon Valley Interchange -
DataTech Node 010 .... (408) 732-9190 IMSW
Edward Svoboda; (3;11M); Apple CP/M pgms; (south SF bay area)

OxGate-001 Saratoga .... (408) 867-1243 IMSW
Paul Traina; (3BV;2.4M); (south SF bay area)

CrosNest II (DataTech Node 014)..... (415) 341-9336 IMSW
Wilbur H. Smith; (3;2.8M); (San Mateo)
CDOS, CP/M hardware/software tipes/bulletins/educational
utilities and communications software (SF Bay area)

RBBS of Marin County .... (415) 383-0473 IMSW
Jim Ayers; M-F 5P-8:30A wknd 24 hrs; (1-7;10M);
Now up with 10 meg drives A:-E: user areas 1-2
w/ SIGM and CP/MUG pgms; (SF bay area)

Rich & Famous RCP/M .... (415) 552-9968 IMSW
Stephen Price Ralph Nishimi; (3;760K); games communications;
(San Francisco)

DataTech Network Hq. System .... (415) 595-0541 IMSW
Edward Huang; (3BV;1M); Hub of DataTech Network. Heath/Zenith
/TRS-80 utilities and communications software.   (SF Bay Area)

Napa Valley RBBS/RCPM .... (707) 257-6502 W
Dave Austin; (1-7;1 2M); Features: Apple Atari Compupro
Kaypro Osborne TRS CP/M software; interest in BDS/Aztec C
dBase II Ham Radio; (Napa)

Southern California

Los Angeles RCP/M .... (213) 296-5927 IMSW
Bob McCown; (1-7;2.5M); System features catalog of the
latest CP/M Apple Atari TRS-80 and IBM PC software; (West LA)

PatVac .... (213) 306-1172 IMSW
Pavlov's Cat (Harris Boldt Edelman); (3;366K); a magazine
for the Real Programmer whose defenses are down; often abused
by the locals; (Venice)

Granada Engineering Group RCP/M .... (213) 360-5053 IMSW
Webber Hall; (3;1M); (Granada Hills)

The MOG-UR'S HBBS .... (213) 366-1238 IMSW
Tom Tcimpidis; (3B;19M); 11 different boards varied interests.

Database use welcome to all systems operating systems and
users; (San Fernando valley LA area)

South Bay RCPM/RBBS .... (213) 370-3293 IMSW
Phil Wheeler; (usually 24 hrs password request means system
temporarily set-up for sysop use only); (3B;382K); (Torrance)

Temple City RBBS/RCPM .... (213) 445-7058 IMSW
Al Krug; M-F 7P-10P wknd 10A-10P; (3B;1.5M); set up especially
to help distribute ZCPR2 (on disk C and D).

G.F.R.N. Data Exchange (RBBS) ...... (213) 541-2503 IMSW
Skip Hansen; (3BV;2.4M); ham radio-related pgms; (Palos Verdes)

Pasadena RBBS .... (213) 577-9947 IMSW
Rich Berg; (1-73BV;3.98M); Note: system power off until modem
carrier lock. (does not recognize CR's for 15 secs after lock
while system auto boots) Heath H89; (LA area)

Hollywood RCPM/RBBS .... (213) 653-6398 IMSW
Kim Levitt; (no answer when in use); (3B;382K); communications
entertainment; Now supports 300/1200 212A baud; (Los Angeles)

La Canada RCPM/RBBS .... (213) 790-3014 IMSW
Chris Hays; (no answer when in use); (3B;276K); electronics
communications software; (LA area)

Pasadena CBBS .... (213) 799-1632 IMSW
Dick Mead; (1-7;8.3M); (LA area)

Hawthorne RBBS...................... (213) 973-2374
Mike Haefner; (3B;370K?); IBM-PC based system; (LA area)

Barstow RCP/M .... (619) 256-3914 W
Bill Wood; (34BV;5.5M); H89 system. (does not see CR's for
8 secs after carrier detect while system auto boots)

San Diego RCPM .... (619) 273-4354 IMSW
Brian Kantor; (3BV;2.4M); (San Diego)

G.F.R.N. Data Exchange (RBBS) Garden Grove 714) 534-1547 SW
Doug Laing; (3BV;5M); amateur radio Apple/CPM; (Garden Grove)

San Dimas RBBS/RCPM .... (714) 599-2109 MSW
Stu Anthony; M-F 8A-7P weekend 24 hrs (try anytime);
(3B;(1.2M?); Xerox 820-II

AnaHug RCPM/CBBS .... (714) 774-7860 IMSW
Bob Mathias John Secor; (3B;10M); hobby computing ham
electronics hobbyists; Now has 300/1200 212A baud; (Anaheim)

Thousand Oaks Technical RCP/M (RIOS) (805) 492-5472 MSW
Trevor Marshall; (36B;34M); (baud rate set at log on or with
NEWBAUD); active bulletin board; Now has 34MB 15 drives A:-H:
most software in subdirectories use MOUNT to access them.
Most of SIG/M on-line. Drive H: has 16-bit software.

Simi RCP/M .... (805) 527-2219 SW
Pete Mack; M-F 7P-7A wknd 24 hrs; (3-6 B on request;20M);
General interest programs plus special interest in BDS 'C'.
(Simi Valley)

Gil Berry's Simi RBBS .... (805) 527-8668 SW
Gil Berry; M-F 5P-11P wknd 24 hrs; (3;270K); Apple][system;
engineering robotics science music; (Simi Valley)

CP/M-Net (tm) West (The Original) .. (805) 527-9321 SW
Kelly Smith; M-F 7P-7A 7P Fri-7A Mon; (1-7;20M); General
Interest A: SIG/M 76-93 B: & C: ZCPR2 D:; special interest
in Osborne 1 & DEC Rainbow; (Simi Valley)

SIMIAPPLE/RCPM......................... (805) 584-6054
John Damico; M-F 7P-11P wknd 24 hrs; (3;6M); interest in
modem rcpm and amateur radio software. (Simi Valley)
SOUTHWEST
Colorado
Boulder Colorado RCPM .... (303) 499-9169 MSW

Jack Riley; daily 12P-6A hard disk up 7P-12A Wed Sun;
Keyword-based bulletin board high-level language software
graphics numerical analysis & UNIX info MX-80 graphics
typesetting; (1-7BV;32M)

Pinecliffe RMP/M RBBS .... (303) 598-3995 MSW
Craig Baker; Irregular hrs 24 hrs. soon (try anytime);
(3B;16M); Login by using LOGIN program. On-line databases
on such topics as nuclear power Retrieval system MP/M-II mods
interest in active discussions; (Pinecliffe)

Denver CUG-NODE .... (303) 781-4937 MSW
? Sysop; (1-7;1M)

Texas
Dallas RCP/M CBBS .... (214) 931-8274 IMSW
Dave Crane; M-F 6P-8A wknd/holidays 24 hrs; (1-7;2.4M);
pgms for and discussions of application of micros to science &
engineering especially earth sciences

Satsuma RCP/M .... (713) 469-8893 MSW
Charlie Sanborn; 2P-12A daily; (3B;10M); (Houston)

Westchase RCP/M .... (713) 789-3355 MSW
James Cahill; (3B;11M); (Houston)
El Paso Texas Apple UG RBBS/RCPM ... (915) 533-2202 MSW
Frank Wancho; (1-7;12M);

El Paso RCPM/CBBS .... (915) 598-1668 MSW
Sigi Kluger; (3B;3M) Files on B: are rotated every other day.
Interest in N* and latest releases.

Utah
Northern Utah CP/M U/G RBBS .... (801) 776-5024 MSW
Brett Berg; (346BV;3M); Big Board II CPMUG library;
(Roy UT)

NORTHWEST

Alaska

Anchorage Alaska RCPM .... (907) 337-1984
Thomas Hill; 11P-9A daily; (3;12.4M)

Alberta,Canada

Edmonton RCPM .... (403) 454-6093
Dave McCrady; (no answer when in use); (3BV;3.8M)

British Columbia,Canada

Frog Hollow CBBS/RCPM .... (604) 937-0906
David Bowerman; (1-7;1.2M); (Vancouver)

Montana
Helena Valley RBBS/RCPM .... (406) 443-2768 W
Marion Thompson; (no answer when in use); (3B;1.2M); Photo-
typesetting service special interest in S-100; (Helena)

Oregon

Chuck Forsberg's RCPM .... (503) 621-3193 SW
Chuck Forsberg; (3BV;??K); (Oregon)

Beaverton Oregon RCPM .... (503) 641-7276 SW
Dave Morgan; (1-7;26M); Special Interst in Computer Art;
(Oregon)

Washington

Olympia RCPM .... (206) 357-7400 W
Tim Linehan; (3B-1/7 on request;16M)

Yelm RBBS & CP/M .... cb (206) 458-3086 W
Dave Stanhope; (1-7;250K); (Olympia)

Terminal Computers RCPM/RBBS........ (509) 927-0367 W
Bruce Jorgens & David Schmidt; (3;3M); Interest in C
and dBASE II software. (Spokane)

OVERSEAS

Australia

SOFTWARE TOOLS RCPM ..... 61-2-997-1018 (Australia)
Bill Bolton; (300 baud CCITT V21 standard;4.8M); (Sydney)

MICOM CBBS .... 61-3-762-5088 (Australia)
Peter Jetson; (300 baud CCITT V21 standard;500K); (Melbourne)

If you look at all the different states represented and even the foreign countries, you can tell how small the world becomes in a telecommunications environment. The predominant operating system in the 8-bit world is CP/M. That fact is reflected in the listing of all those bulletin boards. Just look at all those CP/M systems in use. In addition, CP/M has to have the largest software base of any home computer, and I would not be surprised at all, if the trend of combining 8-bit and 16-bit processors in the same computer, continues.

Now, what can you do if you happen to own one of those 16-bit PC systems, but you want to run all that nice CP/M software? You can do what all those Apple users did. They went out and got themselves a CP/M board and a copy of the CP/M operating system and now had access to software that they could not use before. Check Appendix A to determine if you can get a CP/M board for your make of computer. If you own an Apple and you want to get a CP/M board, look at imported boards and save yourself a bundle. If you have not bought a computer yet or are contemplating buying another one, look closely at the dual purpose models made by CompuPro, they make the COMPUPRO 10; Zenith/ Heath make the ZF-120-22 All-in-One, a nicely packaged offering; and I am sure there are many more.

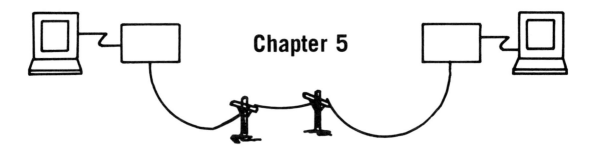

Chapter 5

On-Line With Another Computer

The sign of a successful bulletin board is the busy signal—plain and easy! With the arrival of the IBM PC a great new class of PC bulletin boards has sprung up across the land, and many of the PC owners have gone and equipped their machines with telecommunication capabilities, mostly by adding a modem board. I have differentiated between external and internal modems, the internal ones normally occupying a slot in the chassis of their respective computer, and the external ones being attached to a serial port of the terminal/computer.

The software that is mostly encountered consists of a BASIC program that was adapted from the Apple computer and allows the selection of the telecommunications functions using a menu. Other software is compatible with the XMODEM protocol and allows the transmission of binary program files, usually identified by the .COM extension. Here is where you put to practice what you have learned.

PALOS VERDES BULLETIN BOARD

I am calling the Palos Verdes, California bulletin board using XMODEM programs at (213) 541-2503. The phone rings, and fortunately it is not busy. My dialog with the Palos Verdes bulletin board begins:

```
BOOTING...

G.F.R.N. Data Exchange System.

A FREE service to personal computing enthusiasts

Please log on by entering:
```

Your FIRST name: lou

Your LAST name (or your callsign if you are a Ham): haas

City,State: los angeles, california

Welcome LOU HAAS from LOS ANGELES,CALIFORNIA

Is any of this WRONG? : no

Logged in as LOU HAAS

Logged in at 05:27:00 AM on 09/27/83

You are caller # 22965

There are 486 active messages in the BBS

The next message number will be 1955

*** User Survey ***

You need not answer any question if would rather not do so.

We are just curious about our audience.

What kind of terminal or computer are you using? Hazeltine 1510

Where did you learn of this system

(If a BBS, which one)? Pasadena BBS

Do you work with computers professionally? yes

What is your profession-

(student,military,accountant,etc)? writer

How old are you (roughly)? 39,+

Are you a ham radio operator (call)? no

Thank you very much!

Do you want to read how to use the system(Y/N)?: y

Type ctrl-S to pause, ctrl-K to abort.

How to use the system:

Once you exit from this logon program, you will be communicating with the CP/M operating system. It will signify its readiness for input by typing A>
CPM expects you to type a command, which will then be executed. If what you type is echoed back to you followed by '?', then it isn't a valid command.
Commands are really instructions to CPM to load a program from disk and execute it. Those files whose name ends in .COM are commands. An example is BBS.COM which is executed by typing simply BBS (This is the Bulletin Board system, by the way).
Two very important commands on this system are HELP and TEACH.

The HELP command will list for you a few commands and control characters that will refresh your memory.
The TEACH command will list available documentation on programs, commands, and other things worth knowing. Check it from time to time, as more information is being added regularly.
The SOFTWARE EXCHANGE portion of this system works as follows:
On this system there are two disks, known as A: and B:. They contain many source files of contributed

72

programs. None of these are compiled (ie, you can't run them here) because you are supposed to load them on to your system and execute them there.

The TEACH TRANSFER command will tell you how to get files to your system from here, and vice-versa.

To see a list of files on the system, type DIR (This will list the files on the current disk. To see what's on the other disk, use DIR B:).

Files which end in .BAS are basic source files, files which end in .ASM are 8080 or Z80 assembler source files. (For more on other types of files, see the TEACH command.)

This system uses the MODEM/XMODEM programs to transfer files. MODEM runs on your system, XMODEM runs here. Together they will allow you to transfer files from here to your system, or from your system to here. See TEACH to find out how they work BEFORE YOU USE THEM!!!

If you have a CPM system, but don't have the MODEM program, you may use the MBOOT program to get the MODEM program onto your system. See TEACH TRANSFER for instructions.

For APPLE people: a 40 character screen is too narrow for some of the programs that you will find on this

system. I have tried to keep output to <= 64 characters
in width, but some programs assume 80 columns.

This system, new as it is, is still rather busy. Feel
free to make as much of it as you want, but try to be
considerate of other users.

Do you want to use the Bulletin Board System now? (Y/N): y

Message Subsystem.

(Minibbs version 2.5 [modified])

You are logged in as LOU HAAS

486 active messages.

You are caller # 22965

Next msg will be # 1855

Functions supported:

E - Enter message   Q - Quick scan   C - exit to CP/M

R - Read message   K - Kill message   G - Goodbye

X - eXpert (on/off)   S - Scan messages

Ctrl-K to abort, Ctrl-S to pause

Commands may be strung together, separated by semicolons.

For sequential retrieval, use '+' or '-' after Msg #.

For example, 'R;123+' reads message # 123 and all following.

Function (C,E,G,K,Q,R,S,X or ?): q

Msg # (7- 1854) to start (or <CR> to abort): 1800
1803 MA BELL DOES LOVE YOU!

74

1804 MA BELL'S LOVE (CONT)

1805 MA BELL'S LOVE (CONT)

1806 MOON LOCATOR PROGRAM

1807 STOCK MKT/COMMODITY SFTWR

1808 M100 VS NEC

1812 SETUP BBS

1820 "EUROPEAN STANDARDS"?

1823 FORTH DISK

1824 SEARCH FOR BBS

1825 WATT

1826 STK/COMD SOFTWARE

<<<End of messages>>>

Function (C,E,G,K,Q,R,S,X or ?): r

Msg # (7- 1854) to read, H for Help, or <CR> to abort: 1803,+

Msg # 1803, 09/18/83 from WALLY ROBERTS

To ALL 'MA BELL DOES LOVE YOU!'

The recent skirmish that some modem users had with Southwestern Bell over possible inane surcharges for hooking a modem to a voice-grade telephone circuit, should have demonstrated to the perceptive person the total arrogance and self-decreed image of omnipotence that is suffered upon us by that "thick gray line"--those executives of Ma Bell, all in their pin-stripe suits. In case any might think that such arrogance is limited to the executive suites of Southwestern Bell, let me set the record straight: Pacific Telephone Company currently has three major rate cases before the California Public Utilities Commission (PUC), which have been consolidated by the Commission into essentially one case. This case is unprecedented in its magnitude of proposed rate increases and rate restructuring because of the impending breakup of

-continued-

Msg # 1804, 09/18/83 from WALLY ROBERTS
To ALL 'MA BELL'S LOVE (CONT)'
the Bell System which is to occur on January 1, 1984. Accordingly, the PUC hearings and procedures in this case are extremely complex and must, of necessity extend beyond January 1, 1984, so that the case can at least have the hope of being properly heard and considered, for the sake of the rate-payers of California. Well, this is not good enough for the managers of Pacific Telephone, for three times in recent months they have attempted to short= circuit due process at the PUC. Following is an excerpted quote from a PUC decision (Cal PUC Decision No. 83-09= 006) issued on September 7, concerning Pacific's third attempt at such short-circuiting:

"...Despite the long standing relationship between this Commission and PT&T, the utility apparently has   no appreciation of the workings of   the   Commission's

-continued-

Msg # 1805, 09/18/83 from WALLY ROBERTS

To ALL 'MA BELL'S LOVE (CONT)'

decision-making process.   The Commission is its own best
judge of the minimum time required for this process.   For
PT&T to continue to persevere, and to repeat for the third
time, its proposal that the Commission's long-standing
decision-making process be short circuited, is taxing the
patience and forbearance of the Commission and is forcing
it to spend time that could be more profitably used to
resolve the issues of the proceeding.   PT&T's proposal
presupposes that its case is so compelling that its
ratification by the Commission is a foregone conclusion.
Such is not the case..."

I hope, sports fans, that the foregoing removes any
doubts you might have had about the benevolence of our
very   own   and beloved Pacific Telephone & Telegraph
Company.   If you think they are lovable now, just wait
until next year!

Msg # 1806, 09/18/83 from DAVE G8ADM

To ALL 'MOON LOCATOR PROGRAM'

Please help with the moon locator program in Basic on
your system. Line 1600 has a bracket missing there are

two possible locations for this. Please advise.

Lines 1760 and 1770 have GOTO's to a non existent line shown as 2178, I think this should be 2170.

Having corrected these errors it still does not work. The time on the display does not increment.

If anyone can help please leave a message for DAVE G8ADM calling from ENGLAND. I use Microsoft Basic. 73's

Msg # 1807, 09/18/83 from BOB WA0TZM

To ALL 'STOCK MKT/COMMODITY SFTWR'

I am looking for any software system which can give me access to stock and/or commodity software at a reasonable price. I am also looking for any programs for this purpose.

Msg # 1808, 09/19/83 from JOHN LEARY

To ALL 'M100 VS NEC'

WSJ ADVERTS SHOW NEC VARIANT M100

WITH RAM-PACKS, AND DISK INTERFACE

...ANYONE HAVE AN NEC PORTABLE?

...WHAT IS COMPATIBLE BETWEEN THE

TWO, AND WHAT IS NOT?

LEAVE MSG HERE PLS

        THANKS

        JL

<<<Message 1809 is private>>>

<<<Message 1810 is private>>>

<<< Message 1811 Has been deleted >>>

Msg # 1812, 09/20/83 from OMAR HAJJAR

To SYSTEM OPERATOR 'SETUP BBS'

I WANT TO KNOW WHAT FILES DO I NEED TO OPEN A BBS

SYSTEM LIKE YOURS , SOMETHING SIMPLE. WHICH FILES DO

I NEED AND PLEASE GIVE ME A GENERAL IDEA OF HOW TO

START. I HOPE THAT YOU COULD HELP? ALSO WHAT MODEM MAKE

DO YOU USE ???   THANKS

<<< Message 1813 Has been deleted >>>

<<<Message 1814 is private>>>

<<<Message 1815 is private>>>

<<<Message 1816 is private>>>

<<<Message 1817 is private>>>

<<<Message 1818 is private>>>

<<< Message 1819 Has been deleted >>>

Msg # 1820, 09/21/83 from BOB W9HBF

To ALL '"EUROPEAN STANDARDS"? '

Can anyone help me figure out how to do transcontinental

communications with London or Geneva? I don't know how

to readjust to properly hit European phone lines

am OK throughout North American and Hawaii, but can't get

connections elsewhere. Have UDS 212A/D modem and DEC-mate

II (VT-100) system.

If you have ideas or can help, please leave message
here, or call me at 312/329-9292 X561 collect ASAP.
Ask for Bob Brown.

    Many thanks!!!!!!!!!!

<<<Message 1821 is private>>>

<<< Message 1822 Has been deleted >>>

Msg # 1823, 09/22/83 from BARRY COLE

To JERRY BERKSTRESSER 'FORTH DISK'

Bootstrapping in an editor is possible but tricky. I have
a screen editor and a short procedure using DDT and a
2 line program you type into forth to do it. Let me know
your system type if you need help.

Msg # 1824, 09/22/83 from SHAWN HAVERLY

To ALL 'SEARCH FOR BBS'

HI THERE

I AM IN SEARCH FOR A GOOD BBS PROGRAM. IF YOU
WOULD HAPPEN TO HAVE ANY INFO. PLEASE LET ME KNOW VIA
THIS BOARD. THANK YOU FOR YOU TIME.

THANKS....SHAWN HAVERLY

Msg # 1825, 09/23/83 from WATT HATER

To ALL 'WATT'

JAMES WATT HAS GOT TO GO !

Msg # 1826, 09/23/83 from JOHN BOLLINGER

```
To BOB WAOTZM 'STK/COMD SOFTWARE'

HI BOB GIVE ME A CALL IF WANT TO TALK ABOUT MARKET SOFT

WARE.

    JOHN BOLLINGER   213-659-8300/VOICE

<<< Message 1827 Through, 1829 Have been deleted >>>

<<<End of messages>>>

Function (C,E,G,K,Q,R,S,X or ?): g

Want to leave any comments (Y/N/R)? n

LOU HAAS Logged out at 05:35:58 AM

May the Force be with you.

PLEASE BE SURE YOU HANG UP!!!!
```

Well, this was quite a trip! I started out by signing on to the BBS, answered a number of questions, then requested a rundown on systems features, quick-scanned available messages, using the Q prompt, and then retrieved all messages from message number 1800 on up. Instead of retrieving one message at the time, it was selected to get all of them by the command: R 1800,+. This saves many a keystroke.

CLEO

Its not surprising to see telecommunications put to use in an absolutely positive way. One day I ran across CLEO, a Computerized Listing of Employment Opportunities. I want you to share this gem.

While the Palos Verdes bulletin board is a CP/M oriented board, you must keep in mind that telecommunications are for home computers, and, as the name implies, are strictly for the home. You will find computers with a lot less pizzazz than a CP/M system. So, while I acknowledge the many contributions of early CP/M supporters, I can not dwell on CP/M alone. Therefore, I am dialing onto a bulletin board that very likely uses an ATARI type system. Let's see what a small screen of 32 columns can accomplish.

It was not easy to depict the correct sequence of events, as the following dialog is a bit lengthy. Because a screen-width of 32 columns is used, it makes for a few more pages to show you everything. Also, the system's prompts to the user came out like this:

```
OPTIONS:  1 - 10
HELP
MAIN
MORE
```

but in order to preserve space, I took the liberty to change the lines above to the following format:

```
OPTIONS: 1 - 10, HELP, MAIN, MORE
```

You will see this format used throughout. Another interesting observation about the width on the screen is that quite a few small game consoles can be equipped with telecommunications capabilities, so here are some of their screen widths: ATARI Graduate - 32 columns, Coleco ADAM - 36 columns, and Mattel Intellivision - 20 columns. These game consoles, when equipped with the propper computer add-ons turn into instant home computers, and all of the models mentioned have either built-in (Mattel) or optional (ATARI and Coleco) serial modem connections. Now, back to CLEO.

I dial up (213) 618-8800, get a ring, and here comes CLEO.

```
MAIN MENU

PLEASE CHOOSE YOUR OPTION FROM
THE LIST BELOW

1 BEGIN JOB SEARCH

2 READ ADVTR & READER INFO
3 EXIT CLEO

OPTIONS:  1 - 3, HELP

-->2

USER INFORMATION MENU

1 SUBMIT SYSTEM FEEDBACK
2 READ CLEOS USERS'S GUIDE

3 COMPLETE CLEO SURVEY

4 ADVERTISER INFORMATION

CLEO USER INFORMATION

WELCOME TO CLEO!  THE CLEO
SYSTEM MAINTAINS A COLLECTION
OF HIGH-TECH JOB OPPORTUNITIES.

YOU CAN USE THIS SYSTEM AS YOU
WOULD YOUR DAILY NEWSPAPER TO
```

```
LOCATE JOB ANNOUNCEMENTS THAT
ARE RIGHT FOR YOU.   WHILE USING
CLEO
YOU WILL BE GIVEN THE
CHANCE TO:

PRESS RETURN TO CONTINUE:

1.   SELECT A GROUP OF ADS YOU
WOULD LIKE TO READ.
2.   RESPOND TO SPECIFIC ADS.
3.   RESPOND TO MARKETING SURVEYS
4.   OFFER SUGGESTIONS TO MAKE
CLEO WORK BETTER FOR YOU.

THE FOLLOWING IS OFFERED TO HELP
YOU UNDERSTAND AND EFFECTIVELY
USE THE CLEO SYSTEM.

PRESS RETURN TO CONTINUE:

YOU WILL BE ASKED TO SELECT A
JOB CATEGORY AND JOB TITLE.
THIS IS DONE TO FORM A COLLEC-
TION OF ADS.   YOU MAY THEN


NARROW THIS COLLECTION.
FOR EXAMPLE

IF YOU HAD SELECTED:

JOB CATEGORY: ENGINEER P THRU S
JOB TITLE:    SISYPHEAN
YOU'LL ALSO BE ABLE TO SPECIFY:
```

PRESS RETURN TO CONTINUE:

COMPANY: ROCKHOUNDS
INC.
METRO AREA: LOS ANGELES
REGION: SOUTH BAY/LONG BEACH
DESCRIPTIVE WORD: NEWS
NOTE: IF YOU NARROW YOUR
COLLECTION TOO FAR
AND NO ADS
ARE FOUND
YOU WILL BE SHOWN
THE PREVIOUS GROUP OF ADS THAT
YOU SELECTED.
WHEN YOU BEGIN READING THE JOB
ANNOUNCEMENTS
YOU WILL BE GIVEN
THE FOLLOWING OPTIONS:

PRESS RETURN TO CONTINUE:

B = BEGINNING OF CURRENT AD
C = SEE COMPANY INFORMATION
N = DISPLAY NEXT AD
R = RESPOND TO CURRENT AD
MAIN = RETURN TO MAIN MENU
HELP = GENERAL HELP INFORMATION
MORE = MORE ON CURRENT AD

WHEN USING CLEO
PLEASE KEEP
THESE POINTS IN MIND:

PRESS RETURN TO CONTINUE:

1.   JOB LISTINGS MAY CHANGE
DAILY
AND THE ORDER IN
WHICH YOU SEE ADS MAY
CHANGE EACH TIME YOU DIAL
INTO CLEO.

2.   DUE TO THE GREAT NUMBER OF
PEOPLE WANTING TO READ THE
JOB ADS LISTED IN CLEO

THE TIME ALLOWED FOR EACH
SESSION IS LIMITED.

PRESS RETURN TO CONTINUE:

3.   ANY TIME YOU WISH TO END
YOUR SESSION WITH CLEO

SELECT THE OPTION THAT WILL

RETURN YOU TO THE MAIN MENU.
THEN SELECT THE EXIT OPTION.

GOOD LUCK IN YOUR JOB SEARCH!!!

PRESS RETURN FOR MAIN MENU.
MAIN MENU

PLEASE CHOOSE YOUR OPTION FROM
THE LIST BELOW

1 BEGIN JOB SEARCH
2 READ ADVTR & READER INFO
3 EXIT CLEO

OPTIONS: 1 - 3, HELP

```
-->1

CATEGORIES MENU

1 SALES/MKT/ADM/MGMT/MISC

2 COMPUTERS/DP A THRU P

3 COMPUTERS/DP Q THRU Z

4 ENGINEERS A THRU E

5 ENGINEERS F THRU L

6 ENGINEERS M THRU O

7 ENGINEERS P THRU S

8 ENGINEERS T THRU Z

9 MISC: TRAINING/WRITING/TECHS

10 SCIENCES/MATH/RESEARCH

OPTIONS:  1 - 10, HELP, MAIN, MORE

-->1

TITLES

1 MGR. ENGINEERING MGR.

2 PRODUCT MANAGER

3 SALES ENGINEER

4 TEST AD/TEST AD

OPTIONS:  1 - 4, MAIN, HELP, MORE

-->1

THERE ARE NO ADS MEETING YOUR

REQUIREMENTS.  PLEASE TRY AGAIN.

TITLES

1 MGR. ENGINEERING MGR.

2 PRODUCT MANAGER

3 SALES ENGINEER
```

```
4 TEST AD/TEST AD

OPTIONS:  1 - 4, HELP, MAIN, MORE

-->2

THERE ARE   1  ADS MEETING YOUR

SELECTION CRITERIA.

YOU MAY NOW SEARCH FOR JOBS WITH

SPECIFIC COMPANIES; AND/OR JOBS

IN SPECIFIC GEOGRAPHIC LOCATIONS

AND/OR JOBS CONTAINING DESCRIPT-

IVE KEYWORDS THAT YOU ENTER.

OPTIONS ARE:

1 DISPLAY ALL CURRENT ADS

2 NARROW LIST BY COMPANY

3 BYPASS COMPANY SEARCH

OPTIONS:  1 - 3, HELP, MAIN,

-->1

832410058

PRODUCT MANAGER

SAN JOSE/SANTA CLARA

NANOMETRICS              600

09SEP1983

*********************************

*        PRODUCT MANAGER       *

*          (NANONET)           *

*      WE ARE GROWING...       *
```

```
*      SO CAN YOU!                *

**********************************

***MORE***

OPTIONS:   B, C, N, R, HELP, MAIN, MORE

-->B

832410058

PRODUCT MANAGER

SAN JOSE/SANTA CLARA

NANOMETRICS               600

09SEP1983

**********************************

*         PRODUCT MANAGER        *

*            (NANONET)           *

*      WE ARE GROWING...         *

*      SO CAN YOU!               *

**********************************

***MORE***

OPTIONS:   B, C, N, R, HELP, MAIN, MORE

-->C

NANOMETRICS IS THE LEADER IN

COMPUTER-BASED MEASUREMENT AND

INSPECTION SYSTEMS USED DURING

THE WAFER FABRICATION STAGE OF

THE MANUFACTURE OF INTEGRATED

CIRCUITS.

SHARE IN OUR PROFITS

NANOMETRICS OFFERS EXCELLENT

SALARIES AND AN ATTRACTIVE BENE=

FITS PROGRAM WHICH PROVIDES A

SEMI-ANNUAL CASH PROFIT-SHARING

***MORE***

OPTIONS:   B, C, N, R, HELP, MAIN, MORE

-->MORE

BONUS.   RECENTLY

WE PAID ELI=

GIBLE EMPLOYEES A BONUS OF 12%

OF THEIR EARNINGS.   WE OFFER

MEDICAL

DENTAL AND LIFE INSUR=

ANCE

A SOUND RETIREMENT PLAN

AND OUTSTANDING OPPORTUNITIES

FOR INDIVIDUAL CONTRIBUTION AND

PERSONAL GROWTH.

**********************************

*                                *

*          NANOMETRICS           *

*                                *

**********************************

***MORE***

-->MORE

INSTRUMENTATION MANUFACTURED IN

SILICON VALLEY FOR SEMICONDUCTOR

MEASUREMENT AND INSPECTION.

***END OF COMPANY TEXT***

OPTIONS:   B, C, N, R, HELP, MAIN
```

--->MAIN

MAIN MENU

PLEASE CHOOSE YOUR OPTION FROM
THE LIST BELOW

1 BEGIN JOB SEARCH

2 READ ADVTR & READER INFO

3 EXIT CLEO

OPTIONS: 1 - 3, HELP

->1

CATEGORIES MENU

1 SALES/MKT/ADM/MGMT/MISC

2 COMPUTERS/DP A THRU P

3 COMPUTERS/DP Q THRU Z

4 ENGINEERS A THRU E

5 ENGINEERS F THRU L

6 ENGINEERS M THRU O

7 ENGINEERS P THRU S

8 ENGINEERS T THRU Z

9 MISC: TRAINING/WRITING/TECHS

10 SCIENCES/MATH/RESEARCH

OPTIONS: 1 - 10, HELP, MAIN, MORE
-->2

TITLES

1 AVIONICS COMPUTER

2 CAM

3 COMMUNICATIONS SYSTEMS

4 DESIGNER

5 H/W AND/OR S/W ENGINEER

6 OPERATIONS

7 PERSONAL COMPUTER ANALYST

8 PLANNING/CAPACITY/ANALYSIS

9 PRODUCT SUPPORT ANALYST

10 PROGRAMMER/ANALYST/BUSINESS

11 PROGRAMMER/ANALYST/SCIENCE

OPTIONS: 1 - 11, HELP, MAIN, MORE
-->10

THERE ARE   5   ADS MEETING YOUR
SELECTION CRITERIA.

YOU MAY NOW SEARCH FOR JOBS WITH
SPECIFIC COMPANIES; AND/OR JOBS
IN SPECIFIC GEOGRAPHIC LOCATIONS
AND/OR JOBS CONTAINING DESCRIPT-
IVE KEYWORDS THAT YOU ENTER.
OPTIONS ARE:

1 DISPLAY ALL CURRENT ADS

2 NARROW LIST BY COMPANY

3 BYPASS COMPANY SEARCH

OPTIONS: 1 - 3, HELP, MAIN

-->1

832660017

PROGRAMMER/ANALYST/BUSINESS

SAN FRANCISCO BAY CITIES

BENETICS CORPORATION   062

21SEP1983

PRODUCT SUPPORT ANALYST

GROWTH IS OUR GOAL; IF IT IS
PART OF YOUR PLANS
THEN JOIN US

FIREFIGHTERS APPLY . . .

MORE

OPTIONS: B, C, N, R, HELP, MAIN, MORE

-->MORE

GENERALISTS NEEDED: UNIX AND C.
BE INVOLVED IN ALL PRODUCT AREAS
DESIGN AND IMPLEMENT TEST PLAN &
INTERACT WITH CUSTOMER SERVICE &
DEVELOPMENT STAFF. YOUR RESPON-
SIBILITIES INCLUDE DEVELOPING
SYSTEM & PRODUCT UTILITIES
AS
WELL AS TESTING APPLICATIONS SW
TO ASSURE QUALITY. PROVIDE IN-
TERNAL TRAINING; DESIGN & MAIN-
TAIN REMOTE DIAGNOSTICS & PER-
FORM SW CONFIGURATION & INSTALL-
ATION. 2-4 YRS. EXPERIENCE.

MORE

OPTIONS: B, C, N, R, HELP, MAIN, MORE

-->MORE

FOR PROMPT CONSIDERATION
PLEASE
FILL OUT THE CLEO MINI-APP OR
SEND YOUR RESUME TO:

STEVEN LIST

PRODUCT SUPPORT MGR

BENETICS CORP.

335 E. MIDDLEFIELD ROAD

MOUNTAIN VIEW

CA.

94043

BENETICS IS AN EQUAL OPPORTUNITY

EMPLOYER M/F. U.S. CITIZENSHIP

OR PERMANENT RESIDENT VISA IS

REQUIRED.

END OF AD

OPTIONS: B, C, N, R, HELP, MAIN

-->MAIN

MAIN MENU

PLEASE CHOOSE YOUR OPTION FROM
THE LIST BELOW

1 BEGIN JOB SEARCH
2 READ ADVTR & READER INFO
3 EXIT CLEO

 OPTIONS: 1 - 3, HELP

-->HELP

SELECT ITEM APPROPRIATE
TO YOUR OPTION LINE

01-XX=MENU ITEM SELECTION

HELP=PRINT THIS MESSAGE

MAIN=RETURN TO MAIN MENU

MORE=DISPLAY MORE INFORMATION

OR REFRESH THE SCREEN

ALL= DISPLAY ALL AREAS OR

ALL COMPANIES

OPTIONS: 1 - 3, HELP

-->1

CATEGORIES MENU

1 SALES/MKT/ADM/MGMT/MISC

2 COMPUTERS/DP A THRU P

3 COMPUTERS/DP Q THRU Z

4 ENGINEERS A THRU E

5 ENGINEERS F THRU L

6 ENGINEERS M THRU O

7 ENGINEERS P THRU S

8 ENGINEERS T THRU Z

9 MISC: TRAINING/WRITING/TECHS

10 SCIENCES/MATH/RESEARCH

OPTIONS: 1 - 10, HELP, MAIN, MORE

-->9

TITLES

1 PRECISION MECH INSPECTOR

2 TECHNICAL STAFF

3 TECHNICIANS

4 TRAINING SPECIALISTS

OPTIONS: 1 - 4, HELP, MAIN, MORE

-->ALL

YOU HAVE SELECTED AN INVALID

OPTION. PLEASE TRY AGAIN.

OPTIONS: 1 - 4, HELP, MAIN, MORE

-->1

THERE ARE   1 ADS MEETING YOUR

SELECTION CRITERIA.

YOU MAY NOW SEARCH FOR JOBS WITH

SPECIFIC COMPANIES; AND/OR JOBS

IN SPECIFIC GEOGRAPHIC LOCATIONS

AND/OR JOBS CONTAINING DESCRIPT-

IVE KEYWORDS THAT YOU ENTER.

OPTIONS ARE:

1 DISPLAY ALL CURRENT ADS

2 NARROW LIST BY COMPANY

3 BYPASS COMPANY SEARCH

OPTIONS: 1 - 3, HELP

-->1

832380009

PRECISION MECH INSPECTOR

SAN JOSE/SANTA CLARA

NANOMETRICS   600

09SEP1983

****
*   PRECISION   *
*   MECHANICAL INSPECTOR   *
*   WE ARE GROWING...   *
*   SO CAN YOU!   *

```
*********************************
***MORE***
OPTIONS:   B, C, N, R, HELP, MAIN, MORE
-->MAIN

MAIN MENU

PLEASE CHOOSE YOUR OPTION FROM
THE LIST BELOW

1 BEGIN JOB SEARCH
2 READ ADVTR & READER INFO
3 EXIT CLEO

OPTIONS:   1 -   3, HELP

-->2
USER INFORMATION MENU

1 SUBMIT SYSTEM FEEDBACK
2 READ CLEO USER'S GUIDE
3 COMPLETE CLEO SURVEY
4 ADVERTISER INFORMATION

OPTIONS:   1 - 4, HELP, MAIN
-->1

WE WOULD APPRECIATE ANY
FEEDBACK YOU HAVE FOR THE
ENHANCEMENT OF CLEO.   YOU MAY
GIVE US YOUR NAME IF DESIRED OR
PRESS RETURN TO CONTINUE.
NAME:
ENTER YOUR REMARKS .   PLEASE
LIMIT YOURSELF TO NINE LINES
```

```
(UP TO 32 CHARACTERS PER LINE).
CHARACTERS IN EXCESS OF 32 WILL
BE TRUNCATED.   IF YOUR REMARKS
ARE FEWER THAN NINE LINES
PRESS
RETURN AT THE BEGINNING
OF A LINE
1..............16..............32
-->^C    (interrupted here)

MAIN MENU

PLEASE CHOOSE YOUR OPTION FROM
THE LIST BELOW

1 BEGIN JOB SEARCH
2 READ ADVTR & READER INFO
3 EXIT CLEO

OPTIONS:   1 -   3, HELP

-->$

YOU HAVE SELECTED AN INVALID
 OPTION.   PLEASE TRY AGAIN.

OPTIONS:   1 -   3, HELP
-->1
CATEGORIES MENU
1 SALES/MKT/ADM/MGMT/MISC
2 COMPUTERS/DP A THRU P
3 COMPUTERS/DP Q THRU Z
4 ENGINEERS A THRU E
5 ENGINEERS F THRU L
```

6 ENGINEERS M THRU O

7 ENGINEERS P THRU S

8 ENGINEERS T THRU Z

9 MISC: TRAINING/WRITING/TECHS

10 SCIENCES/MATH/RESEARCH

OPTIONS: 1 - 10, HELP, MAIN, MORE

-->3

TITLES

1 REALTIME

2 SOFTWARE DESIGN

3 SOFTWARE DEVELOPMENT

4 SOFTWARE ENGINEER

5 SOFTWARE TECHNICIAN

6 SYSTEMS ANALYSIS/DESIGN

7 SYSTEMS DEVELOPMENT

8 SYSTEMS PROGRAMMER

OPTIONS: 1 - 10, HELP, MAIN, MORE

--->8

THERE ARE   4 ADS MEETING YOUR
SELECTION CRITERIA.

YOU MAY NOW SEARCH FOR JOBS WITH
SPECIFIC COMPANIES; AND/OR JOBS
IN SPECIFIC GEOGRAPHIC LOCATIONS
AND/OR JOBS CONTAINING DESCRIPT-
IVE KEYWORDS THAT YOU ENTER.
OPTIONS ARE:

1 DISPLAY ALL CURRENT ADS

2 NARROW LIST BY COMPANY

3 BYPASS COMPANY SEARCH

OPTIONS: 1 - 3, HELP

-->1

832640008

SYSTEMS PROGRAMMER

ORANGE COUNTY

TELOS CONSULTING   906

22SEP1983

****
*   *
*   SOFTWARE & SYSTEMS   *
*   PROGRAMMERS/ENGINEERS   *
*   *
****
MORE
OPTIONS: B, C, N, R, HELP, MAIN, MORE
-->MORE
THERE IS A POSITIVE ALTERNATIVE
TO YOUR CAREER PATH - THE -
PROFESSIONAL CONSULTING FIELD.
TELOS CONSULTING SERVICES OFFERS
SECURITY
LIBERAL BENEFITS &
CHALLENGING ASSIGNMENTS.

ORANGE COUNTY/SAN DIEGO COUNTY
-REALTIME SYSTEMS
-DATA BASE MANAGEMENT SYSTEMS

-MICRO OPERATING SYSTEMS

-NAVAL SYSTEMS

MORE

OPTIONS: B, C, N, R, HELP, MAIN, MORE

--->MORE

-INTELLIGENCE APPLICATIONS

-MISSILE SYSTEMS

CALL FRAN EVERY (714) 992-6801

OR SEND RESUME TO:

801 E. CHAPMAN AVE.

FULLERTON

CA.

92631

EOE

***

END OF AD

OPTIONS: B, C, N, R, HELP, MAIN, MORE

--->$

YOU HAVE SELECTED AN INVALID

OPTION. PLEASE TRY AGAIN.

END OF AD

OPTIONS: B, C, N, R, HELP, MAIN, MORE

--->B

832640008

SYSTEMS PROGRAMMER

ORANGE COUNTY

TELOS CONSULTING   906

22SEP1983

****

*   *

*   SOFTWARE & SYSTEMS   *

*   PROGRAMMERS/ENGINEERS   *

*   *

****

MORE

OPTIONS: B, C, N, R, HELP, MAIN, MORE

--->N

832310008

SYSTEMS PROGRAMMER

LOS ANGELES

XEROX CORP.   992

PRINTING SYSTEMS GROUP

01OCT1983

EXPERIENCED PROFESSIONALS ARE

SOUGHT BY A WORLD ELECTRONIC

PRINTING LEADER TO BECOME

CONSULTING MEMBERS OF THE

PROGRAMMING & ENGINEERING STAFF.

MORE

OPTIONS: B, C, N, R, HELP, MAIN, MORE

--->MORE

THOSE SELECTED WILL POSSESS

HARDWARE/SOFTWARE ARCHITECTURE

KNOWLEDGE COMBINED WITH STRONG

EXPERIENCE IN NETWORK AND DIS-

TRIBUTED SYSTEMS ARCHITECTURE.
FAMILIARITY WITH SEVERAL OF THE
FOLLOWING DESIRED: VLS1 DESIGN

IMAGINAL & VECTOR GRAPHICS

USER INTERFACES WITH XEROX AND
COMMERCIALLY AVAILABLE MICRO-
PROCESSOR SYSTEMS
AND MODELING
AND SIMULATION TECHNIQUES.

MORE

OPTIONS: B, C, N, R, HELP, MAIN, MORE
-->MORE
BS/MS IN COMPUTER SCIENCE OR
EQUIVALENT AND 10 YEARS EXPER-
IENCE IN SYSTEMS SOFTWARE AND
OPERATING SYSTEMS IS REQUIRED.
QUALIFIED CANDIDATES ARE INVI-
TED TO COMPLETE THE CLEO MINI-
APP AND FORWARD THEIR RESUME TO
DENISE SENEGAL

PRINTING SYSTEMS
GROUP
   DEPT. CL
880 APOLLO ST.

P3-26
EL SEGUNDO
CA.
90245.

XEROX IS AN AFFIRMATIVE ACTION
EMPLOYER.
END OF AD
OPTIONS: B, C, N, R, HELP, MAIN, MORE
-->N
832590028
SYSTEMS PROGRAMMER
VENTURA COUNTY
GRUMMAN AEROSPACE CORP.   334

13SEP1983

****
. . .A CHALLENGE WITH A CAREER
AT GRUMMAN AEROSPACE

SYSTEM PROGRAMMERS
****
MORE

OPTIONS: B, C, N, R, HELP, MAIN, MORE
-->MORE
WORK IN BEAUTIFUL VENTURA COUN-
TY
A GREAT PLACE TO LIVE. . .

EXPERIENCE REQUIREMENTS INCLUDE:
AYK 14
8085
CMS2M
PLM
ASSEMBLY LANGUAGE
REAL-TIME APPLICATIONS

PROGRAMMING

CODE DESIGN/PROGRAMMING/

CHECKOUT

MORE

OPTIONS: B, C, N, R, HELP, MAIN, MORE

-->MORE

INTEGRATION/SPECIFICATION

QUALIFIED CANDIDATES ARE INVITED

TO FILL OUT THE CLEO MINI-APP OR

FORWARD THEIR RESUMES FOR CON-

SIDERATION TO:

JOE C. RIVERA

GRUMMAN AEROSPACE CORPORATION

BOX 42232

POINT MUGU

CALIFORNIA 93042

AN EQUAL OPPORTUNITY EMPLOYER.

U.S. CITIZENSHIP IS REQUIRED.

FOR MORE INFORMATION

PRESS C .

END OF AD

OPTIONS: B, C, N, R, HELP, MAIN, MORE

-->C

GRUMMAN AEROSPACE CORPORATION

AT PONT MUGU

CALIFORNIA

IS

50 MILES NORTH OF LOS ANGELES

AND 40 MILES SOUTH OF SANTA

BARBARA

ON THE PACIFIC OCEAN.

OPPORTUNITIES FOR A CHALLENGING

CAREER IN DESIGN TEST & ANALYSIS

OF ADVANCED AIRBORNE SYSTEMS -

F14A

EA6B -

GRUMMAN OFFERS YOU EXCELLENT

COMPANY BENEFITS

WHICH INCLUDE

MORE

OPTIONS: B, C, N, R, HELP, MAIN, MORE

-->MORE

MEDICAL AND LIFE INSURANCE

AND

DENTAL PLAN; PENSION AND INVEST-

MENT PLANS

PAID HOLIDAYS AND

VACATION; PAID ABSENCE ALLOW-

ANCE AND TUITION REIMBURSEMENT.

DISCOVER VENTURA COUNTY

A

BEAUTIFUL PLACE TO LIVE

WHETHER IN ONE OF THE MANY

SMALL TOWN COMMUNITIES OR THE

METROPOLITAN CITIES OF THE

COUNTY. . .

MORE

OPTIONS: B, C, N, R, HELP, MAIN, MORE

NOT JUST ANOTHER JOB OFFER. . .

BUT A CHALLENGE WITH A CAREER.

END OF COMPANY TEXT

OPTIONS: B, C, N, R, HELP, MAIN, MORE

-->N

 832590032

SYSTEMS PROGRAMMER

LOS ANGELES

COMPANY NOT DISCLOSED

17SEP1983

PROGRAMMER

AN OPPORTUNITY EXISTS FOR YOU TO

GROW WITH AN AGGRESSIVE VENTURE

CAPITAL COMPANY OWNED BY A

MAJOR COMMUNICATIONS CORPORATION

MORE

OPTIONS: B, C, N, R, HELP, MAIN, MORE

-->MORE

THE REQUIREMENTS ARE NOT FORMID-

ABLE IF YOU ARE FAMILIAR WITH

DEC SOFTWARE. YOU WILL BE

WORKING ON AND SHOULD BE ABLE TO

UNDERSTAND THE DEC VMS OPERATING

SYSTEM AND HAVE THE ABILITY TO

PERFORM NEW VERSION INSTALLA-

TIONS. YOU SHOULD BE ABLE TO

TAKE FORMAL APPLICATION SPECS

AND CONVERT THEM INTO WORKING

CODE AND THEN BE ABLE TO PRO-

VIDE APPROPRIATE USER AND

OPERATIONAL PROCEDURES AND

MORE

OPTIONS: B, C, N, R, HELP, MAIN, MORE

-->MORE

MORE

ASSOCIATED DOCUMENTATION.

THE PERSON SELECTED SHOULD HAVE

EXCELLENT COMMUNICATION ABILI-

TIES

BOTH WRITTEN AND ORAL.

THE REWARDS ARE GREAT! YOU

COULD BE WORKING IN A SMALL

OFFICE

CONVENIENTLY LOCATED

CLOSE TO THE SAN DIEGO FREEWAY

IN TORRANCE. YOU WILL HAVE ALL

THE BENEFITS OF A LARGE CORPORA-

TION AT YOUR DISPOSAL INCLUDING

MORE

OPTIONS: B, C, N, R, HELP, MAIN, MORE

-->MORE

HEALTH AND DENTAL INSURANCE.

TO RECEIVE A PROMPT RESPONSE

PLEASE FILL OUT THE CLEO MINI-

APP OR WRITE TO BOX 101

 C/O

CLEO

2164 W. 190TH STREET

TORRANCE

CA.

90504.   EQUAL

OPPORTUNITY EMPLOYER M/F/H/V.

END OF AD

OPTIONS: B, C, N, R, HELP, MAIN, MORE

-->N

THERE ARE NO MORE ADS IN THIS

COLLECTION

OPTIONS: 1 - 10, HELP, MAIN

-->R

THE RESPONSE FORM WILL SUPPLY

THE AD ID NUMBER.   YOU WILL BE

PROMPTED FOR CONTACT INFORMATION

AND ABBREVIATED OCCUPATIONAL

INFORMATION.

ALL INFORMATION IS OPTIONAL

AND CONFIDENTIAL. PRESS RETURN

TO SKIP AN ITEM.

832590032

NAME:

STREET:

CITY:

STATE:

ZIP CODE:

HOME PHONE:

BUSINESS PHONE:

WHAT LEVEL AND TYPE OF DEGREE

DO YOU HAVE?

OCCUPATION:

BRIEFLY DESCRIBE YOUR PRESENT

OCCUPATION (TWO 32 SPACES LINES

ARE AVAILABLE FOR YOUR USE).

HOW MANY YEARS EXPERIENCE DO YOU

HAVE IN YOUR PRESENT OCCUPATION?

WHAT PROJECTS ARE YOU CURRENTLY

WORKING ON? (ONE 32 SPACE LINE

IS AVAILABLE FOR YOUR USE).

BEST TIME TO CONTACT:

832590032

SYSTEMS PROGRAMMER

LOS ANGELES

COMPANY NOT DISCLOSED

17SEP1983

PROGRAMMER

AN OPPORTUNITY EXISTS FOR YOU TO

```
GROW WITH AN AGGRESSIVE VENTURE

CAPITAL COMPANY OWNED BY A

MAJOR COMMUNICATIONS CORPORATION

***MORE***

OPTIONS:  B, C, N, R, HELP, MAIN, MORE

-->MAIN

MAIN MENU

PLEASE CHOOSE YOUR OPTION FROM

THE LIST BELOW


1 BEGIN JOB SEARCH

2 READ ADVTR & READER INFO

3 EXIT CLEO

OPTIONS:  1 - 3, HELP


-->3
```

```
**********

THANK YOU FOR USING CLEO.  WE

HOPE YOU HAVE FOUND OUR LISTINGS

HELPFUL.  REMEMBER

THE JOBS

LIST CHANGES DAILY.  WE HOPE

YOU WILL USE CLEO AGAIN SOON.

GOOD DAY.
```

What one can do with 32 columns! A nice sign of ingenuity, and best of all, the screens flick by so fast that you almost do not notice the smaller line width. The system probably has many counterparts in many other areas of the country, so find the closest one near you and go job shopping. I think, now that you have learned how to get around in different bulletin boards, it is time to examine some of their files. I will do that in the next chapter.

Chapter 6

Bulletin Board Files

Once you are on-line with another computer, you will want to browse through its files. In this chapter, I will take you through the files of several different types of bulletin boards. I am sure that you will be impressed by the amount and the variety of software available.

CP/M BULLETIN BOARDS

One of the busiest boards is the Palos Verdes Bulletin Board, operated by Skip Hansen. It has been on-line for quite a number of years and is oriented towards ham operators.

Filefind

After you are lucky enough to get through on (213) 541-2503 and you have successfully signed on, the command FILEFIND allows you to get a listing of all available files. This well organized board shows the following files in response to filefind (to allow you to distinguish my inputs from the bulletin boards responses, I am preceeding my inputs with this prompt:-->):

```
--->filefind

A00:DIR      .COM   A00:TYPE     .COM   A00:CHAT     .COM

A00:XMODEM   .COM   A00:LIPM52   .AQM   A00:PACKET   .BIB

A00:MODEM221.AQM    A00:AX25     .DQC   A00:BYE      .COM

A00:TY       .COM   A00:LOGON    .COM   A00:CRCK     .COM

A00:FILEFIND.COM    A00:HELP     .COM   A00:BYE77    .AQM
```

```
A00:MBOOT    .DOC    A00:CIA      .BQS    A00:D-27A    .AQM

A00:LIB85    .LIB    A00:MEMR     .OBJ    A00:CPDOS    .BAS

A00:CPDOS    .DOC    A00:SEQIO2   .LQB    A00:DECXHAM  .ASM

A00:PINUP    .PQC    A00:PINUP2   .PQC    A00:DISZILOG .DOC

A00:DISZILOG.OBJ     A00:DRAGON   .DOC    A00:DRAGON   .PQC

A00:DU-V77   .DOC    A00:DU-V77   .OBJ    A00:ELIZA    .BAS

A00:ENTBBS24.BQS     A00:FBAD-V54.AQM     A00:FORMHAM  .ASM

A00:FREAK    .TXT    A00:MODEM75  .AQM    A00:HAMMING  .DOC

A00:HAMPROGS.DOC     A00:INSUR    .TXT    A00:MODEM75  .DQC

A00:MODEM75  .LQB    A00:DISKMENU.DOC     A00:MBOOT3   .ASM

A00:MFT45    .AQM    A00:MINIBBS  .BQS    A00:PACKET   .RQL

A00:SYSTEM   .DOC    A00:PROTOCOL.DQC     A00:RESOURCE.DQC

A00:RESOURCE.OBJ     A00:XMODEM50.AQM     A00:MOONLOC5.BAS

A00:MORSE    .ASM    A00:BBS      .COM    A00:RCPM-040.LQT

A00:LIPMODS  .TXT    A00:TIPMO5   .AQM    A00:TIPMO5   .DQC

A00:TWEETY   .PQC    A00:PINUP1   .PQC    A00:PRACTICE.ASM

A00:RANDTEXT.BAS     A00:USQ-19   .OBJ    A00:TURNKEY1.AQM

A00:TEACH    .AQM    A00:TTY      .AQM    A00:RTTY     .AQM

A00:SNAGLPUS.PIC     A00:SNOOPY   .PIC    A00:SQ-15    .OBJ

A00:SQ/USQ   .HIS    A00:SQUEEZER.DQC     A00:TURNKEY1.DOC

A00:TEACH    .COM    A00:TIME-QT  .ASM    A00:UNSP30   .AQM

A00:UNSP30   .DQC    A00:ZCHESS   .OBJ    A00:AUTOLOAD.ASM

A00:CODE     .BAS    A00:CPM-BKSP.ASM     A01:BAS      .DOC

A01:@        .DOC    A01:POWER    .COM    A01:DIR      .DOC

A01:FILENAME.DOC     A01:HAMPROGS.DOC     A01:HELP     .DOC

A01:TRANSFER.DOC     A15:COUNTERS.BBS     A15:USERS    .BBS
```

```
A15:SUMMARY .BBS   A15:MESSAGES.BBS   A15:CALLER  .
A15:CALLERS .BBS   A15:LOG     .SYS   A15:SURVEY  .BBS
A15:COMMENTS.BBS
```

COMMENT: The files residing on drive A: have been
         subdivided into three user areas. Thus A00 means
         drive A:, user 00. The other users are A01: and
         A15. Under CP/M version 2.0 and higher one can
         divide each drive into 16 user areas - 00 to 15.

COMMENT: No additional -->filefind is given here, one -->
         filefind lists the directories on all drives, on
         this system we find two drives, A: and B:.


```
B00:23MATCHE.BAS   B00:60MINS  .TQT   B00:6503     .TXT
B00:80-103A .DCH   B00:ATARICPM.DQC   B00:DISK76F .OBJ
B00:USQ     .DOC   B00:ADVENTUR.OBJ   B00:ADVENTUR.WQK
B00:APMD1201.DOC   B00:APMD1201.OBJ   B00:APMD300 .OBJ
B00:APMEMMAP.NEW   B00:APZCPR  .DOC   B00:ARCHIVE .AQM
B00:AUTOST  .OSZ   B00:BARBIE  .FQC   B00:BDLOC   .OBJ
B00:BEAM    .BQS   B00:BIORY   .BAS   B00:BISHOW14.AQM
B00:BOMB    .TQT   B00:BOMB1   .TQT   B00:BUDGET  .BAS
B00:BUFFER  .DOC   B00:BUFFER  .LIB   B00:CCPPATCH.ASM
B00:CHASE   .BAS   B00:CHDIR   .CQ    B00:CHDIR   .MQG
B00:SQ/USQ  .LBR   B00:COPYFAST.AQM   B00:CPM-DEC .DOC
B00:CPMTODEC.OBJ   B00:CPMUTIL .ASM   B00:CRCK3   .ASM
```

```
BOO:CRCSUBS  .LIB    BOO:DATABASE.BQS    BOO:DBFORMAT.BAS

BOO:DECISION.BQS     BOO:DECTOCPM.OBJ    BOO:DISK74   .DOC

BOO:DIAL10   .DOC    BOO:PCPI/CCP.TQT    BOO:DISKMENU.DOC

BOO:DU/MAP   .DOC    BOO:DX       .OBJ   BOO:ERAQ     .MQC

BOO:EX       .DQC    BOO:EX       .OBJ   BOO:EXPANDO  .RQM

BOO:FILEFND8.AQM     BOO:FLIGHT   .BAS   BOO:FMAP3    .ASM

BOO:HAMCALC  .BQS    BOO:HAMHELP  .BAS   BOO:HP125MDM.HLP

BOO:ICOPY    .ASM    BOO:IDIR     .ASM   BOO:USQ      .EXE

BOO:KINGDOM  .BAS    BOO:KPRO-BY2.HQP    BOO:LABLE    .DOC

BOO:LABLE    .OBJ    BOO:LISTDEC  .OBJ   BOO:LOWER    .ASM

BOO:LOWPASS  .BAS    BOO:LU211    .DQC   BOO:LU211    .OBJ


BOO:MAKEADV  .BQS    BOO:MAZE     .BAS   BOO:MDM707   .DQC

BOO:MDM707   .INF    BOO:MDM707   .OBJ   BOO:MDM707   .SET

BOO:MEMTST   .ASM    BOO:MIND     .BAS   BOO:MLIST501.AQM

BOO:MONA     .PQC    BOO:NEWCAT28.DQC    BOO:NEWCAT29.AQM

BOO:OTHEL    .BAS    BOO:YAM/H89 .OBJ    BOO:BIGBURST.AQM

BOO:CUCU     .TLS    BOO:PACMAN   .DQT   BOO:PACMAN   .AQM

BOO:DIAL     .OBJ    BOO:PINUP4   .PQC   BOO:PINUP5   .PQC

BOO:PIPPTCH2.AQM     BOO:POEM     .TXT   BOO:POKER    .BAS

BOO:PRINT    .ASM    BOO:PRNT     .ASM   BOO:PUZZLE   .BAS

BOO:QT-TIME .BAS     BOO:QUEST    .BQS   BOO:RTE      .ASM

BOO:RTMLD    .ASM    BOO:SAD-TALE.TXT    BOO:SHOOT    .OBJ

BOO:SAP36    .AQM    BOO:SD-48A   .AQM   BOO:SECTION .AQM

BOO:SEXELECT.TXT     BOO:STARTREK.DOC    BOO:STARTREK.PQC

BOO:SUB      .OBJ    BOO:SUB-FIX .DOC    BOO:SUPSUB   .DQC

BOO:SWEEP35 .OBJ     BOO:SYSTAT   .AQM   BOO:TEST1A   .ASM
```

```
BOO:TEST2     .ASM    BOO:TIGER     .PQC    BOO:TINYBAS .DQC

BOO:TINYBAS .OBJ      BOO:TREK2-1 .BAS      BOO:TYPE17   .OBJ

BOO:UNDEL     .DOC    BOO:UNDEL    .OBJ     BOO:UNERA    .ASM

BOO:UNSP30   .OBJ     BOO:USRDFLT2.CQP      BOO:WARI      .BAS

BOO:WARMBOOT.ASM      BOO:WORDMAZE.BAS      BOO:WORDMX   .DOC

BOO:XD       .AQM     BOO:XMAS      .PQC    BOO:Z80-OPS .ASM

BOO:Z80ASM   .OBJ     BOO:Z80DOC   .DOC     BOO:Z80MAIN .AQM

BOO:Z80OPCDS.ASM      BOO:Z80SUBS .AQM      BOO:ZCMD      .AQM

BOO:ZCMD     .MSG     BOO:OVERLORD.OBJ      BOO:MORGANA .PQC

BOO:YOW      .OBJ     BOO:OVERLORD.DOC      BOO:DOCTOR   .OBJ

BOO:HELP-DTR.OBJ      BOO:ZCPRBLOC.AQM      BOO:ZESOURCE.DOC

BOO:ZESOURCE.OBJ      BOO:ZZSOURCE.OBJ      BOO:Z19PAT3 .ASM

BOO:NOCWID   .DQC     BOO:OLD      .TXT     BOO:WEIRD    .PIC

BOO:GROUCHO .PQC      BOO:PLANE    .PQC     BOO:OSDDAUTO.DOC

BOO:CATXRF12.DOC      BOO:CATXRF12.OBJ      BOO:OSDDAUTO.OBJ

BOO:NCAT31   .BUG     BOO:ELIZA    .BAS     BOO:TYPE     .OBJ
```

This was the end of - -> filefind, a very useful command if you want to get a quick overview of what is on a bulletin board. Filefind, itself, as well as the Palos Verdes bulletin board are both implemented under the CP/M operating system. On some other boards not running under CP/M and the bulletin board software used here, you may have to use DIR for Directory, or as the board advises.

You may have noticed that both file name and file extension or file type are used in the CP/M notation, which consists of filename XXXXXXXX eight characters long followed by a file extension/ file type XXX that is three characters long. Combining file name and file extension/type, we get a picture of XXXXXXXX.XXX. As it is impractical to use the full filename and file extension/type for every file, you will find in most instances that not all available positions are being used. The first file on drive A00 is DIR.COM. The file name is DIR, which stands for directory, and the file type is .COM, which stands for COMpiled. Here you are dealing with a machine-language file resident on the BBS. Any .COM file is a read only file and can not be copied. Any .COM file that the BBS operator is willing to let you copy, will have an extension of .OBJ. I will show you how to transfer files in all detail in Chapter 7. If you are interested in the different types of file extensions/types encountered on drive A:, here is a quick summary.

.AQM—means really .ASM but the Q means file was squeezed to conserve both storage space on the BBS disc and to speed up transmission, thus

saving transmission cost. Files of the type Q, and mostly the middle letter of the extension/type will be a "Q", have to be unsqueezed by you so you can read them in their expanded form. To get a preview of a squeezed file use the command TYPE-SQUEEZE. For details on how to use SQUEEZE, UNSQUEEZE, and TYPESQUEEZE see Chapter 10. Oh, sorry, .ASM is a program file to be assembled for translation into a .COM file by an assembler.

.BQS—This stands for a BASIC program file, which has been squeezed.

.COM—This is a machine-language program that you can execute, usually output from an assembler.

.DQF—.DIF, for a very clever way of updating a file to its newest version. A program called SSED is used to take the old version of a file and to apply the file .DIF, which had been squeezed in our sample, to come up with the new version. For the gory details, see Chapter 10.

.DQC—.DOC, documentation, your friend and helper. A lot of fine documentation on this bulletin board system is well worth your attention. Here is a quick sample: squeezed version, .DQC, we find AX25, MODEM75, PROTOCOL, RESPONSE, TIPMOS, SQUEEZER, and UNSP30. In the unsqueezed version, .DOC, we find: DPDOS, DISKMENU, DISZILOG, DRAGON, DU-V77, HAMMING, HAMPROGS, SYSTEM, and TURNKEY. This documentation covers BBS software, utility programs, HELP files, a spooler, systems software, games, hamprograms, and a disassembler. What a selection! Does this not sound like all that stuff you were always looking for? Up

and at 'em! Sounds like some exciting sessions coming up!

.HQP—.HLP, HELP files, what great stuff. If you want to find out what you and a home computer really can do, go and find as many files with the extension .HLP as you can find. A terrific companion and the program that uses HELP files is called HELP.COM. Together HELP.COM and SUBJECT.HLP files allow you to get into the detail of many intricate processors, languages, and utility software programs imaginable. A good sample of how to use HELP.COM and .HLP files is given in Chapter 10.

.LBR—This is a compendium of programs and documentation, normally collected by subject matter and contained in one super-file with the .LBR extension. Very useful for archiving your own files, such as correspondence, and so forth.

.MAC—or .MQC are program files to be assembled by the Macroassembler MAC or RMAC.

.MQG—or .MSG, just as the name implies, a little message (or is it a long one?)

.OBJ—these are .COM files that you can transfer to your own system using XMODEM, see Chapter 7 or .COM above.

.TQT—A friend of .DOC — .TXT files contain usually data files used in conjunction with a program.

WhatsNew

There are more ways to determine what is going on on a bulletin board. In addition to filefind -->, a nice feature of many bulletin boards is the whatsnew--> feature.

```
A0>whatsnew-->


WHATSNEW VER 2.7A

CTL-S PAUSES, CTL-C ABORTS
```

---: NEW FILES SINCE 5/23/83 :

A: LIPM52 .AQM : LIB85   .LIB : DISKMENU.DOC : RCPM-040.LQT

A: LIPMODS .TXT :

---: DELETED FILES SINCE 5/23/83 :

A: LIPM05 .AQM : RCPM-037.LQT :

AO>b:-->

BO>whatsnew-->

WHATSNEW VER 2.7A

CTL-S PAUSES, CTL-C ABORTS

---: NEW FILES SINCE 5/22/83 :

B: ATARICPM.DQC : DISK76F .OBJ : USQ   .DOC : ADVENTUR.OBJ :

B: ADVENTUR.WQK : BDLOC   .OBJ : BOMB   .TQT : BOMB1   .TQT :

B: SQ/USQ .LBR : DECISION.BQS : DIAL10 .DOC : PCPI/CCP.TQT :

B: DISKMENU.DOC : USQ   .EXE : LABLE   .DOC : LABLE   .OBJ :

B: YAM/H89 .OBJ : BIGBURST.AQM : CUCU   .TLS : PACMAN   .DQT :

B: PACMAN .AQM : DIAL   .OBJ : SHOOT   .OBJ : UNSP30   .OBJ :

B: XMAS   .PQC : ZCMD   .AQM : ZCMD   .MSG : OVERLORD.OBJ :

B: MORGANA .PQC : YOW   .OBJ : OVERLORD.DOC : DOCTOR   .OBJ :

B: HELP-DTR.OBJ : Z19PAT3 .ASM : NOCWID .DQC : OLD   .TXT :

B: WEIRD   .PIC : GROUCHO .PQC : PLANE   .PQC : OSDDAUTO.DOC

B: CATXRF12.DOC : CATXRF12.OBJ : OSDDAUTO.OBJ : NCAT31   .BUG :

B: ELIZA   .BAS : TYPE   .OBJ :

```
--: DELETED FILES SINCE 5/22/83 :

B: PACUTIL .CQ  : DECISION.BAS : JRT-PAS .FIX : PACMAN   .C   :

B: PAC-ID  .LIB : ADVEN80 .DQC : ADVEN80 .MQC : PACMAN95.OBJ :

B: BOMB    .TXT : ZCPR    .DQC : BOMB1   .TXT : ZCPR     .AQM :

B: DISK74B .OBJ : PACMONST.C   : ZCPR    .MSG : CLOCK    .PAS :

B: SAMPADV .AQV : PACDEFS .H   : PACMAN  .DOC : CHEAP    .64K :

B: DATE    .BAS :
```

This helpful feature is another nice way to find out what has transpired since you last browsed through the files of your favorite board. Whatsnew brings to your attention all the subjects that may be of interest to you, in a compact format without having to sort through all the past files.

Directory

The last and final form of the directory search is to just plain issue a DIR--> Remember that file DIR.COM in the beginning of the directory. Again, all the files for the selected drive are listed. If you want the B: drive, you must issue another DIR-->.

```
A0>dir-->

AUTOLOAD.ASM  4k : AX25     .DQC 26k : BBS      .COM 18k :

BYE      .COM  4k : BYE77    .AQM 46k : CHAT     .COM  2k :

CIA      .BQS 12k : CODE     .BAS  2k : CPDOS    .BAS  6k :

CPDOS    .DOC  4k : CPM-BKSP.ASM   2k : CRCK     .COM  2k :

D-27A    .AQM 14k : DECXHAM  .ASM  4k : DIR      .COM  2k :

DISKMENU.DOC   4k : DISZILOG.DOC   2k : DISZILOG.OBJ 10k :

DRAGON   .DOC  2k : DRAGON   .PQC  4k : DU-V77   .DOC  8k :

DU-V77   .OBJ  6k : ELIZA    .BAS  8k : ENTBBS24.BQS  8k :

FBAD-V54.AQM  24k : FILEFIND.COM   6k : FORMHAM  .ASM  4k :

FREAK    .TXT  4k : HAMMING  .DOC  4k : HAMPROGS.DOC  2k :

HELP     .COM  2k : INSUR    .TXT  4k : LIB85    .LIB  2k :

LIPM52   .AQM 32k : LIPMODS  .TXT  4k : LOGON    .COM 12k :

MBOOT    .DOC  4k : MBOOT3   .ASM  8k : MEMR     .OBJ  4k :
```

```
MFT45    .AQM  14k : MINIBBS .BQS  14k : MODEM221.AQM  54k :

MODEM75 .AQM  46k : MODEM75 .DQC  10k : MODEM75 .LQB  10k :

MOONLOC5.BAS   6k : MORSE   .ASM   8k : PACKET   .BIB   6k :

PACKET  .RQL   6k : PINUP   .PQC   4k : PINUP1  .PQC   6k :

PINUP2  .PQC   4k : PRACTICE.ASM   8k : PROTOCOL.DQC   6k :

RANDTEXT.BAS   2k : RCPM-040.LQT  16k : RESOURCE.DQC  18k :

RESOURCE.OBJ   6k : RTTY    .AQM  14k : SEQIO2  .LQB   8k :

SNAGLPUS.PIC   4k : SNOOPY  .PIC   4k : SQ-15   .OBJ  14k :

SQ/USQ  .HIS   8k : SQUEEZER.DQC  14k : SYSTEM  .DOC   2k :

TEACH   .AQM   6k : TEACH   .COM   2k : TIME-QT .ASM   6k :

TIPMO5  .AQM  20k : TIPMO5  .DQC   6k : TTY     .AQM   6k :

TURNKEY1.AQM   4k : TURNKEY1.DOC   4k : TWEETY  .PQC   2k :

TY      .COM   2k : TYPE    .COM  10k : UNSP30  .AQM  12k :

UNSP30  .DQC   6k : USQ-19  .OBJ  12k : XMODEM  .COM   4k :

XMODEM50.AQM  34k : ZCHESS  .OBJ   8k
```

```
A: Total of 772k in 83 files with 0k space remaining.
```

The message at the end of the directory listing of drive A gives you the appropriate size, the number of files, and the amount of space remaining. In this sample it is a full house! By going through the process of giving you the contents of drive B;, please observe that the program DIR.COM, invoked by the command DIR-->, gives us a different format than the program FILEFIND.COM. Filefind gives us the contents of all drives, differentiates between drive and user, and is only required once. The command DIR-->, however, has to be used for each drive separately. It gives all users on a drive if the drive is split up in more than one user area. You will find this quite convenient.

```
B0>dir-->

23MATCHE.BAS   2k : 60MINS  .TQT   8k : 6503    .TXT   2k :

80-103A .DCH   2k : ADVENTUR.OBJ  22k : ADVENTUR.WQK  24k :

APMD1201.DOC   2k : APMD1201.OBJ   8k : APMD300 .OBJ   8k :

APMEMMAP.NEW   6k : APZCPR  .DOC   4k : ARCHIVE .AQM  18k :
```

ATARICPM.DOC 6k	AUTOST .OSZ 4k	BARBIE .PQC 4k
BDLOC .OBJ 2k	BEAM .BQS 12k	BIGBURST.AQM 8k
BIORY .BAS 4k	BISHOW14.AQM 8k	BOMB .TQT 6k
BOMB1 .TQT 4k	BUDGET .BAS 10k	BUFFER .DOC 2k
BUFFER .LIB 6k	CATXRF12.DOC 6k	CATXRF12.OBJ 6k
CCPPATCH.ASM 2k	CHASE .BAS 4k	CHDIR .CQ 10k
CHDIR .MQG 4k	COPYFAST.AQM 16k	CPM-DEC .DOC 6k
CPMTODEC.OBJ 4k	CPMUTIL .ASM 8k	CRCK3 .ASM 8k
CRCSUBS .LIB 6k	CUCU .TLS 8k	DATABASE.BQS 10k
DBFORMAT.BAS 4k	DECISION.BQS 4k	DECTOCPM.OBJ 4k
DIAL .OBJ 8k	DIAL10 .DOC 6k	DISK74 .DOC 4k
DISK76F .OBJ 4k	DISKMENU.DOC 10k	DOCTOR .OBJ 8k
DU/MAP .DOC 2k	DX .OBJ 2k	ELIZA .BAS 0k
ERAQ .MQC 8k	EX .DQC 4k	EX .OBJ 2k
EXPANDO .RQM 4k	FILEFND8.AQM 10k	FLIGHT .BAS 2k
FMAP3 .ASM 8k	GROUCHO .PQC 2k	HAMCALC .BQS 8k
HAMHELP .BAS 6k	HELP-DTR.OBJ 10k	HP125MDM.HLP 2k
ICOPY .ASM 8k	IDIR .ASM 6k	KINGDOM .BAS 10k
KPRO-BY2.HQP 4k	LABLE .DOC 2k	LABLE .OBJ 10k
LISTDEC .OBJ 4k	LOWER .ASM 4k	LOWPASS .BAS 4k
LU211 .DQC 18k	LU211 .OBJ 18k	MAKEADV .BQS 6k
MAZE .BAS 4k	MDM707 .DQC 20k	MDM707 .INF 6k
MDM707 .OBJ 18k	MDM707 .SET 8k	MEMTST .ASM 4k
MIND .BAS 2k	MLIST501.AQM 10k	MONA .PQC 8k
MORGANA .PQC 2k	NCAT31 .BUG 2k	NEWCAT28.DQC 12k
NEWCAT29.AQM 22k	NOCWID .DQC 8k	OLD .TXT 2k

```
OSDDAUTO.DOC    2k :  OSDDAUTO.OBJ    2k :  OTHEL    .BAS    6k :

OVERLORD.DOC    2k :  OVERLORD.OBJ    4k :  PACMAN   .AQM   18k :

PACMAN   .DQT   2k :  PCPI/CCP.TQT    4k :  PINUP4   .PQC    4k :

PINUP5   .PQC   4k :  PIPPTCH2.AQM    6k :  PLANE    .PQC    2k :

POEM     .TXT   2k :  POKER    .BAS  10k :  PRINT    .ASM    8k :

PRNT     .ASM   6k :  PUZZLE   .BAS   4k :  QT-TIME .BAS     4k :

QUEST    .BQS   8k :  RTE      .ASM   8k :  RTMLD    .ASM    4k :

SAD-TALE.TXT    2k :  SAP36    .AQM   8k :  SD-48A   .AQM   42k :

SECTION .AQM    8k :  SEXELECT.TXT    2k :  SHOOT    .OBJ   10k :

SQ/USQ   .LBR  36k :  STARTREK.DOC    2k :  STARTREK.PQC   18k :

SUB      .OBJ   4k :  SUB-FIX .DOC    4k :  SUPSUB   .DQC    4k :

SWEEP35  .OBJ  28k :  SYSTAT   .AQM   6k :  TEST1A   .ASM    4k :

TEST2    .ASM   2k :  TIGER    .PQC   4k :  TINYBAS .DQC     8k :

TINYBAS  .OBJ   4k :  TREK2-1 .BAS    8k :  TYPE     .OBJ    0k :

TYPE17   .OBJ  10k :  UNDEL    .DOC   4k :  UNDEL    .OBJ    4k :

UNERA    .ASM   6k :  UNSP30   .OBJ   2k :  USQ      .DOC    2k :

USQ      .EXE  28k :  USRDFLT2.CQP   10k :  WARI     .BAS    4k :

WARMBOOT.ASM    4k :  WEIRD    .PIC   2k :  WORDMAZE.BAS     6k :

WORDMX   .DOC   2k :  XD       .AQM  18k :  XMAS     .PQC    6k :

YAM/H89 .OBJ   28k :  YOW      .OBJ   2k :  Z19PAT3 .ASM     6k :

Z80-OPS .ASM    8k :  Z80ASM   .OBJ  10k :  Z80DOC   .DOC    4k :

Z80MAIN .AQM   18k :  Z80OPCDS.ASM    4k :  Z80SUBS .AQM     8k :

ZCMD     .AQM  44k :  ZCMD     .MSG   2k :  ZCPRBLOC.AQM     2k :

ZESOURCE.DOC    4k :  ZESOURCE.OBJ    8k :  ZZSOURCE.OBJ     8k :

B: Total of 1202k in 162 files with 2k space remaining.

B0>
```

Wild Card Symbols

To spare you to go through the entire directory using the DIR.COM program or the routine FILEFIND.COM there a is shortcut for the CP/M world: the use of wild card symbols. *.* in CP/M'ese means all files and all extensions. This is also true in other DEC computer languages. It is likely that the original version of CP/M was written on a DEC PDP computer. In lieu of the actual 8080 chip that had no input/output peripherals at the time other than punched paper tape, one used on 8080 simulator, a means of writing software later used on

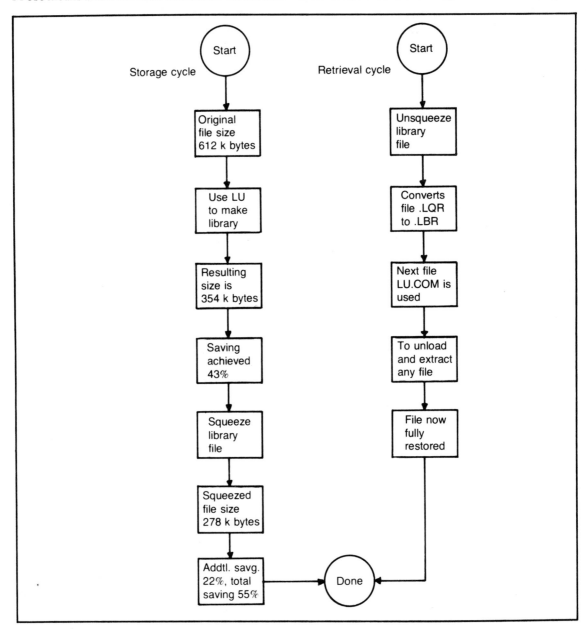

Fig. 6-1. Economical file archiving.

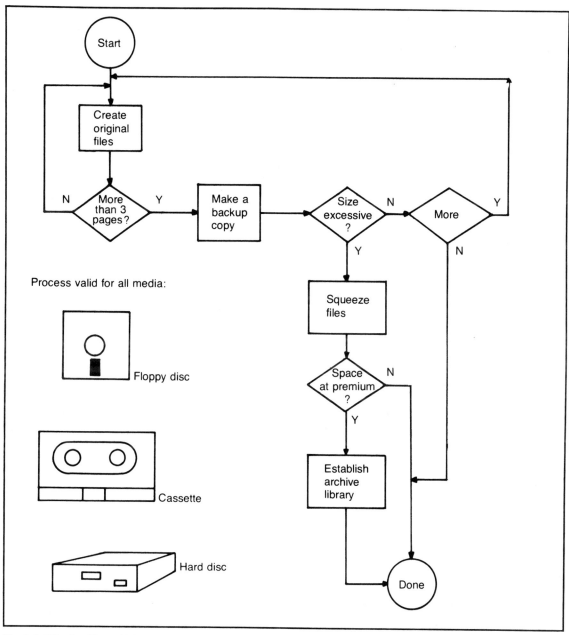

Fig. 6-2. Effective file archiving.

another computer or chip. W *.* then means all files with the beginning letter of W, no matter what follows, and no matter what extension. The second wild card character is the question mark. *.?Q? means all files with the second letter of Q in the extension. Issuing the command: DIR--> ham*.* on drive B: of the Palos Verdes bulletin board would then yield for us the following extract:

B:> : HAMCALC .BQS 8 K : HAMHELP .BAS 6 K :

: HAMMING .DOC 2 K :

and show us that three files have qualified for our request.

If you wanted to know all the files with the extension .BAS, squeezed or unsqueezed, on a given drive, the use of *.B?S, with the wild card character "?", would give us both the .BAS and the .BQS files. This is powerful stuff, so use it to your advantage.

File Handling Utilites

The directory of another very successful board contains a sample of the kind of utility software that is available in the public domain. The particular directory shown here describes a multitude of software, that can be used on many systems and contains excellent documentation. My commentary follows the directory. Figure 6-1 and Fig. 6-2 also illustrate efficient file handling techniques.

-FILUTIL.U01	0k		ARCHIVE	.AQ6	18k		ARCHIVE	.AQM	18k
BANNER	.AQM	8k	BUFFER	.DQC	2k	BUFFER	.LQB	4k
CAT	.OBJ	2k	CAT2	.OBJ	2k	CATALOG	.DQC	4k
CDOSCOPY.ZQO	10k	CMPRLEX	.OBJ	2k	CMPRLEX	.ZQO	8k
COMPARE	.MQC	4k	CPMTOPAS.PQS	8k	CPMXFER	.DQC	2k
CPMXFER	.OBJ	4k	CPYFIL15.MQC	8k	CPYFST40.DQC	22k
CPYFST43.AQM	28k	CRCK42B	.AQM	8k	CRCK45	.OBJ	4k
D-29	.AQM	18k	DATABASE.BQS	10k	DBFORMAT.BAS	4k
DF	.DQC	2k	DF	.OBJ	10k	DICCRE10.OBJ	2k
DIF2	.OBJ	16k	DIF2	.RQO	4k	DIRR	.DOC	4k
DIRR	.OBJ	4k	DISPLAY	.DQC	2k	DISPLAY	.OBJ	2k
DISPLAYP.AQM	2k	DX4	.OBJ	2k	EPRINT	.AQM	12k
EPRINT	.DQC	4k	ERAQ	.MQC	8k	FILE-XT2.AQM	6k
FILFND11.AQM	12k	FILTER11.MQC	4k	FIND-20	.AQM	10k
FIND-20	.DQC	2k	FIXTEX10.AQM	14k	FLAGS	.DQC	2k
FLAGS12	.AQM	8k	FMAP40	.DQC	2k	FMAP40	.OBJ	2k
GENPTS	.BQS	2k	GRAPHIX	.BQS	2k	IDUMP421.AQM	4k
INDEX101.DQC	6k	INDEX101.OBJ	12k	LDIR	.CQ	6k
LDIR	.MQG	2k	LDIR	.OBJ	6k	LIBRIES	.DOC	2k
LIBRIES	.LBR	60k	LISTT	.DQC	4k	LISTT	.OBJ	2k

```
LRUN      .OBJ    2k    LU       .DOC   14k    LU        .OBJ   18k

LU111-FX.SQB    2k    MACROS   .TOP    6k    MASTHEAD.AQM    4k

MDIR8/17.AQM    8k    MFT45    .AQM   12k    MLIST50 .AQM   10k

MX-80    .TOP    4k    MX-PLOT .BOS    6k    MX80GRAF.DOC    2k

NCAT32   .DOC    4k    NCAT32   .OBJ    8k    NCAT32   .SQT    4k

NEWCAT28.DOC   12k    NEWCAT29.AQM   22k    PASTOCPM.AQM    8k

PRINT234.AQM   26k    PRNTSQ   .OBJ   10k    PTSRCNVT.AQM    4k

PTSRCNVT.DOC    2k    PTSRCNVT.OBJ    2k    RENAME   .AQM   18k

RT11     .DOC    6k    RT11     .OBJ   14k    RUN80    .DOC    6k

RUN80-V2.AQM   22k    SORTV    .DOC    2k    SORTV-12.AQM   10k

SP-ED    .DOC    6k    SP-ED11 .OBJ   10k    SPELL    .DOC    2k

SPELL-11.AQM   18k    SPELL-11.DOC    2k    SPELL-11.OBJ    4k

SPTTIME .AQM    6k    SQ-16    .OBJ   16k    SQUEEZER.DOC   16k

SSED2    .OBJ   12k    SWEEP35 .DOC    8k    SWEEP35 .OBJ   28k

SWEEP36 .OBJ   28k    SYSLBHLP.LBR   58k    SYSLBS21.WQ    28k

SYSLIB   .WQ    68k    TBPRNT12.MOC    8k    TLIST    .AQM   14k

TYPE1380.OBJ   10k    TYPE15   .DOC    2k    TYPE15   .OBJ   10k

USQ-19   .OBJ   12k    VDMSAVE .AQM    4k    WASH-12 .AQM   22k

WASH-14 .OBJ    4k    WCOUNT   .OBJ    6k    XCAT37   .DOC    4k

XCAT37   .OBJ    4k    XDIR2-51.AQM   66k    XDIR2-51.MOG    4k

XDIR3    .MOC   24k
```

```
Drive C, user 1 contains 1262K in 125 files with 2328K free
```

Quite a few of the programs listed mean absolutely nothing to me. Some of them give you an idea of what they are doing. I am very familiar with quite a few of them. As a matter of fact, I use some of them constantly.

ARCHIVE is a series of programs that allow you to store and retrieve program and data types. The BANNER program allows you to print block letters on a line printer. CATALOG belongs to a series similar to ARCHIVE, COMPARE allows you to check the contents of two files and list all dissimilarities, and CPMTOPAS is a file transfer program, to which the other half is called, you quessed it, PASTOCPM.

CPYFAST allows disc to disc copy using a fast read/write mode. DIF does like COMPARE, and DISPLAY allows you to use the same syntax as the CP/M editor to display a screen full of text at the time. The FIND series work in conjunction with the CAT/NCAT series, and they let you archive your discs and allow you to find filenames and extensions.

LDIR allows the listing of filenames contained in a type .LBR file. LISTT, a welcome addition to anyones utility library, allows you to start listing a long file anyplace, and if you ever printed lines 5,666 to 7,600 a file that has 9,000 entries, you can appreciate the time saved when you finally have a program that allows you to do so near the end instead of way up front. LISTT does not show you one line before the one you ask for, a real eye-saver!

LU, library utility, goes with the FIND, CAT, and NCAT series of programs. See the comment

under CAT. MX-80 must be print routines enhancing the use of that fine printer from Epson. SORTV is supposedly a screaming sort in the public domain that is supposed to handle files which have records of variable length—sorry, I have not used that one.

SQUEEZE, UNSQUEEZE, TYPESQUEEZE, and PRINTSQUEEZE are all part of a family of programs described that allow you to compress file space by squeezing programs and data files for storage. SWEEP and WASH do much the same as a program called DISC, they display the contents of disc file directories and allow you to display individual files, rename them, copy, and delete. Finally, the DIF and SSED programs allow you to update files, as described in Chapter 10 also. XDIR and XCAT, I believe, belong to the CAT/NCAT family of archiving tools. So there you are, an impressive array of utilities that comes in very handy on many occasions, and don't forget, the price is right!

Communications, Utilities, Languages, And Games

Let's take a look at the RCP/M board in Pasadena, California.

```
--->USER 3
C3>--->DIR

-COMMS    .UO3   0k   APBOOT   .OBJ   2k   APBYE782.AQM   38k
APMBOOT  .AQM   6k   APMD1200.DOC   2k   APMD1201.OBJ   8k
APMD300  .OBJ   8k   APMDM221.OBJ   8k   APPLFLIP.AQM   4k
APPLMODM.AQM  24k   APVIDEX  .AQM   2k   APXMOD50.AQM   32k
BY2-IO   .LBR  36k   BYE      .DOC   8k   BYE2     .DOC   4k
BYE2-12  .AQM  36k   BYE79    .AQM  54k   BYE79    .FQX   4k
BYE79H89.AQM  54k   BYEXX    .BUG   2k   CHAT19   .AQM   8k
COMM7    .DOC   6k   COMM7    .HQS   8k   COMM7    .PRO   2k
COMM7    .TQT   8k   COMM714  .AQM  74k   COMM7CAL.OBJ   2k
DBBS     .DOC   6k   DBBS     .FIX   2k   DBBS     .LBR  24k
```

```
DIALMM2 .OBJ    2k    ENTBBS24.BQS    8k    FLIP7    .AQM    4k

HAMLINK4.AQM   16k    INITBAUD.SUB    4k    LMODEM16.AQM   22k

M797AC89.AQM   12k    MBOOT3  .AQM    6k    MCNFG797.AQM   10k

MENU    .RQS    2k    MINBBS26.BQS   16k    MODEM220.AQM   52k

MODEM2XX.FQX    2k    MODEM797.AQM   58k    MODEM797.HQS   14k

MODEM797.IQF    4k    MODEM797.LQB   14k    MODEM797.OBJ   16k

MODEM797.SQT    4k    MODMPROT.OQ1    6k    MTN22   .DQC    6k

MTN22B  .OBJ   16k    MTNMSGS .OVR   18k    NEWBD23 .AQM    6k

NEWCOM  .1Q     2k    OBSMODEM.DOC    4k    OBSMODEM.OQJ   10k

QSBPLINK.AQM   10k    OTERM4  .DQC   28k    OTERM404.NQE    2k

OTERM404.OQJ   28k    OTERM405.SQB    2k    OTSETUP4.DQC    2k

PACKET  .LBR   36k    PIPMOD  .AQM    2k    PIPMOD  .DQC    6k

PLINK   .DQC    2k    PLINK67 .AQM   22k    RBBS-RTN.OQ1   12k

RBBS-USE.DQC    8k    RBBS30  .AQC   20k    RBBS30  .DQC    2k

RBSUTL31.AQC    8k    ROOM    .LBR   44k    ROOM    .MSG    2k

RTTY    .AQM   14k    SECURTY2.AQM    4k    SENDOUT7.AQM    6k

SIGNON  .MQG    2k    SIGNON-1.LBR   66k    SIGNON-2.LBR   62k

SMODEM  .DQC   16k    SMODEM39.MQC   50k    XMODEM60.AQM   34k

XMODEM60.HQS   10k

Drive C, user 3 contains 1306K in 85 files with 2328K free
```

That looks suspiciously like hard disc storage. That kind of storage can be put on a floppy disk, but they are not selling those as yet! By now you should have recognized that the category of -COMMS means communications. Let's see what the next category is all about.

```
C3>-->USER 4

C4>-->DIR

-DIAGS  .UO4    Ok    BGMEMTST.AQM    2k    BRNWASH .MQC   20k
```

```
CPMONIT .AQM   12k     CPMONIT .DQC    4k     CPUDIAG .AQM   10k

DU-V77  .AQM   30k     DU-V77  .DQC    4k     DU-V7778.DQF    2k

DUU10/23.OBJ    8k     FINDBD54.AQM   24k     FINDBD54.BQG    2k

FINDBD54.OBJ    2k     MNEMON21.AQM   16k     MONITOR .PQS    8k

UMPIRE  .DQC    2k     UMPIRE  .OBJ    2k     WORM21  .AQM    6k

XAMN    .OBJ   28k     Z80MT   .AQM    6k
```

Drive C, user 4 contains 188K in 20 files with 2328K free

This was a file of utility programs.

```
C4>--->USER 5

C5>--->DIR

-LANGSYS.UO5   0k     ALGOL/M .LBR   50k     F80-BUG .FQX    2k

FIGFORTH.AQM   40k     FIGFORTH.DQC    6k     FIGFORTH.OBJ    8k

FORTH11 .AQM   24k     FORTH11 .DQC    2k     INIT4TH .AQM    6k

PILOT   .LBR   36k     U-LISP  .AQC    8k     ZPILOT  .OBJ    2k

ZPILOT  .ZOO    6k
```

Drive C, user 5 contains 190K in 13 files with 2328K free

Here you are looking at language systems. The file contains six different languages.

```
C5>--->USER 6

C6>--->DIR

-GAMES  .UO6   0k     ADVEN80 .LBR   48k     ADVENTUR.LBR   80k

ALIENS  .DIF    2k     ALIENS11.CQ    14k     ALIENS11.DQC    2k

ALIENS11.OBJ   14k     AMAZING .BQS    4k     BANG    .BQS    4k

BIO     .BQS    4k     BIOCAL83.AQC    6k     BIOSIN  .BQS    6k

BIOSUM  .BQS    6k     BIRTHDAY.BQS    4k     BLURG   .BQS    2k

CAL     .DQC    2k     CAL     .OBJ    6k     CALENDAR.BQS    2k
```

114

```
CARDTRK  .AQC    4k    CHESFOR  .DOC    2k    CHESFOR  .OBJ   26k

CHESS    .PQI   14k    CHESS    .PQS   52k    CHESS41  .DOC    2k

CHESS41  .FQR   16k    CHESS41  .OBJ   26k    CHINC    .BQS    2k

DEEPSPCE .BQS    6k    EAC      .DQC    4k    EAC      .OBJ   28k

ELIZA    .BQS    6k    FANCFONT .LBR   44k    GAMMON   .BQS   10k

GIANT3   .BQS    4k    GOLDI    .PLT    2k    HAMLOG   .FOR    2k

HANOI    .AQG    2k    HP35     .DOC    4k    HUNT     .DOC    2k

HUNT     .OBJ   32k    LIFE8    .AQM   12k    LIFE8    .DOC    2k

MONOPLY  .BQS   18k    MONSTER  .BQS    6k    MONSTER  .DOC    4k

NUKETANK .H19   10k    OZCLOCK  .BQS    8k    PACMAN   .DOC    2k

PACMAN89 .OBJ   18k    PACMAN95 .OBJ   18k    PLICHESS .OBJ   18k

PONG41   .AQM    6k    POSTER   .BQS   12k    PRACTICE .AQM    6k

ROSE     .BQS    2k    STAR     .BQS   24k    STAR     .OBJ   36k

STARWARS .BQS   10k    TAX81    .BQS   10k    TCTCTO   .LQP    4k

TEACH    .AQM    6k    TVIGAMMO .BQS   10k    WORDPUZL .BQS    4k

ZCHESS   .DOC    2k    ZCHESS   .OBJ    8k    ZILCH    .BQS    6k

Drive C, user 6 contains 758K in 66 files with 2328K free

C6>
```

Thank you, Pasadena, this last directory has more games than Carter has liver pills, as my good friend Paul would say! The game category is entirely up to your imagination. Have fun.

A PC BULLETIN BOARD

Here is what you will find if you log-on to a PC bulletin board. By all means, do not forget that you do not need a PC or a PC look-alike. Any terminal or home computer with communications can access most boards. The sign-on has been skipped to come right to the file transfer function and to the inventory of available files. This is the IBM PC board: A file transfer protocol is set up to work with IBM Asynchronous Communications Support, but any properly programmed computer can utilize the download feature. When prompted for "Name of file on host to be transmitted" enter one of the filenames listed below. The next prompt will ask IBM Asynchronous Support users to hit a function key and other users to hit their <ENTER> or <RETURN> keys. At this point, a carriage return will result in a message "Starting File Transmission. . ." followed by the file, and ending with "File transmission complete . . .", 5 bells, and the PC BBS command prompt. Program your computer accordingly. The files in the following list are available for transfer. Files with an extension of .HEX must be converted to .COM or .EXE files with the HEXCNVRT.BAS program before execution.

FILENAME		SIZE	DESCRIPTION
CONFIG	HEX	41472	Convert to .EXE for summary of system configuration
IBMODEM	BAS	14214	Terminal program for I.B.M. PC
IBMODEM	DOC	4736	Documentation for above file
MYCOMM	BAS	10463	Terminal program for I.B.M. PC
XMODEM	BAS	9702	File transfer between I.B.M. PCs w/error checking
RV-EDIT	BAS	12416	BASIC full screen editor
RV-EDIT	DOC	9824	Documentation for above file
SPOOLER1	HEX	1664	DOS print spooler for Mono/Printer Adapter
SPOOLER1	DOC	649	Documentation for above file
SPOOLER2	HEX	1920	DOS print spooler for Printer Adapter
SPOOLER2	DOC	363	Documentation for above file
T	HEX	3546	Generate a printer form feed from DOS
T	DOC	490	Documentation for above file
PRT	HEX	76672	Send files to a serial printer with lots of options
PRT	DOC	10495	Documentation for above file
DISPLAY	BAS	4480	Create screen graphs
DISPLYIN	BAS	1084	Use with DISPLAY.BAS
DISPLAY	DOC	722	Documentation for above 2 files

DISPSMPL	DAT	128	Sample data file for DISPLAY.BAS
DISP	TST	256	Sample data file for DISPLAY.BAS
PRINTER	BAS	4736	Prints paginated listings of text files
DEFINE	BAS	6396	Define graphics characters for later use
DEFINE	DOC	896	Documentation for above file
GCOPY	BAS	6016	Copy files from within BASIC
COREDUMP	BAS	1408	Display memory contents on screen
PC-FILE	HEX	89856	Comprehensive Relational Database manager
PC-FILE	DOC	55808	Documentation for above file
PC-SORT	HEX	50816	Use with PC-FILE
PC-EXPOR	HEX	44416	Use with PC-FILE
PRT	CTL	39	Use with PC-FILE
PRT40	CTL	21	Use with PC-FILE
PRT80	CTL	17	Use with PC-FILE
PEEKPOKE	DOC	3072	PEEK and POKE information for the PC
ONEFOR	HEX	8064	Fast Format Utility
ONEFOR	DOC	3328	Documentation for above file
TWOFOR	BAT	38	Batch file for ONEFOR
SEARCH	BAS	3328	Search for strings in text files
SEARCH	DOC	348	Documentation for above file
BAT	HEX	6400	Batch file utility
BATPRINT	DOC	35328	Documentation for above file (Epson Ctrl Codes)
BATDEMO	BAT	4037	Demo file for BAT
BEEP	HEX	384	Convert to BEEP.COM for BEEP within

DOS

PCLIST	BAS	3072	BASIC program listings to Epson printer
SELSORT1	BAS	4224	Visicalc sort utility
LABELEPS	BAS	2816	Print labels on Epson printers
COMPRESS	BAS	4608	Remove remarks and spaces from BASIC programs
PRTITALX	BAS	3072	Italics on Epson printers
DIFPROC1	BAS	4224	Visicalc DIF file utility
PROFILER	BAS	2304	Times BASIC program execution
PROFDEMO	BAS	768	PROFILER demo
747	BAS	33408	747 Flight Simulator for PC with graphics card
CLOCK	BAS	13824	Digital Clock with tick-tock & chime
ALGEBRA	BAS	5504	Graphics demo (requires graphics card)
DESIGN	BAS	17280	Graphics demo (requires graphics card)
FREE4	HEX	13056	Electronic Disk (160K)
FREE4	DOC	3023	Documentation for above file
FREE5	HEX	3840	Reset program
FREE5	DOC	3020	Documentation for above file
HIDEFILE	BAS	12800	Hide/Unhide disk files from directory
DIR	BAS	7936	Sorted directory from BASIC
SOFTSTSW	BAS	640	Switch between color & mono screens from BASIC
MODEM	HEX	19840	Convert to .COM for MODEM communications program
NECPRINT	BAS	14208	Utility for NEC 8023A printer

NECPRINT	DOC	5248	Documentation for above file
PC-TALK	DOC	119681	Documentation for following file
PC-TALK	BAS	45440	The newest version of the PC terminal program
PCTKREM	MRG	3584	PC-TALK remarks to be merged with PC-TALK.BAS
BLACKJAK	BAS	11051	An I.B.M. PC Blackjack game
CHESS	BAS	21139	An I.B.M. PC Chess game
CONV-VC	DOC	702	Documentation for the following file
CONV-VC	HEX	3717	Un copy-protect Visicalc
DATABASE	BAS	15037	Keeps track of your disks and files on them
DESCRIPT	DOC	726	The file that prints when you ask for description
DISKRTN	DOC	503	Documentation for the following file
DISKRTN	HEX	20085	A series of menu-driven disk utilities
EATME	BAS	12416	Pacman-like game for the PC
FINPAK	BAS	16565	A series of financial programs
FK	DOC	4643	Documentation for the following file
FK	HEX	4245	Define PC function keys in DOS
HELPFILE	DOC	1218	The file that prints when you ask for 'HELP'
HEXCNVRT	BAS	9212	Converts .HEX files to .COM or .EXE and vice-versa
HOST	BAS	14172	Use with SMARTMODEM to download files from remote area

```
HOST      DOC      379    Documentation for above file

INTERMOD  BAS     2659    Determine intermod frequencies after
                          entering others

MAIL1     BAS    24091    A mailing list management program

MAIL1     DOC     2816    Documentation for above file

MAILHELP  DOC     2176    Summary of PC BBS Mailbox Commands

MEMORY    DOC     2688    Documentation for the following file

MEMORY    HEX     3043    Change your DIP switches from the keyboard

NEWS      DOC    varies   PC BBS News

PONG      BAS     6137    A Pong-type game for the PC

SDIR      DOC      543    Documentation for following file

SDIR      HEX     2684    A sorted disk directory with options

STARTREK  BAS    25090    A Startrek game for the PC

SYSTAT    DOC     1050    Documentation for the following file

SYSTAT    HEX     2925    Get information about your disks
                          and configuration

TOWERS    BAS     2896    The Towers of Hanoi game for the PC

TUNE      DOC      716    Documentation for the following file

TUNE      HEX      813    Play one of five different tunes in DOS

UNPROTCT  DOC     1226    Documentation for the following file

UNPROTCT  HEX      284    Unprotect "protected" BASIC programs

UNWS      HEX     5828    Remove high-order bits from Wordstar
                          files.
```

Now, isn't that one of the nicest accumulations of software that you have ever seen? And this is just a smidgen of what is available in public domain software. What is even more exciting is the fact that the IBM and look-alike PC world is rapidly filling up their boards with excellent software.

AN ATARI BULLETIN BOARD

To give you an idea of another bulletin board, here are the files that you can get for the ATARI computer from an ATARI bulletin board:

```
WHAT IS YOUR CHOICE ?

(A,B,C,D,E,F,G,H,I,K,L)

(O,P,Q,R,S,T,U,W,X,?) >?

/CTRL=^/ ^S PAUSE, ^Q RESUME, ^X QUIT


            * FUNCTIONS *


        A..........ASCII/ATASCII SWITCH

        B...............PRINT BULLETINS

        C................PRINT CALLERS

        D..............DOWNLOAD A FILE

        E..............ENTER A MESSAGE

        F......LIST DOWNLOAD FILE NAMES

        G.......GOOD-BYE (LEAVE SYSTEM)

        H......EXPLANATION OF FUNCTIONS

        I.......INDEX OF DOWNLOAD FILES

        K......DELETE YOUR OLD MESSAGES

        L.....LINE FEED SWITCH (ON/OFF)

        O.........OTHER BULLETIN BOARDS

        P......PAGE AND CHAT WITH SYSOP

        Q.....QUICK SUMMARY OF MESSAGES

        R.............RETRIEVE MESSAGES

        S............SUMMARIZE MESSAGES

        T.................TIME AND DATE

        U................UPLOAD A FILE

        W.........PRINT WELCOME MESSAGE

        X............EXPERT USER SWITCH
```

121

```
?..............PRINTS THIS LIST

        *** END OF FILE ***

(A,B,C,D,E,F,G,H,I,K,L)

(O,P,Q,R,S,T,U,W,X,?) >-->I

/CTRL=^/ ^S PAUSE, ^Q RESUME, ^X QUIT


        SOME SHORT DESCRIPTIONS OF FILES

    HAWKMEN - FANTASY SPACE BATTLE

    RUNWAY  - CAN YOU LAND THIS PLANE?

    GRAVITY - KEEP THE BALL 'IN LINE'

    DISASMBL- MEM.DUMP/DISASSEMBLER

    DOODLE  - DRAW IN GR.9,10,11

    ERAMTEST - MEMORY CHECKER-BINARY

    TORTURE - USE PORTS 2 AND 3

    LIVEWIRE- FROM ANALOG-BINARY LOAD

    NEWXMOD - WE THINK IT'S BETTER THAN

            THE COMMERCIAL TERM.PROGS.

    AUTOGEN - LATEST VERSION/DIALER

    DSKTRNFR- ATARI DISK TRANSFER

    SECTUTIL- ACCESS TO 720 AND MORE

    ANMSCOPE- GRAPHICS DEMO - BINARY

        ***MORE COMING LATER***

        *** END OF FILE ***
```

Did you get the comment on the file NEWXMOD? NEWXMOD of course is the good old XMODEM program that you will use to talk to most of the bulletin boards. WE THINK IT'S BETTER THAN THE COMMERCIAL TERM. PROGS. Nice comment, you ought to check that out! Again, as you can see, it does not matter what computer you have, there is plenty of software out there for you, and best of all, it is absolutely free!

Well, I hope that you found browsing the directories of several real bulletin boards very exciting. What you have to learn now is how to download files so that you can add goodies to your own files and get the subject matter that you are really interested in. It is very interesting to see the wide range of subjects on many boards. The orientation of many boards is on certain subjects, and you can spend a lot of time learning new and interesting subjects. The organization of the files on many boards reflects the breadth and depth of software out there.

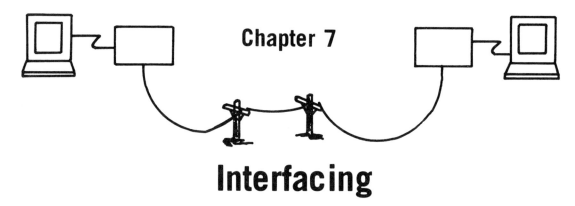

Chapter 7

Interfacing

In a recent conversation with Ward Christiansen, he explained how Irv Hoff took over the implementation of some ideas passed on to him on the MODEM part of the XMODEM programs and that the latest implementation known to him is now MDM712. He also acknowledged the contributions made by Dave Jaffe on BYE, mentioning that Dave wrote the original implementation of the MODEM program for the D.C. Hayes 80-103A modem board for the S-100 bus, while Ward himself was responsible for the implementation of MODEM on the PMMI modem board for the S-100 bus.

Then he told the story of how a commercial version of his code was surrounded by some window dressing and the same communications program that you can get on many bulletin boards for free and was offered to the unknowing for $400. Upon Ward's interference, the pirates acknowledged the origins of much of the code and halved the price of their product. What kind of pennance is that? The moral, of course is: always beware and let someone knowledgeable advise you when you buy software that may already exist in the public do-main. This moral also holds true for hardware as you will see.

THE S-100 BUS

Mentioning the S-100 bus brings us to a viable product that has been with us since those famous days in December of the year 1974, when a company called MITS of Albuquerque, New Mexico, published a do-it-yourself project for a home computer called Altair in the magazine Popular Electronics and sold you the parts that allowed you to build your own home computer using the Intel 8080 chip. The *S-100 bus* is a system connecting electrical signals that uses a 100-pin socket to make contact with 100 connectors (50 on each side) of any S-100 compatible board. The uniform layout of board and sockets allows a variety of manufacturers to produce S-100 products. These products can be plugged into the mainframe, a name that is used to describe a box that contains a power supply, a system for cooling whatever is in that box, and what is referred to as a *mother board*, the cage holding all those sockets into which you put the S-100 board level products. Much of the S-100 real-estate is populated with a tremendous variety of quality but, unfortunately, also a few bad products.

The advantages of the S-100 bus far outweigh the price, which is higher than if you would buy an integrated computer which may have slots for accepting expansion boards but does not conform to a standard. The advantages of the S-100 are that you can go out and buy high quality products and that you can acquire a system that is tailor made to your needs. By changing boards, you can instantly change the makeup of the compute power at your disposal.

Let us look at an example. Suppose you own a Z-80 system with two dual sided 8-inch floppy discs and 64 K of memory. This is a nice single user CP/M system. At your disposal are 1 million characters of on-line storage (certainly beats those little Mickey Mouse drives), but you still need more. To boot you want PC compatibility, but you are not willing to pay those inflated prices when buying a box that brings you yesterday's technology tomorrow. And, with hard disc prices coming down, and with memory getting a lot cheaper, you have plans to expand your system. Fantasy and fiction? Not at all.

Just take a look at the recent ads of a long established, reliable supplier of products for the S-100 bus, the CompuPro designs of a company called Goodbout Electronics of Oakland, California. In their catalog, they offer a large variety of individual S-100 boards and systems populated with those boards. Look at their memory boards. A board with the name of M-Drive/H allows you to substitute 512 K bytes of memory for a disc up to a maximum of 4 megabytes, that's 4 million bytes that can be put on a system by just adding additional boards. This will really speed up processing, especially word processing and other memory intensive computer applications. And if you like to get things done in a hurry, speeds never before available to you can now be attained. Additionally, multiusers are no problem. Dual capabilities of 8-bit and 16-bit computers are at your disposal on one and the same S-100 board. They've got it all!

Now you see why a lot of highly knowledgeable

and quite experienced users in the world of microcomputer processing demand a product often not available from the manufacturers of conventional microcomputers. The S-100 bus allows you to mix and match S-100 boards as required. If you have a 10 slot motherboard, a minimum configuration may consist of the following boards for a single user system: computer board, memory board, and disc controller. These boards occupy 3 out of ten or more available slots and there is plenty of room left for all kinds of expansion.

BUYER BEWARE

The "bad" referred to belongs to a class of product that exists on the fringes of many legitimate S-100 houses, such as Cromemco, Goodbout, Ithaca Intersystems, SD Systems, and others. The shifty operator buys boards in kit form and sells them assembled and tested. Assembled and tested by whom? That's where the catch comes in.

In case you do want the best, there are classes of boards that sell at a premium above similar boards from the same manufacturer. From the Goodbout company they are burned-in for 200 hours under a program called Certified System Component (CSC). They give you an extra extended warranty of two years instead of the one year guarantee on their other products. You must carefully weigh the small additional charge of such superior products when compared to the piece of mind that it buys.

The only other manufacturer that can provide you such comfort is one that has a computer such as the one you are using close by. In the event of an outage of your own computer, you can then run most of your critical applications on another machine that is compatible with the one you were using while your's is being repaired. That may not be the case with all of the S-100 products, but most of the manufacturers of S-100 products have reliable dealers that offer walk-in depot service or can provide you with access to an alternate computer during repairs.

OTHER BUSES

The S-100 bus is not the only bus, nor is it the

first one. One of the early other efforts centered around the S-50 bus, an effort that never took off and is way behind the S-100 bus in both number of designs and number of manufacturers using the basic structure. In the rapidly changing minicomputer world there are a number of different schemes to connect board level products. The multi-bus is an Intel product. In the 6809 world there is the S-50 bus used by Smokesignal Broadcasting. A Uni-Bus is from DEC, the Digital Equipment Corporation. Prolog has a bus called Standard. Also in the 6809 world and from Motorola are the Exor-Bus for 8-bit applications, the VME-Bus for 16- and 32-bit use, and on the high end the Motorola Versa-Bus for 32-bit applications.

These are but a few samples of using economical and standardized systems to interconnect board level products. The early efforts and contributions of the S-100 bus have been recognized. The S-100 bus has been defined and made a standard that is identified as the IEEE 696 bus. Coming from the Institute of Electric and Electronic Engineers, that is a fine compliment. The reason to describe the S-100 capabilities to such a level of detail is plain: many users have accomplished to obtain reliable data processing capabilities at costs below that or equal to systems with little or no expansion capabilities.

If you want to know about the best products that the 8- and 16-bit world has to offer, you might as well be informed. Other successful and reputable manufacturers of S-100 products include Morrow Designs of San Leandro, California, Cromemco of Mountain View, California, Ithaca Intersystems, of Ithaca, New York, and SD Systems of Dallas, Texas. The best informed magazine on the S-100 bus is Microsystems, the CP/M user's journal.

Information Services

One of the more compelling reasons to use Information Services is the speed and ease with which one can access data that would take impossible amounts of time to accumulate otherwise. For those of you that have ever clipped newspaper quotes of financial information, you probably remember the day the thunderstorm hit your newspaper's printing presses, and your favorite summaries were blankety blank. Alternative? Go to library, copy other paper's columns, or go to stockbroker hoping to find missing information. Now you can do much better; with a computer or terminal, a modem (either built in or external), telephone access via acoustic or direct coupler, and the necessary software, you can have minimum access capability to the three important information services summarized in Table 8-1. Examine their differences and look at what the individual choices are.

DOW JONES

For those of you with financial interests of important proportions, nothing but the premier service of the high world of Finance will do: the Dow Jones Financial Service. This service comes in three different classes: Standard, Blue Chip, and Executive. Each class depends on the amount of time spent on the system. The rates are on a sliding scale; the more you use, the lower the hourly rate. Besides different base charges for each class of service and each location using the service, the information offered is broken down into four different categories:

- ☐ DJ Business and Economic News.
- ☐ DJ Quotes.
- ☐ Financial and Investment Services.
- ☐ General News and Information Services.

The DJ provides access to all the news that will appear in the Wall Street Journal and to corporate news stores and disclosures. The advantage here is to have access to this kind of information early and selectively.

Table 8-1. Summary of the Three Important Information Services.

Attribute	Compu-Serve	Dow-Jones	Source
Startup fee	none *1	$50 *2	$100 *3
How do you get started?	Buy a start-up kit	Get an application	Get an application
Where do you call?	1-800-848-8199	1-800-257-5114	1-800-336-3300
Modems supported	300 - 1200	300 - 1200	300 - 1200
300 baud service rate per hour during prime time —all rates approximated—	$22.50	$24 to $74	$20.75
300 baud service rate per hour during non prime time	$8.75 to $10.75	$7.80 to $54	$5.75 to $8.75
1200 baud - prime time	$35	$34.80 to $125.80	$25.75
1200 baud -non prime time	$17.50	$13.25 to $91.80	$10.75
minimum charges	2 hrs. mo. for prime service	Blue Chip: $75/yr/loc. Executive: $50/mo/loc.	maint. & usage $10/ mo. each access $.25
Estimated number of subscribers 1982 revenue, millions	38,000 $40	60,000 $50	27,000 $7
Other charges	communications esp. Alaska and Hawaii, storage, line printer, billing	lower rates for Blue Chip and execut-ive class service	rates app. 60% higher for the source plus service, storage
Remarks	*1 $39 buys starter kit, includes all manuals and 5 hrs. Use best buy for the dollar!	*2 offers free intro. for all users, the premier service of finance!	3* startup fee in-cludes all manuals, fine system oriented to education!

All investment decisions can now be made on-line all during the day. Your fingers need not get black on your local evening paper. They will examine all those closing prices and averages on-line. The significance of access to the DJ service combined with new terminals is important in that it gives investors a degree of mobility; they can use their TRS-80 Portable Computer, anyplace that there is a phone to plug into. The name Dow Jones, closely associated with the Wall Street Journal and Baron's, does not disappoint in its electronic version. Eighty categories of news, free text search by words, dates of numbers, current quotes with the customary 15 minute delay while the market is open, money market summaries, four of the most recent transcripts of the popular Wall $treet Week program, and Wall Street Journal Highlights, among others, make this the premier financial information service.

COMPUSERVE

The next service is a good all around information service that was established by a group of professionals that grew up in the cutthroat world of commercial timesharing. Companies used to access computepower this way when it was not practical to buy or lease their own. This compute power was sold like advertising time on radio or tv; anything reasonable goes! Needless to say that if you survive in such an environment, you got to be good.

What's so good about CompuServe? When you talk to people that have compared this service to others they have used, they will mostly recommend CompuServe if they come out of the programming environment. That's like the airline captain who, when he was asked why he likes the DC10, replied: "Because it flies like an airplane is supposed to!" The offering of CompuServe consists of a variety of services, too many to report upon in all the detail that will do them justice. An excellent idea is to use the higher level languages offered here to save time and money: for the cost of a Fortran or other compiler for your own computer, you can do a lot of Fortran work faster and cheaper on their big number crunchers. This is also true for evaluating other exotic languages; instead of going out and trying to get a demonstration, you can decide in armchair comfort what is suited for your particular needs.

Electronic mail is a terrific way to stay in touch with your friends, and with free access to 64 K characters of mass storage a month, it is a terrific way to exchange software. Specific bulletin boards also exist. One of the most active is the CP/M one. How does EMail work? You simply access the main menu, work your way to the EMail menu, and then you are ready to be guided by the service on how to send and receive your EMail. Like on most services, once you are familiar with the prompts issued by the system to help you through a given process, you can reduce the prompts to a minimum.

Other offerings are of course financial quotations, shopping, banking, and electronic forums, where parties of similar interests *chew the rag* ala ham radio. The different hobbies are categorized by club. In addition to these conference calls, there are games and for the newshounds access to the CBS news wire on a 24 hour basis.

THE SOURCE

How to work smarter and faster instead of harder and longer: Go to the Source! Quite a well thought out slogan. Their offerings, include news, financial quotes, mail, bulletin boards, electronic mail, games, access to higher level languages, shopping, and electronic travel service by letting you shop for rates that suit you and by accessing the Mobil Travel Guide. The orientation towards education is based upon access to instructional programs that include geometry, spelling, mathematics, poetry, and foreign languages.

ADDITIONAL INFORMATION

Here, as a convenience, are the mailing addresses of these three services. Write to them for more specific details of their offerings.

COMPUSERVE
5000 ARLINGTON CENTRE BLD.
COLUMBUS, OHIO 44320

DOW JONES NEWS SERVICES
P.O. BOX 300
PRINCETON, NEW JERSEY 08540

THE SOURCE
1616 ANDERSON ROAD
McLEAN, VIRGINIA 22102

A final word on specials. In cooperation with Radio Shack, if you buy a COCO MC10, you will get FREE access to one hour of service on both CompuServe and the Source. And finally an ownership note: H&R Block owns CompuServe, and the Source belongs to Readers Digest. And don't forget, // INTRO is free for all users of the Dow Jones.

Chapter 9

Apple and IBM Software

Documentation for two telecommunications packages are detailed in this chapter. The SMART-MODEM package is for use with the smartmodem and the Apple or other Z80 computers. PC-Talk III is for the IBM PC. The documentation presented here is quite exhaustive. Should you copy the programs from an on-line source, you will already have a hard copy of the documentation.

APPLE'S SMARTMODEM

This is the modem program for the Apple and other computers that have a Z80 CP/M board and are using an external smartmodem. If your smartmodem is connected to the serial RS-232 port of a DISK JOCKEY controller with primary address (D000H) and your system is 32 K or better then no modifications are needed to SMO-DEM36.MAC. The elementary I/O routines take advantage of the firmware on the DJ board. If you are using another board, then alterations are needed in the source file. Note: SMODEM.ASM is

modified for use with Digital Research's MAC macro assembler, not for use with Microsoft's M80. See the .ASM file, and set the appropriate equates for your I/O. Enhancements were added to the original program to take advantage of smartmodem's auto-dial feature Escape to Command Mode and On-Hook features. These features include . . .

☐ Kill a disc file.

☐ Terminal mode/Echo mode toggle.

☐ List device toggle (terminal mode).

☐ Send/receive object code informal file (terminal mode).

☐ CRC-(cycle redundancy check option).

☐ Auto line-feed is generated in the Echo mode.

☐ Greatly enhanced menu.

☐ Display number of file sectors in decimal and hex during SEND/RECEIVE file.

☐ XON-XOFF recognition in transfer informal file mode.

□ Double sized telephone directory - 52 entries.

□ The telephone directory is a separate file. This allows fast editing without the need to recompile or reedit the modem programs.

□ Auto-dial from internal directory to SMARTMODEM.

□ Direct dial from program initiation or from menu.

□ All macros are included in the source listing.

SMODEM3 Menu Commands - In Menu Mode

WRT - Write informal file to disc
DEL - Erase informal file from disc
RET - Return to terminal mode (no data loss)
DSC - Disconnect phone (SMARTMODEM)
CAL - Auto dial from list (SMARTMODEM)
XPR - Expert mode (toggle menu on/off)
DIR - Directory <drive>
CPM - Exit to CP/M
K - Kill disc file [fn.ext]
S . . . - Send CP/M file [fn.ext]
R . . . - Receive CP/M file [fn.ext]
T - Terminal mode <fn.ext>
E - Terminal mode with echo

Commands - In Terminal Mode

no messages
^O - Off line-exit to menu
^Z - END of file
^S - XOFF character
^Q - XON character
^P - Printer (toggle on/off)
^T - Transmit informal file
^R - Receive informal file
^E - Terminal/Echo (toggle on/off)
^D - Disconnect phone (SMARTMODEM)
^X - Cancel send/receive

Secondary Options

. . .B - Batch file mode
. . .S - Show as sent
. . .V - View as sent/received
. . .R - Show as received
. . .Q - Quiet
. . .T - Return to terminal mode
. . .E - Return to echo mode
. . .D - Disconnect phone
. . .C - CRC check/not checksum
        (receive option only)
. . .A - Answer Mode (& offhook)
. . .O - Orig. Mode (& offhook)

Commands in Menu Mode

WRT, Write Informal File To Disc. For the purpose of definition an *informal file* is one which is setup for receiving or transmitting data without data validity checks in the terminal mode. When data has been saved to an informal file, the file must be closed before continuing with other options. The WRT command writes all remaining buffered data to the disc and then closes the file. Information will be lost if this is not done.

DEL, Delete Informal File. This command will delete the informal file and it won't be saved on the disc. All information held in memory from previous saves will be erased.

RET, Return to Terminal Mode. The RET command is used to reenter the terminal mode with no data loss. If information has been saved to an informal file the user may reenter the menu mode but all saved data will be lost if a return to the terminal mode is made with the T or E options. Using the RET allows reentry to the terminal mode and preserves all saved information.

DSC, Disconnect (smartmodem). When disconnect is initiated the HAYES default escape code "+++" is first sent to the modem to reenter the command state. Then the *on-hook* command ATH is sent. This causes the modem to hang up. The program then enters the menu mode.

CAL,C, Auto-Dial (smartmodem). The auto-dial feature allows the user to call a number automatically from one of several phone directories. Auto-dial primary option may be used in three different ways when initiating SMODEM3: e.g., initiate and ask for directory name.

1. SMODEM3 C
                    ^(primary option)
    Initiate and load the default directory PHONE.001 then dial the number associated with the directory letter M.
2. SMODEM3 C M
                    ^(directory-letter)
    Initiate and dial the given number.
3. SMODEM3 C 231-1898
                    ^(any number)
    Auto-dial may also be used from the MENU mode with CAL. The commands are exactly the same except the code CAL is used instead of the C primary option. If the command CAL is used alone SMODEM will ask for a directory name. When the phone directory is up any number in the directory may be dialed by entering a directory-letter and pressing return. Or any number may be typed in the command line. The dial command ATD and the selected number are automatically sent to the SMARTMODEM. If you wish to cancel a call while the phone is ringing, press return. The NO CARRIER message will be sent and SMARTMODEM will go to an on hook (hang-up) state. To redial the same number give the command A/. All the standard HAYES commands can be issued while in the terminal mode. A second opinion for dialing a number is from the terminal mode using the standard SMARTMODEM dial command. Simply type ATD <phone number>.

Telephone Directory

    Directories may be given any name and kept on any disc but there must always be a Default directory with the name PHONE.001 on the default drive. SMODEM automatically loads this file if a direct dial is called for. Phone directories may be set up in two different ways; (see the models below). These models could be saved to separate files and used as actual directories. More may be set up by duplicating the model over and over. Only the entries need be changed.
    XPR,X, Expert Mode. If the X option is included in the command line when SMODEM is initiated, it will come up with the menu display

turned off. You can enter the expert mode at any time with the XPR option.
    DIR <d:>, Directory. This option prints the specified disc directory to the screen.
    CPM, Reenter CP/M. This option terminates the modem program and returns to the CP/M operating system.
    K file name, Kill a Disc File. Files may be deleted from the disc without leaving the modem program. CP/M rules apply.
e.g., >>K file.name
        >>K *.ASM
        >>K B:file.A?M

Primary And Secondary Options

    There are eight primary options in SMODEM. Originate and Answer options are not used since SMARTMODEM handles these automatically. A primary option may be included in a command line when initiating SMODEM or while in the menu mode but only one is allowed. The exception is with T, M, and E. They may be used as secondary options during send or receive.

S. . . Send a file	R. . . Receive a file
T. . . Terminal mode	E. . . Echo mode
X. . . Expert mode	C. . . Auto-dial mode
M. . . Menu mode	K. . . Kill a CP/M file

    There are twelve secondary options. These options may be entered in a command line when initiating SMODEM or while in the menu mode. More than one secondary option may be included in a command line. If the (CRC) option is used, then a maximum of six may be included. As you can see, T, M, and E are also used as secondary options.

. . .S Print to screen/sending
. . .R Print to screen/receiving
. . .V Print send & receive
. . .Q Don't print messages
. . .T Return to Terminal mode
. . .E Return to echo mode
. . .D Disconnect
. . .B Batch files mode

. . .C (CRC) request
    cyc. redundancy check
    (option in receive only)
. . .M Return to menu mode
. . .A Answer tone connect
    to phone line
. . .O Originate tone connect
    to phone line

Sending/Receiving Formal Files

The classification FORMAL means that all transmitted data will be checked for validity against received data. There are two data-check options available. If a primary option is used in a command line when initiating SMODEM, it must be the first character following the same SMODEM3 with one space preceding it. Secondary options immediately follow the primary with no spaces. Secondary options may be entered in any order.

e.g., SMODEM SQT B:file.name

          ^

      (primary option)

The above command line means:

    SMODEM . . . Intiate SMODEM3

    S . . . Send a file

    Q . . . Don't print any system messages on the screen

    T . . . After the file is sent go to the terminal mode

    B: . . . The file is on drive B:

    file.name . . . The name of the file to be sent

The B batch file secondary option may only be used from the menu mode. It may not be included in a command line during initiation of SMODEM3. Command lines entered from the menu mode are virtually the same except the word SMODEM is not typed.

e.g., >>RRD file.name

        ^

      (primary option)

The above command line means:

    R . . . Receive a file

    R . . . Type the file to screen as it is being received

D. . .Disconnect the phone after the file is received

    file.name. . .The name of the received file. (The file.name doesn't have to match the sender's. Ambiguous reference in file.name is not allowed with the receive option, as opposed to the send option)

When sending a batch of files ambiguous references may be used according to the rules of CP/M.

e.g., > > SBST *.BAS

    S. . .Send files

    B. . .Batch mode

    S. . .Print files to the screen as they're being sent

    T. . .When through enter the terminal mode

    *.BAS. . .Send all the files on the default disc with the extention of 'BAS'.

e.g., >>SBCM file.name1 file.name2. . .n

    S. . .Send files

    B. . .Batch mode

    M. . .Enter the menu mode after all files are sent

    file.name. . .The list of files to be sent.

When receiving files in batch mode the file names are not specified. They are sent by the sender. SMODEM automatically receives and uses these names on the disc.

e.g., >>RBCE

    R. . .Receive files

    B. . .Batch mode

    C. . .Send a (CRC) character redundancy request to the sender specifying a (CRC) check of data instead of the default CHECKSUM method.

    E. . .Go to the echo mode after all files have been received.

Sending/Receiving Informal Files

Files may be sent or received from the terminal mode. The classification informal implies that data validity checks are not made on transmitted data. (You take your chances.) To save data to an informal file, a file.name must first be specified in the menu mode while giving the T terminal command. The user is then asked if the received data is object code. (All data is either object code or

ASCII.)

e.g., >>T file.name

Once in the terminal mode any incoming data may be saved to this file by simply pressing the ^R receive toggle. Data may be intermittently saved by toggling on or off. As soon as all desired data is saved the file must be closed with the WRT command from the menu mode. Incoming material may be temporarily stopped and started by issuing the ^S XOFF and ^Q XON commands. To send an informal file the ^T transmit command is given from the terminal mode.

e.g., ^T

Following this command the user is asked if the file to be sent is object code then prompted for the file.name. The data is sent immediately following a carriage return, so care must be taken to prepare the proper information.

Primary Options Summary

S, Send A File. Send CP/M files individually or in batch mode using CHECKSUMS or CRC checks.

R, Receive A File. Receive CP/M files individually or in batch mode using CHECKSUMS or CRC checks.

T <file.name>, Terminal Mode. Enter terminal mode (without echo.). If <file.name> is specified then an informal file is set up and data may be saved to this file using the (Receive)^R' toggle.

E, Echo Mode. Enter echo mode. Echo all characters back to the sender. Auto line feeds are sent following each carriage return. Both terminals may not be in echo mode at the same time or SMODEM will go belly up.

X, Expert Mode. This mode suppresses the menu display upon initiation of SMODEM.

C <command>, Auto-Dial (SMART-MODEM). Dial a number directly or display the telephone directory and wait for command.

Secondary Options Summary

A, ANSWER TONE. Selecting this option tells the smartmodem to go online using answer (higher frequency) tones.

O, Option Tone. Selecting this option tells the smartmodem to go online using originate (lower frequency) tones. If neither A or O are specified SMODEM will assume you are already on-line and begin whatever command you gave it.

S, Show File As Sent. Selecting this option will display the file being sent on the screen.

R, Show File As Received. This option will display the file being received on the screen.

V, Show File. Display sent or received file on the screen.

*Q*uiet Mode. Suppress all system messages; (don't display on the screen).

T, *T*erminal Mode. Enter the terminal mode, <file.name> may not be specified when using T as a secondary option.

D, Disconnect (SMARTMODEM). Issue the Escape code to the HAYES smartmodem, then hang up the telephone and reenter the menu mode.

B, Batch Mode. This option is used to send multiple files. File names can be individually specified in the command line or they can be specified using ambiguous file names (CP/M convention). Individual file names are sent to the receiver first then the file contents until all files are sent.

C, (CRC) cycle redundancy check. SMODEM defaults to a checksum method of checking data validity during send/receive. Although quite accurate it is not virtually error free. The secondary option C may be included in the command line to force a (CRC) check of data. The (CRC) method is 99.99% error proof. The only restrictions are:

☐ Both sender and receiver must use one of the MODEM series programs that have the (CRC) option.

☐ The (CRC) option may only be included in a RECEIVE command line.

If SMODEM3 detects a request for (CRC) during a SEND file, it automatically switches over and informs the operator with a screen message.

Terminal Mode Options

^O, Off-Line. This command will allow reentry to the menu mode without disconnecting the phone.

^Z, End of File. This command sends an end of file ASCII character.

^S, XOFF. The XOFF character tells the sending computer to stop data transmission temporarily. (The sender must recognize XON/XOFF protocol). XOFF is used in conjunction with the XON.

^Q, XON. The XON character tells the sending computer to resume data transmission.

^E, Terminal/Echo (toggle). Switching between Terminal mode and Echo mode can be accomplished by pressing ^E. A message is printed to warn if ECHO ON or ECHO OFF.

^P, Printer (Toggle). All incoming data may be sent to the printer while in terminal mode. This feature does not operate while receiving a file using the R (receive) primary option. A message is printed warning if PRINTER ON or PRINTER OFF.

^T, Transmit Informal File. This command will send a disc file informally (without error checking). After pressing ^T the user is prompted for the file.name and for whether or not the file being sent is object code. The file is immediately sent following the cancel key ^X.

Object code files may be SAVED or SENT while in the terminal mode. The user is prompted during informal file transfer/receive as to whether an object code file is being transmitted. There are no checks to ensure data validity therefore this feature should only be used when it is not possible to use the R (receive) or S (send) primary options.

^R, Receive Informal File (toggle). The receive toggle may be used only if a <file.name> was specified when entering the terminal mode, e.g., T <file.name>. Alternately pressing R turns the save feature ON and OFF and the user is prompted with SAVE ON or SAVE OFF message. When the save function is ON, data is simultaneously saved and printed on the screen and each line is preceded by a colon. (The colon is not sent to the file.)

^E, Echo Mode (toggle). Alternately pressing this key toggles between the terminal mode and echo mode. The user is prompted with an ECHO ON or ECHO OFF message.

^D, Disconnect (smartmodem). This key sends the SMARTMODEM default escape code +++ then issues the command 'ATH' causing the modem to go to an on-hook state (hang up).

^X, Cancel Send/Receive. This key may be used to cancel files being sent or received in the informal mode or files being sent using the primary option S. Files being received with the primary option R can't be cancelled by the receiver. This ensures that line noise doesn't inadvertently stop transmission.

Phone Directory, Two Entries Per Line

The directory itself begins with the letter A and ends with the $. The first character in the file must be A. (No CR/LF pairs preceding it.) Figure 9-1 illustrates a two column directory.

Phone Directory, One Entry Per Line

There must be exactly 31 characters per line including the CR/LF pair. Other than that the rules are the same as the directory above.

```
12345678901234567890123456789010
A  Adam Amadous....................423-1191
B  Bernard Butcher .................322-0198
C  etc. . .                                 ^^
$                                            ¦ ¦
```
(last 2 spaces represent CR/LF pairs)

The length of line in the second directory may be made longer but alterations must be made in the dial routines in the program file. Caution: All Numbers in the directory line will be sent to SMARTMODEM. Only the numbers to be dialed should be present.

In Summary

This program does not include some of the

```
A Erwin                          B Walter
Aikele....499-2908               Blaettel....981-1532
C Molecular                      D Bob
Computg..839-4561                Dalhover.......266-9110
E Conn TRS                       F Frank  Di
North Y...667-9981               Pasquale..733-7949
G Grace                          H Bob Hale..........
Gallagher....421-1922            273- 3011
I IBC .....231-0981              J Joyce.............
K KKGO                           546-7642
615-0116                         L Lisa..............
M Jason · · · · · ·              352-1424
Michael.826-5394                 N Jerry
O Otto                           Nicklin......374-9916
Frank ....452-0197               P P.M.I.CBBS
Q Queens                         (Punter).624-5431
BBSNY .352-4676                  R Norbert
S Sorcerer                       Roth.......216-8778
BBS ......535-9186               T Jason
U Undertaker                     Triegs ....... 223-9238
Paul ......922-7511              V Violinmaker
W Dwight                         George .442-6969
Wilson...231-1898                X Xerox
Y John                           CBBS.........820-5258
Young...418-8114                 Z Egon
y Yucca Valley CC                Zwierlein.....932-3347
. . . . 943-8923                 z Zorba Portables
                                 . . . . 785-5913

a                                b
c                                d

And so on all the way to ...........

$                                ^              ^
^                                |              |
|                                |              |
|                      (two spaces) (carriage return
|                                   line feed pair
(the $ MUST be the last character) not seen but
                                      there)
```

Fig. 9-1. Two-column phone directory.

options that were present in other versions MODEM:

- ☐ Baud rate change.
- ☐ Parity select.
- ☐ Force-send last character typed.
- ☐ Auto-dial source code for the PMMI

modem.

The baud rate and parity select options may be included in other versions. Auto-dial is a built-in feature of SMARTMODEM and is therefore not needed. SMODEM must be assembled with Microsoft's M80 Macro assembler. The assembly commands to create a CP/M .COM file are:

M80 =SMODEM
L80 /P:100
SMODEM
SMODEM/N/E

Other versions have been modified for assembly with Digital Research's MAC macro assembler. See the individual program versions for further instructions. Well, how is that for our Apple friends?

PC-TALK III

When I first saw this program and the accompanying documentation I was very much impressed by the labor of love that went into the preparation of both. I thought that you would enjoy knowing about PC communications, and the only way to do so without having the use of your own home computer is to print a copy for you. So here, reprinted with permission from the Headlands Press, Inc., P.O. Box 862, Tiburon, California, 94920, which holds the copyright © 1983, is the PC-TALK III User's Guide.

The guide consists of a summary of commands, followed by a section on screen, keyboard, and printing. Then follows receiving and transmitting files, after which you will find more file commands. The next section of the users guide tells you about dialing. Thereafter you will learn about parameters and defaults, and input strings. Next you find miscellaneous features and commands, followed by more applications and advanced features.

The guide closes with PC-TALK III file information and a short explanation of communications parameters and the XMODEM protocol. To find out how to obtain the programs you need to run PC-TALK, check the section PC-TALK III File Information for a detailed description of all the modules and check in Appendix A for the correct source.

Starting PC-Talk

First make sure that PC-DOS is loaded so that you see the A> prompt. Place the disc marked "PC-TALK.III" in drive A. Then . . .

—If you have 64K of memory, type 'TALK64' <ENTER>. This will load and run the BASIC file PC-TALK.BAS.

—If you have 128K or more of memory, type 'TALK128' <Enter>. This will load and run the compiled BASIC file PC-TALK.EXE. You can also run PC-TALK.EXE by simply typing 'PC-TALK' <Enter>.

When you see the prompt "===Proceed . . ." PC-TALK is in operation. At this point, you should turn on your modem, if you have not already done so.

—If you have a direct connection modem:
You can proceed to send the appropriate modem commands directly from the keyboard. (Making use of auto-dialing features is described in the documentation under "The Dialing Directory.")

—If you have an acoustic modem:
Dial the phone number you wish, place the telephone receiver in the modem cradle, and switch to 'Data'. Once you have made a connection, you can proceed with keyboard instructions.

At this point, your PC has been set up as a "dumb" terminal, connected with the remote computer. You can send information to the remote computer by typing on the keyboard, and see information sent by the remote computer displayed on your screen. NOTE: IF YOU CAN'T SEE YOUR KEYBOARD INPUT, press Alt-E to put the program into Echo mode.

PC-TALK is capable of doing many "smart" things too, such as receiving and sending disc files, dialing phone calls, and storing commands for future use. All the program features are described in the documentation, which is contained in a file on the program disc called PC-TALK.DOC.
********** PLEASE PRINT AND READ THE DOCUMENTATION! **********
This will save you from having unanswered ques-

tions and greatly increase your enjoyment of the program.
To print the documentation, follow these instructions:

—If you have been provided with two discs, place the working copy of the PC-TALK.DOC disc in drive A.

—If you have been provided with one disc, place the working copy of the PC-TALK.III disc in drive A.

*** Now type 'PRINTDOC' <Enter> and follow the screen prompts. This will print the file PC-TALK.DOC. Please take some time to read through the documentation before trying to use the program.

Screen, Keyboard, And Printing

Echo: Alt-E

With some systems, the remote computer will send back to your screen the characters you type at the keyboard. This is known as "full duplex" communications. In other cases, the remote computer will not send back the characters you type ("half duplex"). You can adjust for either of these situations with the Echo option, which is toggled on and off by pressing Alt-E.

If you can't see your own keyboard input on the screen once communications are in progress, turn on the Echo option (Alt-E). This might make your modem commands appear as double characters, but should produce proper screen output during communications.

If your regular communications input appears as double characters, disable the Echo function by pressing Alt-E.

The Width Alarm: Alt-W

Many remote systems place a limit on the length of a line which can be entered. It can be a nuisance to have to keep track of this limit when typing on the screen.

As you send information using the keyboard, you will notice that the program beeps when you type more than 70 characters on a line. This is the Width alarm feature. It operates like the margin alarm on a typewriter.

The beeps will continue until you press the <Enter> key or until you have typed more than ten additional characters. The beeps are merely reminders—the characters are still sent as typed, even if the alarm sounds.

You can specify a different margin width by pressing Alt-W. If you want to disable the Width alarm, enter 0 (zero) as the value for the margin width.

Printscreen: Shift-PrtSc

At any time during program operation, hitting the Shift key in combination with the PrtSc key will print the contents of the screen to the printer. (This is the regular DOS function).

Simultaneous Printout: Ctrl-PrtSc (or Ctrl-PgUp)

You can also produce simultaneous printout while communications are in progress by pressing Ctrl-PrtsSc or *ctrl-PgUp. A message will indicate "===PRINTOUT ON===" and all subsequent information displayed on the screen will be sent to the printer as well.

You can disable the Printout function by hitting Ctrl-PrtSc or Ctrl-PgUp again. A message "===PRINTOUT OFF===" will be displayed and the Printout function will be toggled off. The Printout function can be turned on and off without disturbing communications.

If the Printout function is invoked when the printer is not turned on, a message "===CHECK PRINTER===" will appear, the function will remain off, and communications will continue.

**Applications Notes

Running the Printout option may slow communications because many printers cannot keep pace with the communications rate. If you are communicating at 1200 baud (described below under "Communications Parameters") you should not try to run simultaneous printout, as you will likely overflow the communications buffer. If this happens, the program will attempt to recover by turning off the Printout function.

A new feature in PC-TALK III buffers the printout to take correct account of backspace characters within each line.

If you happen to run the BASIC interpreter version of the program under BASIC 2.0, the Ctrl-PrtSc key will turn on continuous printing, but not with PC-TALK's support features described above. In this case, you should use the Ctrl-PgUp key to control the Printout function. (Note, however, that if you have enough memory to run BASIC 2.0, you will get better performance by running the compiled version of the program, PC-TALK.EXE. See "Starting PC-TALK", above.)

Screendump: Alt-S

Another new feature in PC-TALK III allows you to dump the contents of the screen to a disc file at any time by pressing Alt-S.

When you start the program, the Screendump file is a file on drive B called SCRNDUMP.PCT. Each time you press Alt-S, the screen contents is appended to that file. The date and time is automatically recorded for each screendump.

You can specify a different Screendump file from within the Default routine (described below). Clearscreen: Alt-C

Pressing Alt-C will clear the screen at any time. This command does not send any character or signal to the remote computer.

Receiving And Transmitting Files

Receiving a File: Alt-R (or PgDn)

The file receiving routine permits you to save information you receive from a remote computer on your own disc files. It operates manually and requires no special protocol.

To start the Receiving routine, press Alt-R. The program will ask for a drive and filename under which to receive the file.

Once the Receiving routine is in operation, you will see a reminder on line 25 of the screen indicating the name of the file being received. From that point on, all information passing through the communications port, whether it is being typed from your keyboard or coming from the remote computer, will be saved to the specified disc file.

To guard against accidentally erasing existing files, if a filename is specified that already exists on the disc, the new input will be appended to the end of the existing file. To terminate receipt of the file, press Alt-R once again. You can receive different files to disc, or keep appending to the same disc file, many times during a communications session.

**Applications and Advanced Features

Certain remote computer systems may send unwanted characters to your computer. If you have need to strip or convert certain characters as they are being received, you can specify those characters with the Strip option described below. PC-TALK can receive binary files without any special file receiving specification. You do have to be careful, however, to open and close your file for receiving so that you do not receive any extraneous characters or messages from the remote computer.

The recommended procedure for receiving binary files is to have the Message option (described below) ON for the receiving computer and OFF for the transmitting computer and for the transmitting computer operator to give the receiving computer ample time to open and close the file. Please note also that if you want to receive a binary file, you must not have any stripping in effect and must be communicating at 8 data bits. (These communications parameters are described below.)

PC-TALK is also capable of receiving files using the XMODEM error-checking protocol. The use of this protocol is described separately below.

Transmitting a File: Alt-T

Just as you can receive information and store it on disc files, you can transmit information from your disc files to the remote computer.

The regular file transmitting routine is "plain vanilla"—it requires no special protocol from the remote computer. It can therefore be used to send your disc files to virtually any other personal computer, to network bulletin boards, and to many large computer systems.

To start the Transmit routine, press Alt-T. The program will then ask for the specification of the file to be transmitted. Once you have given the specification and press the <Enter> key, transmission of the file will proceed.

Once transmission is in progress, you will see the text of your file displayed on the screen. Line 25 of the screen will indicate the name of the file being transmitted and the approximate minutes remaining to complete the transmission. The transmission routine will terminate automatically at the end of the file.

You can terminate transmission manually at any time by pressing Alt-T.

**Applications and Advanced Features

The transmitting routine can be used to send files to personal computers and to network bulletin board services. When you are ready to send your file, start the Transmit routine (Alt-T), specify the file to be sent, and press <Enter>. None of the specification prompts you see on your screen will be sent to the remote computer—only the text of your file.

If the remote computer requires a special character to begin receipt of the file, it should be sent manually via the keyboard prior to giving the Alt-T command.

**File Transmitting Options

PC-TALK offers some advanced transmit options for sending binary files, for pacing transmission, and for transmitting with an error-checking protocol. In each case, the option is invoked by adding an equals sign plus the letters 'b', 'p', or 'x' to the end of the file specification. Each of these options is described below; however, it is recommended that you do not try these options until you are familiar with the basic features of the program.

The Binary transmit option: '=b'

PC-TALK permits transmitting binary files (.COM and .EXE files and BASIC programs not saved in ASCII format). To transmit a binary file, add '=b' to the end of the transmit file specification.

For example, to transmit the file MYF-ILE.COM, you would give the transmit file specification by typing 'MYFILE.COM=b' <Enter>. (It does not matter whether the 'b' is typed in upper or lower case.)

When you transmit using the binary option, the text of the file will not be displayed on the screen.

You must be communicating at 8 data bits (No parity) to transmit a binary file.

The Pacing transmit option: '=p'

Because of the increased performance of this version of PC-TALK, the Transmit routine may operate too fast for some remote computers (such as the Source and many mainframe systems). PC-TALK now offers a Pacing option to slow down transmission of files. This feature will send your file to the remote computer one line at a time, pausing between lines.

To invoke the Pacing option, specify '=p' following the specification of the file to transmit; e.g., 'MYFILE.123=p'. At this point you have two options:

If you want the line pacing to be governed by a time delay, enter a number following the '=p' to indicate how many seconds to pause between transmission of lines of your file.

For example, if you specified "MY-FILE.123=p2', the program would pause approximately two seconds between lines.

You can enter a fractional number, such as '=p.5' for a half-second pause. You should experiment with your remote system to determine the optimum time delay for pacing.

The second line pacing option waits for a prompt from the remote computer before sending the next line. This is invoked by specifying the character(s) for the prompt immediately following the '=p'.

For example, specifying 'MYFILE.123=p?' would cause the program to wait for the receiving computer to send a question mark before the program continued transmitting the next line. You can specify a control character as the prompt; for example, '=p' followed by a control-R would cause '=p' to wait for an ASCII 19.

When paused for a prompt in the line pacing transmit mode, you always have the option of proceeding with transmission manually by hitting the space bar, or terminating transmission by hitting Alt-T.

You can store pacing instructions as one of the parameters in the Dialing Directory (described below).

****Technical Note*

The Pacing option will automatically strip line feed characters (ASCII 10) during transmission. It will also add a space preceding each carriage return (ASCII 13). In other words, each carriage return/line feed sequence (ASCII 13/10) in the file will be transmitted as a space/carriage return (ASCII 32/13). The Pacing routine will then either pause for the specified time delay, or wait for the specified prompt before sending the next line.

If for some reason you want to strip line feeds and pad carriage returns with spaces during transmission, but don't want to pause with either a time delay or to wait for a prompt, just add '=p' to the file spec. The Pacing routine will proceed without stopping. (Please note that if you specify '=p0' as the pacing option, the program will wait for a '0' (zero) from the remote computer before proceeding with the next line.)

The pacing option is a powerful feature that greatly extends the versatility of PC-TALK in communicating with a variety of remote computer systems. However, it is not recommended that you try to use transmit pacing unless you know of a specific need for it.

One common application in which transmit pacing is useful is transmitting files to the Source using Telenet or Tymnet. Depending on how heavily the system is being used, you may find it necessary to pace transmission with a 2- 3-second delay between lines to make sure that your file is properly received by the remote system.

XMODEM Transmitting and Receiving: '=x'

One of the noteworthy features in PC-TALK III is the inclusion of the XMODEM protocol originally developed by Ward Christensen. The purpose of the XMODEM protocol is to guard against inaccuracies in file transfer caused by bad signals on the telephone line. It is a "hand-shaking" and error-checking protocol that ensures accurate transmission and receipt of data and binary files. The protocol is in wide use today among a variety of microcomputer systems.

The XMODEM protocol can be used for both transmitting and receiving files. In each case, you should add '=x' to your file specifications; for example, 'MYFILE.123=x'.

Once you have entered the file spec and pressed <Enter>, you will see a message indicating that the protocol is in effect and the notice, "*** Holding for Start . . ." The rest of the file transfer occurs automatically.

If you are transmitting, line 25 of the screen will indicate how many blocks (of 128 bytes) comprise the file. You will see a message "Sending block # n", followed by the message "- verified" when the remote computer has successfully received that block. The file transfer will proceed, block by block, until the end of the file is reached. The transfer will then terminate automatically.

If you are receiving, you will see the same "*** Holding for Start . . ." notice, followed by messages "Received block # n - verified" as each block is received. You will not see any indication of how long the file is, but the receiving routine will terminate automatically.

If the program detects an error while transferring the file, you will see either a message "**Resending block . . ." in transmit mode, or a variety of error messages in receive mode. In either case, the program will attempt to recover, indicate when the transmission/receipt is verified, and continue with the transfer.

In some cases, the program will not be able to recover, particularly if the line signal is degraded. The transfer will automatically terminate after repeated errors. You can also terminate manually at any time by pressing Alt-R or Alt-T.

If the XMODEM transfer does not succeed, please do not assume that there is something wrong with your computer or with PC-TALK. It is suggested that you hang up, re-establish communi-cations over a new line, and try again.

To operate with the XMODEM protocol, you must be communicating at 8 data bits, No parity (Communications Parameter options 2 or 4—see below). Both computers must have communications software capable of running the XMODEM protocol.

The XMODEM routine in PC-TALK III has been tested with other implementations of the protocol and should give you good results. If the other computer is running PC-TALK III, you can be reasonably assured of a rapid and accurate file transfer.

The XMODEM routine operates automatically. For those who are interested, a brief technical description of how the file transfer takes place can be found in Appendix B at the end of this documentation.

Before leaving the subject of XMODEM, it is appropriate that acknowledgment be given to Ward Christensen, who originated the protocol and who has been a landmark pioneer in computer communications.

A Note on Communications Terminology

The PC-TALK prompts and documentation generally avoid use of the words 'uploading' and 'downloading'. A convention in the mainframe world has been to use 'uploading' to refer to transmitting a file to a remote computer and 'downloading' to refer to receiving a file from a remote computer. In the case of two microcomputers communicating with each other, the notion of 'up' and 'down' seems less appropriate.

For those who feel more comfortable with the mainframe terms, PC-TALK offers the option of using the PgDn key (in addition to Alt-R) to start and stop Receiving a file and the PgUp key (in addition to Alt-T) to start and stop Transmitting a file.

More File Commands
Status Messages: Alt-M

The Message option (invoked with Alt-M) will send messages to the remote computer when receiving and transmitting files.

When receiving a file with the Message option in effect, the message "===READY TO RECEIVE===" will be sent to the remote computer as soon as the receiving routine is in operation and "===FILE RECEIVED===" when the receiving routine is terminated.

During transmission, the messages are "0 '===START OF FILE===" and "65529 '===END OF FILE===" or, if the file was terminated prematurely, "===TRANSMISSION OF FILE TERMINATED===". These messages will appear on the remote computer's terminal, signalled with a "bell" or "beep".

**Applications and Advanced Features*

The best use of the Message function is for the receiving computer to have Messages ON and the transmitting computer to have Messages OFF. That way, the transmitting computer knows when the receiving computer is ready to receive the file.

The numbers in the Transmit messages do make it possible to have the Message function active when transmitting a BASIC file in ASCII format. The messages then become remarks in the transmitted program.

The Message function should not be used when transmitting or receiving files to or from a network or mainframe system. The Receive and Transmit file specification prompts are always displayed on your screen, regardless of whether the Message option is in effect. These local messages are not transmitted and do not interrupt communications.

Viewing a File: Alt-V

PC-TALK permits you to view any file which is on your disc drives while the program is running. This feature makes it possible for you to refer to files on disc while communications are in progress.

To View a file, press Alt-V. The program will ask for file specifications in the same manner as the procedures for transmitting and receiving files.

Once Viewing is in progress, twenty lines of the file will be displayed on the screen at a time. To see more of the file, press the space bar. To cancel the Viewing routine, press Alt-V again.

The text of the file you see displayed on your screen will not be sent to the remote computer.

**Applications and Advanced Features*

If the remote computer sends you information while you are viewing a file, that information will be stored in the communications buffer. A continuous stream of information from the remote computer could overflow the buffer. You should therefore view a file only during a pause in communications.

If you want to read an earlier part of a file that you are receiving, you can terminate receipt of the file with Alt-R and then immediately view it by pressing Alt-V and specifying the file you just received.

Deleting a File: Alt-Y

You can delete any file from your disc(s) while communications are in progress. Press Alt-Y and follow the file specification prompts. You will be shown the first five lines of the file and then asked whether you are sure that you want to delete the file. If you respond 'y' to the prompt, the file will be permanently deleted from your disc. Be careful!

The Logged Drive: Alt-L

For the Transmit, Receive, View, and Delete routines, the program assumes a default "Logged" drive if no drive is given as part of the file specification prompts. Initially, this is drive B.

> For example, if drive B is the Logged drive and you respond to a file specification prompt with just 'MYFILE', the program will automatically look for a file 'B:MYFILE'. If you want to transmit, receive, or view a file on drive A, you should respond to the file specification prompt with 'A:MYFILE'.

To change the Logged drive during program operation, press Alt-L and follow the instructions. The Logged drive can also be changed as part of the Default modification routine (described below).

File Specification Conventions

PC-TALK III uses a standard set of commands for responding to file specification prompts in the Receive, Transmit, View, and Delete routines.

If you do not include a drive indicator as part of the specification (e.g., 'MYFILE.123'), the program will assume that the file is to be located on the Logged drive (see above).

If you would like to see a list of the files presently on the Logged drive, you can type a question mark in place of the file spec. You will be shown a listing of the files on the Logged drive. To see the files on another drive, type a question mark followed by the letter designation of the drive.

> For example, if drive B is the Logged drive and you respond to a file spec prompt with '?', you will be shown a list of the files on drive B. If you respond with '?a', you will be shown a list of the files on drive A.

You can also use the 'wild card' characters '*' and '?' as part of these file listing requests.

> For example, if you respond to the file spec prompt with '?a:*.bas', you will be shown a list of all the files on drive A with the extension '.bas'.

If you decide you do not want to continue with the Receive, Transmit, View, or Delete routines once you have made your initial request with Alt-R, −T, −V, or −D, press <Enter> at the file spec prompt and the routine will be cancelled.

If the Receive, Transmit, or View routines are invoked more than once during a communications session, you can hit the space bar in response to the file spec prompt, and the name of the last file specified for receiving, transmitting, or viewing will appear. You can then either press <Enter> and continue receiving, transmitting or viewing that file, or modify that file spec before pressing <Enter>.

Dialing

The Dialing Directory: Alt-D

The Alt-D command calls up the Dialing Directory, which is one of PC-TALK'S most useful features. The Directory can list up to sixty names and phone numbers, plus communications parameters and echo, message, stripping and pacing instructions for each entry.

The following instructions will first show you how to place names and phone numbers into the Directory and then describe how to use the Directory as part of your standard communications routines.

When the Directory is called up for the first time, all entries will be blank. To add names and phone numbers to the Directory or to revise the Directory later on, enter 'r' at the "Dial entry #:" prompt. (It doesn't matter whether you use lower or upper case.) Then enter the entry number you want to add or revise.

To add/revise entries, type in the name, followed by <Enter>, and the phone number (area code optional), followed by <Enter>. Up to 36 characters may be specified for the phone number; only the rightmost 14 characters will be displayed in the Directory.

You will then be asked whether the communications parameters are "ok". If 300 baud-even parity-seven data bits-one stop bit is acceptable (this is the most common protocol), type 'y' <Enter>. If you respond with 'n', you will be asked to specify communications parameters. The program will not let you dial using invalid parameters. (If you run into trouble, re-specify '300-E-7-1'.)

The reverse entry routine will then ask whether you want to echo characters to the screen (common or inter-personal computer communications, but usually not necessary for public networks such as CompuServe and the Source), and whether you want to send status messages as part of the file Receiving and Transmitting routines (see above). Press <Enter> after responding to each prompt.

The routine will then ask whether you want to strip or convert characters for that entry. It is recommended that you respond with 'n' unless you have a special applications need. (See the explanation of the Stripping option below.)

Finally, the routine will ask whether you want to specify a Pacing instruction for that entry.

If you want to specify a Pacing instruction, enter either a time delay number or a pacing prompt character in response to the "Pacing? p=" prompt.

Respond with 'n' <Enter> if you do not want any pacing in effect for that entry. It is recommended that you do not specify a Pacing instruction unless you know of a specific need for it.

If you make an error specifying a directory entry, type 'n' <Enter> at the final "ok?". You will be taken through the specification routine again. For each parameter, you can either specify a new value or press <Enter> to leave the present value unchanged.

After you have responded with 'y' to the final "ok?" prompt, the Directory will clear, showing the new information you input. The name, phone number, and communications specs will be permanently stored in a separate file on your program disc named PC-TALK.DIR.

Adding to the Directory

As indicated above, specifying communications parameters, echo, message, stripping, and pacing can all be considered advanced features that need not be dealt with the first time you use the program. The following example lists the commands for merely adding a name and phone number to the directory.

1. Press Alt-D. You will see Page 1 of the Directory displayed and the prompt "Dial entry #:".

2. Type 'r' <Enter>. You will see the prompt "Revise/add entry #:".

3. Type '1' <Enter>. You will see the prompt "Name:".

4. Type the name you want for entry #1 (maximum 20 characters) followed by <Enter>. You will see the prompt "Phone number:".

5. Type the phone number you want for entry #1 (maximum 36 characters) followed by <Enter>. You will see the prompt "Communications parameters ok (y/n)?".

6. For this example, the parameters are ok, so type 'y' <Enter>, or just press <Enter>. You will see the prompt "Echo on (y/n)?".

7. Type 'n' <Enter> or just press <Enter>. You will see the prompt "Messages on (y/n)?".

8. Type 'n' <Enter> or just press <Enter>. You will see the prompt "Strip/convert characters (y/n)?".

9. Type 'n' <Enter> or just press <Enter>. You will see the prompt "Pacing? p=".

10. Type 'n' <Enter> or just press <Enter>. You will see the prompt "Is entry #1 ok (y/n)?".

11. Type 'y' <Enter> or just press <Enter>. You will see Page 1 of the Directory re-displayed with the name and phone number you just entered.

12. Repeat the above steps for each name and phone number you want to add to the Directory.

Other Directory Options

Although the Directory has a capacity of sixty entries, the screen will display only fifteen entries at a time. You can "page" forward or back through the directory by entering 'f' or 'b' at the initial "Dial entry #:" prompt.

You can dial any entry, regardless of whether it is displayed. However, you can revise only those entries that are on the displayed page of the Directory.

If you enter 'c' at the "Dial entry #:" prompt, you have the option of clearing Directory entry #s within the range 1-60. You will be asked "Are you sure?" before your selected entries are cleared.

Auto-dialing

The Dialing Directory will automatically dial a Directory entry if your modem supports this function.

The first time the Directory is called up, you will see a notice that says "modem dialing command = ATDT". This is the command used by the D.C. Hayes Smartmodems<tm> for using touch tone dialing.

To specify a different dialing command—such as for pulse dialing or for another auto-dial modem—enter 'r' to revise the Directory and then type 'm' <Enter> at the "Revise/add entry #:" prompt. Then type your desired dialing command, followed by <Enter>. (The Smartmodem command for pulse dialing would be 'ATDP'.)

Whatever modem dialing command you specify will be permanently stored in the Directory file (until revised again).

Once the appropriate dialing command has been entered in the Directory, you can have the program dial phone numbers automatically. Simply type the Directory entry # you wish to call, followed by <Enter>. The phone number listed for that entry will then be dialed.

Long Distance Services: '+#' and '−#'

The Dialing Directory is also able to route calls through supplemental long distance services such as Sprint<tm> and MCI<tm>. Two different service numbers can be stored in the Directory, which are listed in the Directory as '+#' and '−#'.

To add a long distance service number to the Directory, type 'r' <Enter> at the "Dial entry #:" prompt. Then type '+' or '−' plus <Enter> at the "Revise/add entry #:" prompt. You can then specify a long distance number command.

When entering the long distance number, include both your local access number and your i.d. number. Separate the two numbers with your modem's "pause" command indicators (commas on the Smartmodem) so that your i.d. number will not be input until a connection with the access number has been made. The long distance service # might thus appear in the Dialing Directory as: '987 6543, , , , 123456'.

If your long distance service requires a different sequence—such as inputting your account number following the number dialed—you can program a Function key combination for your account number. See "The Function Key Directory" below.

Once a long distance service # has been entered into the Directory, it will reside there permanently (until revised) and display whenever the Directory is called up.

To dial a Directory entry # using the long distance service, input a '+' or a '−' immediately preceding the desired entry #.

For example, to dial Directory entry #3 using the service number listed as '+#', you would type '+3' <Enter> at the "Dial entry #:" prompt.

Manual Dialing: 'm'

You can also use auto-dialing to call phone numbers not stored in the Dialing Directory. From the main Dialing Directory prompt, type 'm' <Enter>. A prompt will then ask for the phone number to be dialed. Type the phone number and press <Enter>, and the number will be dialed automatically.

As in the Dialing Directory, preceding the phone number with '+' or '−' will route the call through one of the supplemental long distance service numbers (if they have been stored in the Directory).

Redialing: Alt-Q

If you have a Hayes Smartmodem<tm>, the last phone number you have dialed can be redialed at any time by pressing Alt-Q, which calls into effect the Redial routine.

The routine will display the time the Redial routine was started and redial the number approximately every minute until a connection is made.

When a connection is made, the program will sound an alarm, prompting you to hit any key to resume communications. You can exit from the auto-redial routine at any time before a connection is made by hitting any key.

You can adapt the Redial routine for longer or shorter delays, or for other modems with auto-dialing features, from within the Default routine described below.

Stripping and Converting Characters

PC-TALK III provides for optional selective stripping and/or converting of characters as they are received during communications. This is an advanced feature.

The program default is not to strip any characters. When you call up the Dialing Directory with Alt-D, the "Strip" column will show "N" for each entry, indicating that no stripping is to take place.

To specify selective stripping as part of the stored parameter for a Directory entry, revise the entry and respond with 'y' to the prompt "Strip/convert string" for that entry. This string should be structured as follows:

Each character to be stripped or converted must be specified with a three-digit representation of its decimal ASCII code, followed by a slash (/), followed by a three-digit representation of the decimal ASCII code to substitute for that character, followed by another slash.

For example, to convert the commonly used end-of-file character Ctrl-Z (ASCII 26) to a space (ASCII 32), the strip/convert string would be '026/032/'. PLEASE NOTE THAT A ZERO SHOULD PRECEDE THE ASCII NUMBER IF IT IS LESS THAN 100.

If you simply want to strip out a character, rather than convert it, enter three zeros as the second part of the string:
'026/000/'.

If you want to strip or convert more than one character, continue with more string specifications.

For example, to strip all ASCII 26's and ASCII 127's and convert each capital A (ASCII 65) to lowercase (ASCII 97), the strip/convert string would be '026/000/127/000/065/097'. Up to 3 characters can be specified for stripping/converting in this manner.

You will have opportunities to correct the newly-specified string within the revise entry routine of the Dialing Directory. (The program pads the strip/convert string with extra slashes.) The strip/convert string will be stored in the Dialing Directory.

When you dial a remote computer with the stripping option in effect, the appropriate characters will be stripped and/or converted during all incoming communications, including files that you receive with the Receive routine. You can not have stripping in effect when you use the XMODEM error-checking protocol (described above).

**Applications Notes

Please note that it is not recommended that you strip or convert characters unless you know of a specific application or need related to the remote computer you are calling.

It is not necessary to specify stripping of line feeds for the purpose of correcting the screen dis-play, as PC-TALK does this automatically. (Line feeds are not automatically stripped during file receiving, however.)

Pacing Instructions

As noted before, you can also store a Pacing instruction as part of each Directory entry. (Pacing is discussed above in connection with transmitting files.) If you have stored a Pacing instruction, the pacing suffix will automatically be added to each transmit file specification.

For example, if you had stored the pacing instruction 'p=2' for the entry you have dialed, and specify a file to transmit simply as 'MYFILE'<Enter>, you will hear a beep and the file will be re-specified as 'MYFILE=p2'. If you press <Enter> at this point, the file will be transmitted with a 2-second pacing delay. Continuing with the above example, if you did not want to transmit using the Pacing option, you could backspace to eliminate the 'p=2' portion of the file spec, press <Enter>, and transmission would proceed without Pacing in effect.

Please note from the above examples that the Pacing instructions stored in the Directory do not automatically transmit every file using Pacing—they merely re-display the Transmit file specs to include the Pacing instruction.

**Applications and Advanced Features

Even if you do not have an auto-dialing modem, you can use the Communications Parameter, Echo, Message, Stripping, and Pacing specifications to customize the program for different applications. Store the name in the Directory and a 'dummy' phone number such as '--' or '<space>'. Store the rest of the specifications. Then "dial" the entry number. Even though no phone number will be dialed, the specifications will have been put into effect.

You should also note that when you place a call through the Dialing Directory, the Communications Parameters and the Echo, Message, Stripping, and

Pacing specifications will remain in effect, even after the call is completed. You might want to set up Directory entry #60 as a 'dummy default' entry to reset certain specifications. You can also reset the program parameters and defaults with the Parameter and Default routines (Alt-P and Alt-F) described below.

**Applications Note: CompuServe and the Source

This version of PC-TALK requires that you place access numbers for CompuServe and the Source as regular entries in the Dialing Directory. This enables you to specify various communications parameters and stripping instructions when calling these networks. (You may want to place several CompuServe or Source entries in your Directory to reflect different parameters, such as 300-baud and 1200-baud entries.)

**Note that some of the Source utilities, such as UPI news, may send an ASCII 26 to mark the ends of articles or messages. If you receive the files with these ASCII 26 characters, DOS will later interpret them as end-of-file markers and you will not be able to view the rest of the file, even though the information might still be there.

If you encounter this problem, you may want to specify stripping of ASCII 26's as part of your Source Dialing Directory entry, or convert them to carriage returns (ASCII 13) or spaces (ASCII 32). In such cases, your strip/convert string should be specified as '026/000' (strip) or '026/013' (convert to carriage return) or '026/032' (convert to space).

The feature of reprogramming the End, Ins, and Del keys for CompuServe and the Source networks has also been eliminated from PC-TALK III. The recommended procedure is to assign whatever commands you regularly use either to permanent Function key strings or to temporary Alt key strings (both of which are described below).

Parameters And Defaults

Communications Parameters: Alt-P

It is not necessary that you understand communications protocols to use PC-TALK, but you might find it helpful to read the brief explanation of communications parameters included as Appendix A at the end of this documentation.

Pressing Alt-P at any time while the program is running will call up a menu which allows you to set the communications parameters to one of four options.

The most common parameters for personal computer communications are 300 baud, even parity, 7 data bits, and 1 stop bit (option 1). These parameters transmit text files as ASCII characters. To transmit binary data, you should communicate with 8 data bits (option 2). This option is also used to transmit "high-bit" encoded files (such as Wordstar<tm> formatted text files).

Options 3 and 4 will transmit text and binary files at 1200 baud.

Option "F" of the Communications Parameters menu permits you to reset the parameters to those specified as the program Defaults (see below).

If you want to specify parameters other than one of the four options, you should first press 'x' to exit to the terminal mode and then invoke the Default routine by pressing Alt-F.

**Applications and Advanced Features:

If either you or the remote computer is receiving unintelligible information on the screen, you are probably using different communications parameters. Sometimes you will be able to change the parameters while communications are in progress, but it may cause a break in communications, depending on the system you are calling and the modems in use.

If you specify 8 data bits, (options 2 or 4), your modem might not give intelligible result codes. Also, if you transmit text files using option 2, as is required to transmit re-formattable Wordstar <tm> files, your screen may display intelligible characters during transmission. The file is being transmitted accurately, however.

Program Defaults: Alt-F

The "defaults" of a program are those values that the program assumes every time it is started. PC-TALK makes a number of such assumptions, which can be changed at any time while the program is running by pressing Alt-F.

When you press Alt-F, the screen will clear and you will see a list of the present program defaults. They are as follows:

Baud rate 300
Parity E
Data bits 7
Stop bits 1

These are the four communications parameters described previously. The permissible baud rates are 75, 110, 150, 300, 600, 1200, 1800, 2400, 4800, and 9600. Parity may be E(ven), O(dd), S(pace), M(ark), or N(one). Data bits may be 4, 5, 6, 7, or 8. Stop bits may be 1 or 2.

Note: If you specify 8 data bits, you must specify N parity. Do not experiment with any of these values unless you have a specific application.

Echo N
Messages N

The default is to have both the Echo and Message functions inactive at program startup. To have either function be active, enter 'Y'.

Note that both functions can be controlled by the Alt-E and Alt-M keys, regardless of how the defaults are set.

Strip #1   0
Replace #1 0
Strip #2   0
Replace #2 0
Strip #3   0
Replace #3 0

These defaults provide the opportunity to strip and/or replace characters as they are received from the remote computer.

The "Strip #" values represent the decimal ASCII values of the characters to be stripped or converted and the corresponding "Replace #" values indicate the ASCII characters to replace them.

A 0 (zero) Strip value indicates that no character is to be stripped or converted. A 0 (zero) Replace value indicates that the strip character is to be replaced by a null (no character).

The values listed in this menu are only the default values for program startup. Stripping can be put into effect via the Dialing Directory, as described in detail above. Stripping is an advanced feature that should not be used without a specific application in mind.

Pacing p= "

This gives you the opportunity of specifying a default pacing instruction, as explained previously. This default is overridden by whatever pacing instructions may be put into effect through the Dialing Directory. The symbol " indicates a null entry.

Logged drive B:
Margin Width 70

Both of these default values can be controlled by the Alt-L and Alt-W commands described previously.

Please note that all of these defaults can be controlled independently through program commands. The values listed in the Default menu represent only the values the program assumes at startup.

In contrast, the following defaults (those listed in the second column of the Default menu) can be set only from within the Default menu.

Screendump file B:SCRNDUMP.PCT

This is the specification of the file that is written to when Alt-S is pressed to activate the Screendump function.

Redial delay 20
Connect prompt CONNECT

These defaults pertain to the Alt-Q Redial function. The "Redial delay" governs the length of time between re-dial attempts (in seconds). The "Connect prompt" specifies the message that the modem sends to indicate that a connection has been made.

These defaults are set to redial every minute

on the Hayes Smartmodems<tm>. They can be adapted to many other auto-dial modems. (Consult your modem manual.)

Line 25 help Y

This default governs whether the brief prompt on line 25 of the screen is displayed. To turn off the prompt, enter 'N'.

Foreground 7
Background 0
High inten. 15

These three values determine how characters are displayed on the screen. If you have a color monitor, you can substitute color values as explained in the IBM BASIC manual. Be careful that you don't assign the same value to Foreground and Background!

Print port   LPT1:
Print init.   "
Print width 80

These three values govern the use of the printer. You can specify 'LPT2:' as an optional printer port, if that is where your printer is connected.

The "Print init." default permits you to send characters to the printer for alternate character fonts. The "Print width" specifies how many columns per line the printer will handle.

For example, to print in condensed type at 132 columns per line on the IBM Matrix Printer, enter <Ctrl>-O (oh) as the Print init. value and '132' as the Print width.

Comm. port COM1:
Comm. init.   ,CS,DS

The first of these defaults permits you to specify 'COM2:' as the communications port.

The second default disables checking of the "Clear to Send" and "Data Set Ready" signals when the communications port is opened. This default should not be changed unless you have a specific application. Consult the IBM BASIC Manual under the OPEN "COM . . . statement for details.

Modem init. "

This provides the option of sending an initializing command to your modem. The " symbol indicates a null entry.

C/R subst. }

This final default specifies which character is to be used to indicate carriage returns when defining Function key and Alt key input strings (see below). This character may be changed at will without altering the actual input string.

The procedure for entering new default values is simple. When you first call up the Default menu, the cursor will be paused next to the default for the baud rate. You can enter new values for all the defaults or leave them unchanged as follows:

—If you want to enter a value, type the new value and then press <Enter>.

—If you want to leave the value unchanged, simply press <Enter>.

—If you want to enter a null (blank) value, type <space> <Enter>.

When you do not want to change any more values, type <Esc> <Enter>. (Pressing the <Esc> key will display a small left arrow on the screen.)

You will then be asked whether the new values you entered are ok. If you do not respond with 'y', you will exit the Default routine and all of the old defaults will remain in effect.

If you indicate that the new values are ok, you will be asked whether you want to make the changed default values permanent. If you respond 'y', your changes will be written to a file called PC-TALK.DEF. The new values will be put into effect, and they will become the new default program values the next time PC-TALK is run.

If you do not want to make the changes permanent, your new values will be put into effect, but the old values will remain as the defaults the next time PC-TALK is run.

**Applications and Advanced Features

The Default routine provides you with a great degree of control over your use of the program. The program will do some checking for invalid default values, but you should be careful when changing the defaults and do so only if you know of a specific need.

If you run into trouble specifying the defaults, you can exit to DOS and simply delete the file PC-TALK.DEF from your program disc. PC-TALK will create a new default file if it does not locate the PC-TALK.DEF file.

Input Strings

The Function Key Directory: Alt-K (or Alt-J)

One of PC-TALK'S other powerful features is the Function Key Directory, which is called up by pressing Alt-K. (To accommodate users of the KEYNOTE program, you can also call up the Function Key Directory with Alt-J.)

The Function Key Directory permits you to assign permanent strings of up to 126 characters to the ten Function keys F1 through F10, and to the combinations of Alt-, Shift-, and Ctrl-F1 through F10. A total of forty keys can thus be assigned permanent strings, which can be used to input i.d. numbers, logon sequences, frequently-used phrases and other text with a single keystroke.

The information in the Function Key Directory is stored in a file called PC-TALK.KEY and is loaded every time PC-TALK is run.

The first time the Function Key Directory is called up, you will see that the keys F1 through F10 have no strings assigned to them. To program a key (or to revise a previously programmed key), press 'r' at the first prompt. You will then be asked to specify which Function key (1 through 10) you assign to that Function key. Type the desired characters, followed by <Enter>. The directory will display the revised input for that key. (If you make an error, press 'r' again and respecify for that key.)

If you want to specify carriage returns as part of the input string, input a "right curly bracket" — the shifted key '}' just to left of the <Ente as the last character of the string.

For example, if you wanted to assign the string 'ABC <Enter> 123 <Enter>' to Function key F1, you would enter the input string as 'ABC}123}'.

The input string may be up to 126 characters in length; only the leftmost 30 characters will be displayed in the directory.

You can "page" forward or revise strings for the key combinations Alt-F1 through Alt-F10, Shift-F1 through Shift-F10, and Ctrl-F1 through Ctrl-F10.

Using the Function Key Assignments

Once any of these forty Function keys or key combinations have been assigned, hitting that key will send the input string directly to the communications port (sending carriage returns in place of '}').

Continuing with the example above, if you pressed F1 during communications, you would send the following to the remote computer:

ABC
123

You can specify a new string for any of the Function keys at any time. If you want to clear the key, type <space> <Enter> as the new input string.

The Alt-K command can be used simply to display the Function Key Directory for reference. You can page through the Directory as needed to confirm your key assignments. To continue with communications, press 'x' at the initial prompt and you will be returned to the regular terminal mode of the program. You can then proceed by pressing any of the Function keys to send an assigned string or proceed by typing information from the keyboard.

IMPORTANT! DO NOT PLACE CONFIDENTIAL ID NUMBERS OR PASSWORDS IN THE FUNCTION KEY DIRECTORY IF OTHERS WILL HAVE ACCESS TO YOUR PROGRAM DISC. When you want to make a copy of PC-TALK for others, do not copy the file PC-TALK.KEY, as this file may contain confidential information.

**Applications and Advanced Features

You can also use the Function keys to store filespecs. Pressing the appropriate key will input the filespec in response to a Receive, Transmit, or View file prompt.

You can include control characters (ASCII 0 through 31) as part of the input string. The program will display these characters as their highlighted letter equivalents (e.g., an ASCII 12 will be displayed as a highlighted letter 'L').

You can change the character used as the carriage return substitute from the right curly bracket to any other character from within the Default specification routine. This carriage return substitute only affects how the string is specified and how it is displayed on the screen; the program always stores a "real" carriage return (ASCII 13). Thus, you can switch back and forth using different characters as the substitute.

A new user of the program does not need to have the PC-TALK.KEY file on his/her disc. If the program does not locate PC-TALK.KEY on the program disc, it will initialize and create a new blank Function key file. The same is true for the file PC-TALK.DIR, which contains the information used by the Dialing Directory.

Temporary Alt Keys: Alt-1 through Alt-0

In addition to the permanent Function key combinations described above, the ten key combinations Alt-1 through Alt-0 can be programmed for temporary custom input while communications are in progress.

Pressing Alt–'=' (Alt-equals) at any time during communications will display a prompt on line 25 of the screen, asking for the key to be programmed. Type any of the numbers 1 through 10.

You will then be prompted to enter the temporary string for that Alt key. All keystrokes entered subsequently will input text for that key, until you press <Enter> (maximum 50 characters). As with the Function key assignments described above, you can use a right curly bracket '}' to include a carriage return as part of the temporary string. Control characters will be displayed as their highlighted letter equivalents.

When a temporary Alt key has been assigned, the program will display the first seven characters of the programmed input on line 25 of the screen and return to normal keyboard operation.

Once an Alt key 1 through 0 has been assigned, pressing it will send the assigned string, just as though it had been typed from the keyboard.

You can change an Alt key assignment at any time by pressing Alt-equals, followed by the number of the key to be respecified and the new assignment.

If you want to clear a key, press Alt-equals, the number of the key, and then type <space> <Enter>. If no Alt-key assignments are in effect, the display on line 25 will disappear.

**NOTE the difference between these Alt key assignments and the Function key assignments described above:

The Alt keys can be easily reprogrammed during communications and are displayed on line 25 of the screen. This makes them convenient for holding temporary input strings needed for quick reference. However, the Alt-key assignments are not saved when the program is terminated.

The Function key assignments, on the other hand, are stored permanently on disk and reloaded each time PC-TALK is run. This makes them convenient for storing i.d. numbers and log-on sequences. However, you cannot continue with communications while you are reassigning the Function keys.

Miscellaneous Features And Commands

Elapsed Time: Alt-Z

At any time during program operation, you can display the elapsed time for the current call by typing Alt-Z. For updated time, hit Alt-Z again. (The elapsed time is reset whenever a new call is made.)

Exit: Alt-X

Pressing Alt-X at any time will give you the option of terminating the program and returning to DOS.

152

Sending a Break Signal: Ctrl-End

Various remote computer systems use different signals to effect a break during communications. For example, the break signal for CompuServe is a Control-C; the Source Break signal is a Control-P. Any key sequence (including all control key combinations) may be sent via the keyboard. Some break sequences may also be programmed via the Function Key Directory.

Some systems require a special "sustained" Break signal. This signal can be sent by hitting the Ctrl and the End keys simultaneously. You will have to experiment, or consult your remote system's documentation to determine the correct Break signal to use.

CAUTION: do not attempt to use the combination of the Ctrl key and the ScrollLock/Break key as this may terminate PC-TALK. Command Summary: Home key.

An on-screen summary of all the PC-TALK program commands described above can be displayed at any time by hitting the Home key.

Toggle Commands

The following keys toggle on/off their respective functions and operate at any time while the program is running:

Alt-T Transmit	Alt-E Echo
Alt-R Receive	Alt-M Messages
Alt-V View	Ctrl-PtrSc Printout

More Applications And Advanced Features

Even though this section is described as "advanced," the following information should be of interest to all users of the program.

XON/XOFF: Alt-0

PC-TALK supports the sending of XON/XOFF signals to the remote computer in the event of a communications buffer overflow (see below), and will trap for XON/XOFF signals sent by the remote computer during transmission of files. The default XON signal is ASCII 17; the default XOFF signal is ASCII 19.

If the remote computer sends an XOFF signal during transmission of a file, the symbol "<<XOFF>>" will be displayed highlighted on the screen until the remote computer sends an "XON" signal, at which time transmission will resume automatically. If transmission has been halted, it may be resumed manually by typing Alt-O (the letter 'oh') at the keyboard.

Communications Errors:
<<>> and <<OVER- FLOW>>

PC-TALK will indicate certain types of errors if they occur during communications. If there is an ambient signal on the line, the program will display the symbol '<<>>' in high intensity. Communications will not be interrupted in most cases, but this symbol should put you on notice that you are sending or receiving corrupted data. On a very noisy line, you may see the symbol repeatedly. You should disconnect and try for a better connection.

With some modems, including the Hayes Smartmodems<tm>, you may see the <<>> symbol when communications are first opened. This should not be a cause for concern, provided you do not see the symbol once communications are in progress.

PC-TALK opens a communications buffer for receiving data through the communications port. In most cases, the program should be able to process data as fast as it is received. If the communications buffer does fill faster than the program can handle the incoming data, you will see the symbol <<OVERFLOW>> on the screen. The program will then try to recover, by sending an XOFF signal to the remote computer, processing the contents of the buffer, and then sending an XON signal.

Two situations should be noted which may cause an overflow condition. If you are running the uncompiled BASIC version of the program at 1200 baud, you may experience an overflow condition if you are making use of the character stripping options, or if the remote computer does not support XON/XOFF.

If you are trying to perform simultaneous printout at 1200 baud, your printer will probably not be able to keep up and eventually the buffer will overflow, even with the .EXE version of the program. PC-TALK will attempt to recover by turning off the print feature.

PC-TALK File Information

PC-TALK III is supplied with the following files:

PC-TALK.BAS—The BASIC source code for the program. It will run on a 64K system using DOS 1.00 or 1.10 and BASIC 1.10.

PC-TALK.EXE—The compiled BASIC version of the program. It will run under DOS 1.00, 1.10, or DOS 2.00 on a system with 128K or more of memory.

PC-TALK.DOC—The text file containing this documentation.

TALK64.BAT—A batch file that runs the 64K version. The file contains the single command 'BASIC PC-TALK/C:1024'. This sets up a 1024-byte communications buffer.

TALK128.BAT—A batch file that runs the 128K version. It contains the single command 'PC-TALK'. The .EXE version can, of course, be run directly from DOS with the command 'PC-TALK' <Enter>.

PRINTDOC.BAT—A batch file with a series of prompts to print the documentation file from DOS.

COPYTALK.BAT—A batch file to aid in making copies of PC-TALK for other users. It will not copy your personal .DIR, .KEY, and .DEF support files.

The first time PC-TALK III is run, the program looks for three support files. If it does not find them, these three files will be created on the program disc:

PC-TALK.DIR—The file that stores Dialing Directory information.

PC-TALK.KEY—The file that stores Function Key information.

PC-TALK.DEF—The file that stores Default Menu information.

Programming Information

One additional file is supplied on the program disc: PCTKREM.MRG. This is a BASIC file saved in ASCII format that contains REMark statements.

It can be MERGED into PC-TALK.BAS to improve the readability of the program. However, once merged, PC-TALK.BAS will no longer run on a system with 64K of memory.

PC-TALK.EXE can be compiled directly from PC-TALK.BAS, as all timing functions are handled independently through the BASIC SOUND and TIME$ functions.

Once PC-TALK.BAS has been saved in ASCII format, it can be compiled using the IBM BASIC Compiler with the following commands:

BASCOM PC-TALK.BAS /E/O/S/C:4096
LINK PC-TALK+IBMCOM

The '4096' argument determines the size of the communications buffer and can be increased if you have sufficient memory. For all but the most demanding applications, however, the 4096-byte buffer should be more than sufficient.

Copying PC-TALK

You are encouraged to make copies of PC-TALK III and distribute them to other users, within the terms of the limited license set forth below. A special batch file has been provided for this purpose.

To copy PC-TALK III, insert the program disc in drive A. From the DOS A> prompt, type 'COPYTALK' <Enter> and follow the prompts. If you do copy PC-TALK for other users, please be sure to provide them with the PC-TALK.DOC and PRINTDOC.BAT files.

Modifying PC-TALK

Please note that this version of PC-TALK makes use of virtually all the memory available on a 64K system when running the interpreter BASIC version (PC-TALK.BAS). Adding any modifications will exceed the memory capacity for 64K machines.

This version of PC-TALK has incorporated the suggestions of many users who made modifications to earlier versions. Some of these earlier modifications were posted on bulletin boards and became, in

154

effect, "standard" modifications to the earlier program.

There are still many more useful modifications which could be made, and we would like to encourage this grassroots improvement process. The only "dangers" are of different people writing modifications which overlap or are inconsistent, and, of course, people unwittingly writing bugs into the program.

You are free to modify PC-TALK as you wish to suit your personal needs. One of the goals in creating PC-TALK was to produce a program in easily modifiable BASIC. We do request, however, that you do not distribute PC-TALK in modified form. The reason for this is that when people have problems or questions, they inevitably contact us, and we have no way of knowing what modifications may have been made.

If you do come up with useful modifications, please keep them as separate MERGE files which can be incorporated into PC-TALK.BAS at the user's option.

To facilitate this process of creating mergeable mods, we would appreciate your sending us copies of your mods (on disc, if they are substantial). In certain cases, we may want to endorse certain mods and "officially" reserve expansion areas for them. Program lines from 10000 up have specifically been reserved for this purpose.

Please understand that our reason for suggesting that we might approve certain modifications is not in any way meant to inhibit your insights or creativity. To the contrary, we're greatly appreciative of the improvements which have been made to the program so far, and we would merely like to make it easier for more people to share in future improvements.

Definition of Communication Parameters

The communications "parameters" are simply values that specify how data is to be sent. The "baud rate" is the speed of transmission—300 baud means 300 bits per second. Since it usually takes 10 bits to transmit one character, 300 baud is a transmission rate of approximately 30 characters per second. A baud rate of 1200 is four times as fast—about 120

characters per second. (Your modem must be able to support the baud rate you select.)

As mentioned, it usually takes a stream of 10 bits to transmit one ASCII character. One of these 10 bits can be designated as a "parity" bit. The value of this bit can be set so that, when added to the other data bits (described below), the sum of the data and parity bits is either even, odd, always one ("mark parity") or always zero ("space parity"). If you have chosen to communicate with 8 data bits rather than 7 data bits (see next paragraph), there is no "room" for a parity bit, and so you must specify "no" parity.

You can choose to communicate with various numbers of data bits. The most common values are 7 data bits, which allow you to send any of the 127 standard ASCII characters, or 8 data bits, which allow you to send an extended ASCII set of 255 characters.

For every character transmitted, the communications program sends 1 "start" bit. You have no option to vary this number. However, you can specify how many "stop" bits are to be sent. There must be at least 1 stop bit, and this is the most common value.

Explanation of the XMODEM Protocol

Once the protocol is put into effect ("Holding for Start . . ."), the transmitter waits for the receiver to send an NAK character (ASCII 21). Meanwhile, the receiver sends NAK signals every ten seconds. Once the transmitter detects an NAK, it starts to send the file in sections of 128 bytes.

Actually, more than 128 bytes are sent for each block. At the beginning of the block is an SOH character (ASCII 01), followed by the ASCII character representing the block number, followed by the ASCII character of the "one's complement" of the block number. Then the 128 bytes of the file are sent. Finally, the block concludes with an ASCII character representing the sum of the ASCII values of the 128 bytes sent (the "checksum" character).

The receiver checks the block to verify that everything is in order. First it makes sure that the block started with an SOH. Then it makes sure that the block number is correct. Then it performs its own calculations on the 128 data bytes and compares its own checksum with the one received from the transmitter. If everything is in order, the receiver sends an ACK character (ASCII 06) to the transmitter, indicating that the next block is to be sent. If the receiver can't verify, it sends an NAK, requesting that the block be sent again. This continues, block by block, until the entire file has been sent and verified. At the end of the file, the transmitter sends an EOT character (ASCII 04). The receiver acknowledges the EOT with an ACK, and the transfer terminates.

Thank You!

While on the subject on user mods, I would like to express my thanks to Larry Jordan, Rich Schinnell, Wes Merchant, Don Winthrow, and the Capital PC Users Group for their many suggestions, contributions, and continued support.

John O'Boyle of United Technologies has been particularly helpful and encouraging in developing version III and in championing the Freeware concept. Thanks also to Phil Ryals of Bank of America and to Joe Doran of GCA Corporation for their programming insights.

Special thanks to Jeremy John Hewes for being my trusty cohort and dear friend from the very beginning and to Larry Magid and Stu Schwartz for their tireless beta testing and for never being satisfied. And thanks to Patricia Navone and Susan Stone for their loyal and excellent work.

Finally, thank you to the entire PC Community for your many words of encouragement and your financial support. PC-TALK and Freeware started as an experiment. It seems to have worked beyond what anyone suspected. I hope that you find this version of PC-TALK to be more useful and just as friendly as the prior versions, and that we continue to find ways to share our adventures in computing.

—Andrew Fluegelman

Chapter 10

Lowering Your Communications Bill

By now you should have gotten the idea that I absolutely adore the most economical way to save a buck. In this chapter, I want to examine a few ways that are available to help you keep your communications bill low and your file transfers high. The most logical place to start is the telephone. But also covered are remote teletypewriting, alternate long distance calling, and even the U.S. Postal Service.

TELEPHONE

Very important rate information is contained in the opening pages of your telephone directory. In our phone book, the world around us is divided in local and ZUM calling areas, the gimmick here is to charge the Zone Usage Measurement. The bad news is from Monday through Friday 8 AM to 5 PM. You guessed it, full throttle—the meter is running as fast as it goes. A little better news starts at 5 PM. On Mondays through Fridays, all calls can be made at a 30% discount. The best news as far as local calls are concerned is from 11 PM to 8 AM and all day on weekends and holidays: the meter slows down 60%.

The companies that lower phone rates by leasing long distance lines and selling you their usage, such as SPRINT, unfortunately do not provide local service at reduced rates. So unless you take up RTTY or the boss lets you use the business lines on the house, you are stuck. The same division of the day for lower rates after 5 PM and on weekends holds true for long distance, except that the amount of the discount differs. For calls within California the discount becomes 30% and 60%, respectively, and for the out of state business they give us 40% and 60%, except for Alaska and Hawaii, of course, where the 60% becomes 55%. The choice then is to call collect, at night, on weekends, or join one of the communications resellers. Many times it is possible to take advantage of different time zones, so don't overlook the fact, that when it is 11 AM in Alaska and Hawaii it is already 5 PM on the Eastern Seaboard.

AMATEUR RADIO

Another approach is to join the amateur radio folks and use RTTY, remote teletypewriting, using the airways and amateur radio gear. For those of you hams a few quick pointers. In volume 41 of the CP/M users group, there is a program file entitled RTTY.ASM but no documentation. Going through my files, I found the following little blurb.

****1RTTY 2001 BY WORSE***
HDOS OR CP/M VERSION

RTTY 2001, WAS WRITTEN BY PERRY, WOSE. THE COMMANDS ARE ALL AVAILABLE WITH A "CONTROL-A" SO LOOK FOR THEM THERE. TO CONFIGURE THE PROGRAM, CALL IT UP, "RTY" AND IT WILL COME UP READY FOR CONFIGURATION. SET ALL THE PARAMETERS TO FIT YOUR SYSTEM, THE TIME, MONTH, AND DAY. FOR AN ASCII PRINTER OUTPUT, PUT IN 0012 FOR THE BAUD RATE FOR 9600 BAUD, OR WHAT EVER YOU ARE USING. FILL ALL THE SPACES IN THE BAUD SPACE.

THE RECEIVED FILE NAMES WILL BE "RTTYCOPY.RYA" TO "RYZ". THE PROGRAM WILL NOT ERASE OR OVERWRITE A PREVIOUS "COPY TO DISK". THE "PACE" NUMBER IS FOR TRANSMIT SPEED ON TRANSMIT, AND IS TAYLORED TO WHAT EVER AVERAGE SPEED YOU CAN KEEP UP WITH. AFTER THE SETTING THE "CONFIGURATION", HIT THE RED KEY, AND UPDATE THE CONFIGURATION. (THIS WRITES A FILE ON THE DISK WITH THE CONFIGURATION YOU JUST SET UP. ANYTIME YOU CHANGE THE CONFIGURATION, HIT EITHER THE F1 KEY TO JUST RUN THE PROGRAM THAT WAY, OR HIT THE RED KEY TO WRITE THE CONFIGURATION BACK TO THE DISK.

PERRY, WOULD LIKE TO KNOW OF ANY BUGS, OR CHANGES THAT WOULD HELP MAKE THE PROGRAM MORE USEFUL, OR CORRECT. PLEASE SEND ANY INFORMATION TO ME, TOM, WONW, FOR RECORD KEEPING AND THEN I WILL GET THE INFORMATION TO PERRY.

MY ADDRESS IS:
T.L. VINSON
RR1, BOX 175

PINE ISLAND, MN
55963
PHONE 507-356-8513

HAVE FUN. IT IS FREE!!!! (FOR ONLY POSTAGE AND A DISK)

Here is some additional info on HAM programs that I came across.

HAM RADIO PROGRAMS DOCUMENTATION
James K. Mills WB9KFP

Ham Radio Special Interest Group Co-ordinator
Chicago Area Computer Hobbyist Exchange
P.O. Box 94864
Schaumburg, IL 60194

BMAINT.BAS and BREPORT.BAS are modifications of Ward Christensen's maillist programs for use by Amateur Radio Clubs. The KEY is now by call-sign instead of by name—this is much more convenient for Amateur Radio Clubs where one usually knows the individual's call-sign better than his name. The keying algorithm is changed not only for the call-sign, but also to allow any number of records up to the maximum of 1920 (15 extents) per disk.

LABELS.BAS is a small BASIC-E program to print return address labels (or whatever you want to use them for). Asks for name, organization, street, city-state and zip. Prints out 2 to 100 labels (you can change the limits).

TEACH.ASM is the predecessor to my own PRACTICE.ASM documented below. TEACH is for those first learning the Morse code. It sends a character, then waits for a response and then another, and so on. It will give you a bar graph of your speed and correctness of responses. Source code is 10 K. Needs hardware to be able to generate tone.

PRACTICE.ASM and RANDTEXT.BAS are for use in order to practice Morse code. Some type of hardware is necessary to generate a tone which can be controlled by the computer.

CODE.BAS is Ward Christensen's MBASIC Morse code receive program. You will need hardware to interface your radio to the computer.

MORSE.ASM is a Morse code send/receive program. Again, hardware interface is required to couple radio to computer. Source code is 8 K.

RTTY.ASM is a Ham RTTY (5-level Baudot Code) send/receive program with some nice features. It was developed from the TTY*.ASM files which are also included on this disk for reference.

Jim Mills WB9KFP

ALTERNATE LONG DISTANCE CALLING

When planning to send and receive data on your home computer, it is prudent to use ITT longer distance, SPRINT, MCI, Western Union Metrophone, or the American Express Expressphone service. In a recent advertisement, MCI claims savings of 50% on a call from Boston to New York, 41% on a call from Miami to Seattle, and 29% on a call from Dallas to Kansas City. While this averages out at about 40% there are, of course, also some hidden factors. Such as access: common sense tells you that if you want to call your mother New Years' Eve or your girlfriend on Thanksgiving, you won't get through, regardless of company. Then the quality of the lines: these calls are switched by computer, so you need a Touch-tone™ phone. Still, two classes of service on MCI, called Full Service and Super Service not only cost you to join, they also cost you to belong, yes in addition to the cost of the call. Oh, yes, American Expressphone is just MCI service and American Express billing you with a respectable discount of an additional 20% and a buck or two off your monthly MCI charge. That's nice.

U.S. POST OFFICE

Now if I tell you that the U.S. Government will help you to lower your communications costs, you may think that I am trying to fool you. But I am not. You see, like most other home computer users, you want to put your telecommunications to good use. The United States Post Office will help you! E-COM is the service, and E—COM stands for Electronic Computer Originated Mail. Now you can have your computer-originated mail sent efficiently and economically via E-COM service from the Postal Service. All you have to do is to let a certified carrier, usually a secretarial service or a printer/ publisher near you, transmit your messages to the Postal Service. Or you can become certified and send your E-COM messages to the Postal Service yourself. There is a minimum of 200 pieces, however. Your message will be assembled into a message, up to two pages, and then sent to its destination by First Class Mail in an attractive blue envelope. The cost? Twenty-six cents for the first page, five cents for the second. That's everything, envelope, stuffing, and postage. If that is not a bargain, I don't know what is. In addition, you can mail your pieces using your own home computer 24 hours a day seven days a week. What a way to announce your next party! That's not all: the messages can be personalized with a unique line of text for each message, or you can send the same message to everyone, or you can send a different message to each address. Publication 235 of the Postal Service tells you where you can contact your E-COM network.

E-COM requires special formats and protocols. The computers that can be used with E-COM are given in the following list.

- ☐ All CP/M compatible systems.
- ☐ IBM PC and compatibles.
- ☐ Radio Shack TRS-80 Model II, III, IV.
- ☐ Apple II, III.
- ☐ Xerox.
- ☐ Cromemco.
- ☐ Osborne I.
- ☐ Televideo TS 802, 802 H, 806, 816.
- ☐ Molecular Computer Supermicro 8, 32, 32X.

For more details get publication DM-506. Should the entrepreneur in you come out and you want to do it yourself, ask for the E-COM User's Guide, handbook DM-501, and the E-COM Information Guide, publication 341 of the U.S. Postal Service. And when was the last time you said something nice about the mails?

MAILGRAM AND EMAIL

Undoubtedly your mailbox has been flooded with offers of new cars, tv sets, and other unbeatable offers that usually expire on midnight Saturday, unless of course, you act immediately. Much of the mail is prepared electronically, some of it even comes camouflaged to look like a check, a telegram, or other attention getter. How many times have you flung the whole pack into the garbage can without looking at it? That is one of the reasons that in today's society better means of written communications are needed.

Both CompuServe and the Source have extensive electronic mail features, and many computerists use access to those systems as a primary means of communications, both socially and for business. One of the most interesting features of the CompuServe network are the Special Interest Groups. SIGs are of special interest to any home computer owner not only because of the number of them (well over fifty) but also because of their areas of interest. For instance, the importance of the announcement of the Radio Shack TRS-80 Model 100 computer by Tandy Corporation was misunderstood by many. It was not on the front page of every paper in town where it should have been.

In a clever move, Radio Shack had programs for their new computer on both the Source and on CompuServe immediately after the machine's introduction. The point: by snooping electronically you can not only find out what is going on in the world of home computers, but you can also get useful software very early and right now!

Going through some of my Model 100 files I find, among others, the list of programs in Fig. 10-1. Impressed? You should be. If you don't think this is for real, I can make a quick believer out of you. Here is the documentation for a program to log-on to the Dow Jones information service.

DWDOC.100

I have designed a program to facilitate logging on to and storing of Dow Jones news data. The program was written to show the communications capabilities of the TRS-80 Model 100. Its features are as follows:

1. Log-on by either the Tymnet or Telemet packet switching network.
2. Auto log-on defineable for people that consistently ask for the same items each time they call Dow Jones.
3. The ability to create a separate file for each individual or group of calls to Dow Jones.
4. Error trapping to:

    a. Prevent use of an auto-log-on file that is incorrect.

    b. Check to see if the auto-log-on file has actually been created.

I have made extensive use of the editing features of BASIC to duplicate subroutines. Efficient programming would dictate that these should be made into GOSUB routines. I was so intrigued by the ability to move blocks that the program has become much longer than it needs to be.

Also many more files than needed were opened using the MAXFILES declaration. This again was done to test the file handling capabilities of the Model 100. The instructions are pretty much self explanatory. Be sure to set STAT to --> M7I1d,xx where xx is either 10 or 20. Two data files are declared during initialization. They are:

1. QUOTE.DO --> Default file to store Dow Jones news.

AIRNAV	.100	5 K :	BYTES	.100	1 K
CTRLDOC	.100	2 K :	CW	.100	2 K
DIR	.100	3 K :	DIR	.DOC	1 K
DIRNEW	.100	3 K :	DISASMBL	.100	2 K
DOREMI	.100	1 K :	DOSORT	.100	2 K
DSMBLR	.100	8 K :	DWDOC	.100	3 K
EXAMIN	.100	1 K :	GRPX	.100	1 K
HEX	.100	2 K :	INVISBL	.100	2 K
KEYWRD	.100	3 K :	LET-80	.100	3 K
M100DOC	.100	5 K :	MEMDP	.100	2 K
MON100	.100	5 K :	MON100	.DOC	2 K
MONIT	.100	3 K :	MONIT	.DOC	1 K
MORSE	.100	3 K :	NAVAID	.DO	2 K
NOTES	.100	1 K :	OPCODE	.100	3 K
P100DOC	.100	2 K :	PGPRT	.100	2 K
PIE	.100	2 K :	PORT	.100	3 K
PRINT	.100	2 K :	RECV	.100	1 K
RENUM	.100	3 K :	RFU-ORIG	.100	6 K
RFUDOC	.100	5 K :	RFUNEW	.100	5 K
RFUNEW	.DOC	1 K :	ROMDP	.100	2 K
SEND	.100	1 K :	SPOUT	.100	2 K
SYSTEMS	.DOC	2 K :	TRIPS	.100	1 K

Fig. 10-1. Model 100 programs.

2. AUTO.DO --> Stores your auto-log-on procedure.

The only problem I have seen is where the connection with Dow Jones occasionally hangs up and gives you no indication of what has happened. As noted on page 30 of the Model 100 manual under Important Note, the telephone line will not be released.

I present you with three challenges:

1. Make better utilization of memory space and condense the program.
2. Write a routine to have the Model 100 dial at a certain time each day using the ON TIME$ GOSUB.
3. Detect that you have indeed become disconnected and issue a CALL 21179.

Craig E. Knouf
Manager Tandy Videotex
70007,512

Well, there you are. Poking around in all those SIGs provides terrific information as well as software for the newest and best kneetop computer on the market, the Radio Shack TRS-80, Model 100 Portable Computer. Take a close look at page 168. It is indeed a beautiful computer, don't you agree? And by using such a beauty you have the whole world of telecommunications laying on your knees.

Appendix A

Suppliers of Telecommunications Hardware And Software

HARDWARE—COMPUTERS
Apple Computer Inc.

An established line with Apple II, Apple *II*e, and Apple III, this company offers an excellent collection of software for games and graphics. Enhanced by sound and color, Apples can be expanded by the use of a CP/M board and thus access the CP/M library of programs. Many peripherals and accesssories are available for this line.

ATARI Home Computers

The addition of four new ATARI XL home computers brings their line to seven models: the four new models 600XL, 800XL, 1400XL, and the 1400XLD, (see Fig. A-1) and the models 400, the 800 and 1200XL. All new models can be equipped with a CP/M option, and the 1400XL and the 1400XLD have built-in modems. Memory capacity is 16 K for the 400 and 600XL, 48 K for the 800, and 64 K for the 800XL, the 1200XL, the 1400XL, and the 1400XLD. ATARI offers a line of three different printers with model 1027 being letter quality (see

Fig. A-2). The CP/M module features access to the world of CP/M software and allows 80 column processing. For telecommunications, ATARI provides the TeleLink. There is an excellent line of home management software and over 1000 service centers. ATARI, Inc. 1399 Moffett Park Drive, Sunnyvale, California 94086.

Coleco Industries

The ADAM is a low-cost approach to CP/M computing with a letter quality daisy wheel printer that is bidirectional at a rate of 120 words per minute. ADAM's price includes a word processor, 80 K of built-in memory, and two joystick controllers. If you already own the Colecovision Video game system, ADAM is available as an expansion module.

Commodore

With models VIC-20 and Commodore 64, the leader in home computer sales and pricing. The VIC-20 comes with 5 K of memory expandable to 32

K. The Commodore 64 has 64 K of standard memory and comes with an optional Z80 microprocessor and the CP/M operating system to allow CP/M compatibility. Software includes the languages Assembler 64, Pilot, and Logo. Other titles include business software for home and office. Extensive peripherals include five printers, five disc drives, hard disc, a cassette recorder and two modems. If you purchase either modem you get a free password and a one-hour subscription to the CompuServe system which features the Commodore Information Network. Commodore, 1200 Wilson Drive, West Chester, Pennsylvania 19380.

Compaq Computer Corporation

The Compaq Portable Computer and Compaq Plus in Fig. A-3 are two portable personal computers, both using the 16-bit Intel 8086 chip and capable of running all software developed for the IBM PC and XT. The operating system for the Portable Computer is MS/DOS and the memory capacity for that model ranges from 128 K to 512 K. It is equipped with 5¼" discs. DOS 2.0 is the operating system for the Compaq Plus, which can be equipped with memory ranging from 128 K to 640 K. In addition to a 5¼" floppy disc drive of 360 K capacity, it comes equipped with 10 megabytes of hard disc. Both models come with built-in modems, and the Compaq Portable can be upgraded to function and perform as a Compaq Plus. The hard disc is a 3½" Winchester implementation. Compaq is at 20333 FM 149, Houston, Texas 77070, and their phone number is (713) 370-7040.

Fig. A-1. The ATARI 600XL, 800XL, 1400XL and 1400XLD home computers. (Courtesy of ATARI Home Computers)

Fig. A-2. The ATARI 1020, 1025, and 1027 Printers. (Courtesy of ATARI Home Computers)

CompuPro

All the nice things that have been said about this company are true: they make a Cadillac if you care to own the best. Their latest offering is the COMPUPRO 10, a dual 8-bit and 16-bit marvel that has five chips for high power: 4 Z-80s and one 8088. The maximum memory of the COMPUPRO 10 is one megabyte, the operating system available is MP/M 8-16 from Digital Research, and the system comes with one hard disc and two 5¼″ dual sided

Fig. A-3. The Compaq Plus Computer. (Courtesy of Compaq Computer Corporation)

double density floppies. The hard disc can be backed up with ¼" cartridge tape, and internal telecommunications via a 1200 baud modem are available. dBase, SuperCalc, and WRITE are some of the software packages endorsed and running on the COMPUPRO 10. To contact them, write to COMPUPRO, 3506 Breakwater Court, Hayward, California 94545.

Heath Company

MSA-1120-21 is the part number for a computer kit for those of you who would like to build their own computer. I am describing the H/Z-100 All-In-One desktop computer that combines dual microprocessors so that you can run both CP/M and PC software by using larger memory, it starts at 128 K and can be expanded up to 768 K. One 380 K disc drive is standard and you can add a second one, and by getting a color chip set you can convert your monitor into an eight color graphics work station. You have your choice of direct connect or acoustically coupled modems, and with an appropriate cable and Heath's CPS telecommunications software you are up and running. For fully assembled Heath products check under Zenith. Heath Company, Benton Harbor, Michigan 49022.

IBM

IBM has skipped the eight-bit computer world and chose to use a larger 16-bit chip, the Intel 8086 instead. The PC, the XT, and the PCjr use MS DOS, PC-DOS, and the CP/M 86 operating systems, and this can cause compatibility problems, as software you purchase at high-cost to run under PC-DOS is very unlikely to run under CP/M 86. But do not despair, if you bought a PC and long for software that is in the public domain, or if you purchased software and would like to keep on using it here is help: you can do as untold others are doing and buy an Apple board or a CP/M board and stick it in your extension slot. This will give you the best of two worlds. You can use the old and experiment with the new! For those of you interested in PC software in the public domain, check out the many PC bulletin boards listed in Chapter 4.

Jade Computer Products

I am a customer of theirs, and I have found great respect for a company that cares. What you should do is get on their mailing list so that when the bargains rain you can avail yourself of them. With five retail locations in California and one in Dallas, Texas, Jade is just the place to look your KAYPRO over. The other day I visited one of their Los Angeles stores and found out that all their accounting was done on a KAYPRO II. I was given a functional, no nonsense invoice made by the mighty K. Page two of their fall catalog features KAYPRO among other fine bargains. You will have a hard time beating their prices. Tell them Lou Haas sent you. Their mailing address is Jade Computer Products, 4901 West Rosecrans Ave., Hawthorne, California 90250. John, I hope this repays, in a small way, all the many favors you and your folks have done for me. Phone (800) 421-5500. In California call (800) 262-1710.

KAYPRO Corporation

Here is the news you like to hear: an excellent trio of products from a company that cares! KAYPRO packs a lot of muscle into small packages. They not only give you an honest value for your money, but the software that is bundled in the package also makes it an excellent buy! All three models, the KAYPRO II, the KAYPRO 4, and the KAYPRO 10 share the same CP/M operating system and are in the 8-bit Z-80 family. The II comes with two single sided double density 5½" floppy discs, the 4 has 2 dual sided double density floppies, and the 10 weighs in with 10 K bytes of hard disc, in addition to a double sided double density 5½" floppy disc. The software is a real smorgasboard: let's take it one computer at time. The KAYPRO II comes with WordStar, The Word Plus, Perfect Writer, Perfect Speller, Perfect Filer, Perfect Calc, Profitplan, Games, CP/M 2.2, Microsoft BASIC, and Uniform. Now go and price all that separately, and you'll be surprised. The KAYPRO 4 in Fig. A-4 comes similarly equipped, and the model 10 features S-BASIC, an advanced, structured BASIC language, M-BASIC, C-BASIC,

Fig. A-4. The KAYPRO 4 Portable Computer. (Courtesy of The KAYPRO Corporation)

Microplan, Superterm, and The Word Plus. For all of you telecommunications fans, Superterm is KAYPRO's own telecommunications software. Up and at 'em! KAYPRO, 533 Stevens Avenue, Solana Beach, California 92075.

Molecular Computer

If you want to use giant computer power on a micro budget, you have only one choice to make, that choice will have to be Molecular. As a price/performance leader in distributed processing, Molecular is way ahead of the competition and can provide a workstation with mega ooomph for miserly bucks. I feel that a SUPERMICRO 8, 32, or 32X is much more than your living room can take, but if you want the best, the way to share high-priced resources such as high speed printers and large capacity disc drives is to use a Molecular. Per station cost is less than any Local Area Network (LAN) connection can do. And look at all the operating systems you can use: N/Star, CP/M 80, CP/M 86, MP/M 80, MP/M 86, and MS-DOS. Up to three hard discs, cartridge backup, 300 and 1200 baud modem capability and use of BYSINC 80/3720, MODEM7, etc. Molecular is a name to remember. Molecular Computer, 251 River Oaks Parkway, San Jose, California 94134. If you have to find their local distributor, call (408) 262-2122.

Morrow Designs

Mentioned earlier as one of the pioneer S-100 computer companies, Morrow's latest offering is a very competitive hard disc desktop, with the monicker MD11. Running with a 4-MHz Z-80 and using 128 K of memory, the MD11 also has a 400 K floppy disc drive, one Centronics and three serial ports. Bundled with software, the owner gets a terminal, the CP/M Plus operating system, and five application packages upon purchase. They are a BASIC, a spread sheet, a spelling checker, a per-

Fig. A-5. The Radio Shack TRS-80 Color Computer. (Courtesy of Radio Shack, a division of Tandy Corp.)

sonal data base manager, and a bookkeeping system. A terrific offer at a good price.

Morrow Designs
600 McCormick St
San Leandro, Ca. 94577

Radio Shack

The 64 K Color Computer shown in Fig. A-5, based on the 6809 chip from Motorola, can be optionally equipped with OS-9 and Extended Disc Basic. Both cassette and up to four 5¼″ floppy disc drives are supported. 300 baud modems can be plugged in externally and the companies own Videotex communications software is used.

The workhorse of home computers has to be the Radio Shack TRS-80 Model 4. Using a Z-80 chip, this 8-bit computer can run using four operating systems: TRSDOS, LDOS, NEWDOS, and CP/M. Up to four 5¼″ floppies and up to four hard discs can be supported on this system. External modems of 300 and 1200 baud are supported and the company's own telecommunications software is Videotex Plus. This model also comes as a portable, designated the 4P. The 4P runs all Model 4 programs and has a 9 inch 24 line display. Compatible with most programs written for the Model III, and, of course, CP/M, the 4P sports 64 K of memory and can be upgraded to 128 K. With dimensions of 16.5 × 13.5 × 9.75 inches, it weighs in at 26 pounds.

Last, I mention the Executive Workstation, the TRS-80 Model 100 Portable Computer shown in Fig. A-6. This little marvel uses a low-power con-

Fig. A-6. The Radio Shack TRS-80 Model 100 Portable Computer. (Courtesy of Radio Shack, a division of Tandy Corp.)

168

suming CMOS chip, the 80C85, and has a memory confiqured in sizes from 8 K up to 32 K. Proprietary software has been poured into silicon. It is all contained in internal chips and consists of BASIC, an appointment calendar, and word processing software. Telecommunications are supported using an internal 300 baud modem and TELCOM, Radio Shack's proprietary telecommunications software for the Model 100. Radio Shack, 1500 One Tandy Tower, Fort Worth, Texas 78102.

Timex Sinclair

The pioneer of the under $100 computer is apparently bringing out two newer versions: the model 1500, a 16 K one pound portable, and the model 2068 a 68 K with color and sound. Both computers have Z-80 chips for CP/M compatibility and can use the Timex Sinclair 2040 Personal Printer which gives you a width of 32 columns. Both computers use cassette tape as their primary data storage device.

Zenith Data Systems

The Z-100 low profile desktop computer, when equipped with a color monitor and hard disc, has both 8-bit and 16-bit capabilities. It has one of the finest graphics displays around. With 11 megabytes of hard disc this powerhouse handles three operating systems: CP/M, CP/M-86, and Z-DOS. As a S-100 bus computer, the Z-100 allows for plenty of expansion with four open slots. Two serial I/O ports operate at speeds from 110 baud to 38400 baud which allow all sorts of communications by attaching external modems. Zenith Data Systems, 1000 North Milwaukee Avenue, Glenview, Illinois 60025.

HARDWARE/MODEMS

Hayes Microcomputer Products

Hayes is a long established modem manufacturer and their current product line consists of five modems: the Hayes Micromodem II, Hayes Micromodem 100, the Smartmodem 300, the Smartmodem 1200, and the Smartmodem 1200B. The Micromodem II is a peripheral card for the Apple II and is compatible with CP/M, and it can be used with both public domain and store bought software. The Micromodem 100 is the Micromodem II on a card for the S-100 bus. It features, like the Micromodem II auto-dialing and answering. The Smartmodem 300 and the Smartmodem 1200 (see Fig. A-7) are external modems that connect to your computer using a RS-232C serial port, and to the phone with a modular jack. Both handle auto-dialing and answering and can be used for Touch Tone™ and pulse dialing. The Smartmodem 1200B is a peripheral card for the IBM PC and XT and has the same features as the previously described model 1200. Hayes Microcomputer Products, Inc., 5923 Peachtree Industrial Bld., Norcoross, Georgia 30092.

Novation, Inc.

Here is a line so complete it is hard to describe. I will start with the sleek looking compact acoustic coupler shown in Fig. A-8 and called the CAT. This unit is sold under different names by others. Their catalog features a CCIT CAT, another acoustic coupler, DCAT, JCAT, 212 AUTOCAT, and SMART CAT, four direct connect modems, Apple CAT II and 212 Apple CAT, two peripheral cards, and finally NOVATION PC1200B SMART MODEM. Quite a list. Novation, Inc., 20409 Prairie Street, Chatsworth, California 91311.

SOFTWARE-PUBLIC DOMAIN

CPMUG CP/M User's Group

1651 Third Ave.
New York, New York 10028

F R E E W A R E User-Supported Software

If you are using this program and finding it of value, your contribution ($35 suggested) will be appreciated.
= = = F r e e w a r e = = =
The Headlands Press, Inc.
Post Office Box 862
Tiburon, CA 94920
Regardless of whether you make a contribution, you are encouraged to copy and share this program.

Fig. A-7. The Hayes Smartmodem. (Courtesy of Hayes Microcomputer Products)

FREEWARE user-supported software is an experiment in distributing computer programs, based on three principles.

First, that the value and utility of software is best assessed by the user on his/her own system. Only after using a program can one really determine whether it serves personal applications, needs, and tastes.

Fig. A-8. The Novation CAT modem. (Courtesy of Novation, Inc.)

Second, that the creation of independent personal computer software can and should be supported by the computing community.

Finally, that copying and networking of programs should be encouraged, rather than restricted. The ease with which software can be distributed outside traditional commercial channels reflects the strength, rather than the weakness, of electronic information.

Anyone may request a copy of a user-supported program by sending a blank, formatted disk to the author of the program. An addressed, postage-paid return mailer must accompany the disk (no exceptions, please). A copy of the program with documentation, will be sent by return mail. The program carries a notice suggesting a contribution to the program's author. Making a contribution is completely voluntary on the part of the user.

Regardless of whether a contribution is made, the user is encouraged to copy and share the program with others. Payment for use is discretionary on the part of each subsequent user.

Will the user-supported concept really work? Up to now, distribution of software has relied either on restricting access (and charging for the cost of doing so), or anonymously casting programs into the public domain. The user-supported concept is a way for the computing community to support and encourage creative work outside the traditional marketplace. This is an experiment in economics more than altruism. Free distribution of software and voluntary payment for its use eliminates the need for money to be spent on marketing, advertising, and copy projection schemes. Users can obtain quality software at reduced cost, while still supporting program authors. And the most useful program survive, based purely on their usefulness. Please join the experiment.

FREEWARE is the trademark of The Headlands Press for its user-supported software, but we invite all software authors to participate in this distribution concept. We would like to publish a FREEWARE CATALOG of user-supported software by program authors who are willing to make their work available on a free, nonrestricted basis. If you would like your program listed, please send a description of the program (including system requirements) and the address to which requests for copies should be sent. Fulfilling requests and suggesting contributions are the sole responsibility of each program author. Listings in the catalog are free.

We welcome your comments about the user-supported concept. Thank you for your support.
Andrew Fluegelman
Freeware

FREEWARE, P.O. Box 862, Tiburon, California 94920

PJS Co.

Software Sales and Rentals
933 S. Santa Fee
Vista, California 92083

S and Y Computing

224 W. Grand Avenue
El Segundo, California 90245

Workman & Associates

112 Marion Avenue
Pasadena, California 91106

SOFTWARE—MODEM MANUFACTURERS

Hayes Terminal Program

For the Apple II and II Plus and Hayes Micromodem II, Smartmodem 300 and Smartmodem 1200. Manages communications, parameters, auto-dial, and file transfer. Captures incoming data to disc and printer.

Smartcom II

Menu driven software with HELP facilities for the IBM PC. It allows storage of calling parameters for up to 25 different auto-dial/auto log-on situations, including phone number, baud rate, passwords and many others. Remote access allows for unattended file transfers.

Novation

PC1200B SMART MODEM with CROSS-TALK XVI Software. Novation and Microstuf, Inc. have combined forces to create a unique communications package for the IBM PC, IBM XT, Columbia, MPC, Columbia Portable, Corona Portable, and Compaq. Crosstalk XVI is an intelligent terminal and file transfer program. It employs all the features of the Novation PC1200B smart modem, including auto-dial, auto-answer, and auto-log-on. Complete control over forty log-ons by simple keystroke, including extensive error checking and facilities for retransmission, capture to disc or printer. Microstuf, Inc. 1845 The Exchange, Atlanta, Georgia 30339.

Appendix B

Reference Literature

With the onslaught of literature taking avalanche proportions and all media inundating us with all sorts of promises, many of which are never kept, it becomes a difficult task to advise on what to read, and what to put in ones reference library.

The initial impact of the IBM PCs will have a rippling effect in that everyone will be jumping on the bandwagon to exploit the situation. Once the product and its look-alikes mature, and this is going to take some time, software will emerge that stands out and will not be bought based on media hype, but on word of mouth. In the 8-bit world the early users of CP/M, C-Basic, WordStar, and The Word didn't buy their software based on Madison Avenue inputs, but on recommendations of other users. To do likewise in home computers will be a difficult task unless one choses the recommended 8-bit CP/M approach. The reason for that is plain: 8-bit CP/M software is plentiful. Much of this excellent software is in the public domain or available as super-buys, such as bundled computers, where the hardware and software are combined. Such offerings of KAYPRO Computers are here to be taken advantage of.

MAGAZINES

The best publication for the serious home computer user is *Byte* magazine, the small systems journal, published by McGraw-Hill. It does a nice job with screening their advertising, and a cursory review quickly tells you, that it also is a very timely magazine. With PCs and compatibles at a crest of popularity, current issues are heavily flavored in that direction. My favorite reading upon receipt of this publication is the User's Column by Jerry Pournelle. His description of life at Chaos Manor is not only fine reading, but his recommendations and comments are timely and to the point. If this monthly diet is too heavy and you would like something on a more frequent basis my recommendation is *InfoWorld*, the Newsweekly for Microcomputer Users. *InfoWorld* enlightens us with excellent reviews and ratings on both hardware and software, and periodically summarizes those reviews.

In the PC arena there are a number of offerings. *PC World* stands out with an excellent column on software called Star-Dot-Star, or *.*, a global exchange of personal computer discoveries, edited by Andrew Fluegelman. A fine magazine that covers the Apple, ATARI, Commodore 64, VIC-20, and Timex/Sinclair waterfront is *Compute!*, the leading magazine of home, educational, and recreational computing. I like their index, which is keyed by the different home computers and thus allows you quick access to whatever is of interest to you. A fine publication for the world of TRS-80 users is *80micro*, a Wayne Green publication. Wayne was into publishing way back in the 70s, his first issue of a magazine, then called *kilobaud, the Computer Hobbyist* Magazine, has a cover date of January 1977! A nostalgic look at the ads of that issue let us remember SWTPC, WAVE MATE, Ohio Scientific Instruments, IMSAI, and the Altair 680 and the Altair 8800b featuring a model 8080A microprocessor and a 100-pin bus structure. Both Bill Goodbout and George Morrow were featured in a column called Around the Industry, and for only $1,450 you could buy a model 33 Teletype with all the trimmings. Good old days! Two publications for the serious CP/M user are *Microsystems*, the CP/M user's journal, and *Lifelines*, the Software Magazine. Both deal with CP/M software, and many advances in hardware for the S-100 bus can be followed by reading *Microsystems*. For the general news on what is happening in home computers and telecommunications you will find regular news features and an excellent column on computers in *Popular Science*.

CATALOGS

If you have decided to make some big purchases it always pays to do some armchair price comparisons, and four catalogs always perform that function in my computer den. For obvious reasons, Heathkit is my perennial favorite. CompuPro gives us excellent information on the high end of products for the S-100 bus, both 8-bit and 16-bit applications, and features single multiuser systems. Radio Shack appeals to us because not only do they publish a regular computer catalog, many times a year, but

they also put out sales catalogs that feature or close out certain products. Also featuring regular and sales catalogs are Jade Computer Products and Priority One Electronics. The Priority One catalogs are sometimes found in the pages of *Byte* magazine, when pull-out sections of many pages are featured.

CONTROLLED CIRCULATION FREEBIES

Many publications offer free copies for qualified subscribers; however most of those that do so in home computers are oriented towards retailers and distributors in the business. If you are a data processing professional, you already have some of these. If not, try to talk yourself into a subscription of *Datamation*, one of the oldest and most respected magazines in Data Processing.

ADDRESSES

BYTE Subscription Dept.
P.O. Box 590
Martinsville, New Jersey 08836

InfoWorld Circulation Department
P.O. Box 837
Framingham, Massachusetts 01701

PC World Subscription Department
P.O. Box 6700
Bergenfield, New Jersey 07621

COMPUTE! Circulation Department
P.O. Box 11747
Philadelphia, Pennsylvania 19101

80 micro Subscription Department
80 Pine Steet
Peterborough, New Hampshire 03458

Microsystems Circulation Department
P.O. Box 2930
Boulder, Colorado 80321

Lifelines
1651 Third Avenue
New York, New York 10028

Popular Science Subscription Department
P.O. Box 2872
Boulder, Colorado 80321

Heath Company
Heathkit Catalog Department
Benton Harbor, Michigan 49022

CompuPro Goodbout Electronics
P.O. Box 2355 Building 725
Oakland Airport, California 94614

Radio Shack
A Division of Tandy Corporation
300 One Tandy Tower
Fort Worth, Texas 76102

Jade Computer Products
4901 West Rosecrans Ave.
Hawthorne, California 90250

Priority One Electronics
9161 Deering Avenue
Chatsworth, California 91311

DATAMATION Circulation Department
875 Third Avenue
New York, New York 10022

Appendix C

Software Aids

Did you ever sit down and cry, because the last time you compiled a Fortran program, you forgot to write down the switch settings. Did you ever want to link a dozen program modules, but forgot to remember the maker of the thing? Well, you can relax.

Software Aids to the rescue! Here, for your computing pleasure are nineteen software summaries for you. Enjoy them, and most of all, use them often.

You will find the individual chapters in alphabetical order and you can use the following index to find them faster.

These modules are mostly CP/M software and are what the user needs to do most of his work in an 8-bit environment. Many of these languages, such as M-BASIC, have also been implemented under operating systems other than CP/M. The language syntax and it's use are thus valid in a lot of different operating environments.

ALGOL/M COMPILER

Although ALGOL/M was modeled after ALGOL-60, no attempt was made to make it a formal subset of ALGOL-60. This was done intentionally in order to provide a language which would to be best suited to the needs of applications programmers using microcomputer systems. However, the basic structure of ALGOL/M is similar enough to ALGOL-60 to allow simple conversion of programs from one language to the other. This was considered particularly important in view of the fact that the standard publication language is ALGOL-60. Therefore, there exists a large source of applications programs and library procedures which can be simply converted to execute under ALGOL/M.

Invoking The ALGOL/M Compiler And Runtime System

ALGOL/M is invoked by typing:

ALGOLM filename $option

where 'filename' is the name of the file 'filename.ALG' which contains the source of the ALGOL/M program. Upon executing this command, ALGOL/M will compile this source program into the pseudo code file 'filename.AIN' which can then be executed by tying—RUNALG filename—where 'filename' is the name of the file 'filename.INT' which contains the ALGOL/M pseudo code.

The options recognized by the ALGOL/M Compiler are:

$A Generate a listing at the terminal.
$E Set Trace Mode for execution under RUNALG.
$AE Do Both of the above.

ALGOL/M Reserved Words

ANDARRAY	BEGIN	CASE
CLOSE	DECIMAL	DO ELSE
ENDFILE	FUNCTION	GO
GOTO	IF	INTEGER
NOT	OF	ONENDFILE
OR	PROCEDURE	READ
STEP	STRING	TAB
THEN	TO	UNTIL
WHILE	WRITE	WRITEON

Type Declarations

ALGOL/M supports three types of variables: integers, decimals, and strings. Integers may be any value between $-16,383$ and $+16,383$. Decimals may be declared with up to 18 digits of precision and strings may be declared as long as 255 characters. The default precision for decimals is ten digits and the default length for strings is ten characters. Decimal and string variable lengths may be integer variables which can be assigned actual values at run-time.

Another form of declaration in ALGOL/M is the array declaration. Arrays may have up to 255 dimensions with each dimension ranging from 0 to $+16,383$. The maximum 8080 microprocessor address space of 63 K bytes limits practical array sizes to something smaller than the maximum. Dimension bounds may be integer variables with the actual values assigned at run-time. Arrays may be of type integer, decimal or string.

Arithmetic Processing

Integer and binary coded decimal arithmetic are supported under ALGOL/M. Integers may be used in decimal expressions and will be converted to decimals at run-time. The integer and decimal comparisons of less-than ($<$), greater-than ($>$), equal-to ($=$), not-equal to ($<>$), less-than-or-equal-to ($<=$), and greater-than-or-equal-to ($>=$) are provided. Additionally, the logical operators AND, OR and NOT are available.

Control Structures

ALGOL/M control structures consist of BEGIN, END, FOR, IF THEN, IF THEN ELSE, WHILE, CASE and GOTO constructs. Function and procedure calls are also used as control structures. ALGOL/M is a block structured language with a block normally bracketed by a BEGIN and an END. Blocks may be nested within other blocks to nine levels. Variables which are declared within a block can only be referenced within that block or a block nested within that block. Once program control proceeds outside of a block in which a variable has been declared, the variable may not be referenced and, in fact, run-time storage space for that variable no longer exists.

Functions, when called, return an integer, decimal or string value depending on the type of the function. Procedures do not return a value when called. Both functions and procedures may have zero or more parameters which are called by value and both may be called recursively.

Input/Output

The ALGOL/M WRITE statement causes output to the console on a new line. The desired output is specified in a write list which is enclosed in parentheses. String constants may be used in a write list and are characterized by being enclosed in quotation marks. Any combination of integer, decimal and string variables or expressions may also be used in a write list. A WRITEON statement is also available which is essentially the same as the WRITE statement except that output continues on the same line as the output from a previous WRITE or WRITEON statement. When a total of 80 characters have been written to the console, a new line is started automatically. A TAB option may also be used in the write list which causes the following item in the write list to be spaced to the right by a specified amount.

Console input is accomplished by the READ statement followed by a read list of any combination of integer, decimal and string variables enclosed in parentheses. If embedded blanks are desired in the input for a string variable, the console input must be enclosed in quotation marks. A READ statement will result in a halt in program execution at run-time until the input values are typed at the console and a carriage return is sent. If the values typed at the console match the read list in number and type, program execution continues. If an error as to number or type of variables from the console occurs, program execution is again halted until values are re-entered on the console.

Disc Access

ALGOL/M programs may read data from, or write data to, one or more disc files which may be located on one or more disc drives. When file input or output is desired, the appropriate READ or WRITE statement is modified by placing a filename identifier immediately after READ or WRITE. The actual name of the file may be assigned to the file name identifier when the program is written or it may be assigned at run-time. Various disc drives are referenced by the letters A through Z. A specific drive may be specified by prefixing the actual file name with the desired drive letter followed by a colon. Additionally, if random file access is desired, the file name identifier may be followed by a comma and an integer constant or variable. This integer value specifies the record within the file which is to be used for input/output.

Prior to the use of a file name identifier in a READ or WRITE statement, the file name identifier must appear in a file declaration statement. The file name identifier can only be referenced within the same block (or a lower block) as the file declaration. Files are normally treated as unblocked sequential files. However, if blocked files are desired, the record length may optionally be specified in brackets after the file name identifier in the file declaration statement.

ALGOL/M Compiler Error Messages

AS   Function/Procedure on left-hand side of assignment statement.
BP   Incorrect bound pair subtype (must be integer).
DE   Disc error; no corrective action can be taken in the program.
DD   Doubly declared identifier, label, variable, etc.
FP   Incorrect file open statement.
IC   Invalid special character.
ID   Subtypes incompatible (decimal values can not be assigned to integer variables).
IO   Integer overflow.
IT   Identifier is not declared as a simple variable or function.
NG   No ALG file found.
NI   Subtype is not integer.
NP   No applicable production exists.
NS   Subtype is not string.
NT   For clause, Step expression, Until clause expressions are not of the same subtype. (must all be integer or decimal).
PC   Number of parameters in procedure call does

not match the number in the procedure declaration.

PD Undeclared parameter.
PM Parameter type does not match the declared type.
SO Stack overflow.
SI Array subscript is not of subtype integer.
TD Subtype has to be integer or decimal.
TM Subtypes do not match or are incompatible.
TO Symbol table overflow.
TS Undeclared subscripted variable.
UD Undeclared identifier.
UF Undeclared file/function.
UL Undeclared label.
UP Undeclared procedure.
US Undeclared simple variable.
VO Varc table overflow. Possibly caused by too many long identifiers.

ALGOL/M Run-Time Error And Warning Messages

ERROR MESSAGES

AB Array subscript out of bounds.
CE Disc file close error.
DB Input field length is larger then the buffer size.
DW Disc file write error.
ER Variable block size write error.
IO Integer overflow (integer value greater than 16383).
IR Record number incorrect or random file is not initialized.
ME Disc file creation error.
NA No AIN file found on directory.
OV Decimal register overflow during arithmetic operation/load.
RE Attempt to read past end of record on blocked file.
RU Attempt to random access a non-blocked file.
SK Stack overflow (no more memory available).

WARNING MESSAGES

AZ Attempt to allocate null decimal or string,

system defaults to 10 digits/characters.
DO Decimal overflow during store operation. The value of the variable is set to 1.0 and execution continues. The variable's allocation size should be increased in it's declaration statement.
DI Disc file variable format error.
DZ Decimal division by zero, result is set to 1.0.
EF End of file on read.
IA Integer addition/subtraction over/under flow result is set to 1.
II Invalid Console Input. Try input again.
IR Record number incorrect or random file is not initialized.
IZ Integer division by zero. Divisor set to 1 and division is completed.
NX Negative exponential. Exponentiation not done.
SO Characters lost during string store.

CP/M ASSEMBLER

Invoking The Assembler

The CP/M Assembler is invoked by typing:

ASM filename or ASM filename.parms

where 'filename' is the name of the file 'filename.ASM' to be assembled. In the case of the first command, the following files are created:

filename.HEX —"HEX" file containing machine code in Intel hex format
filename.PRN —listing file

In the case of the second command, these files are created according to the parameters specified:

ASM filename.pqr

where
    p : A,B,... —designates the disc name which contains the source.
    q : A,B,... —designates the disc name to receive the hex file.
    Z   —skips generation of the hex file.

r : A,B,... —designates the disc name which will receive the print file
X   —outputs the listing to the console
Z   —skips generation of the print file.

Pseudo-Ops

ORG   Set the program or data origin.
END   End program.
EQU   Numeric equate.
SET   Numeric set.
IF   Begin conditional assembly.
ENDIF   End conditional assembly.
DB   Define data bytes.
DW   Define data words
DS   Define data storage area.

In-Line Error Messages

D   Data error: element in data statement cannot be placed in the specified data area.
E   Expression error: expression is ill-formed and cannot be computed at assembly line.
L   Label error: label cannot appear in this context (may be duplicate label).
N   Not implemented: features which will appear in future ASM versions.
O   Overflow: expression is too complicated to compute; simplify.
P   Phase error: label does not have the same value on two subsequent passes through the program.
R   Register error: the value specified as a register is not compatible with the operation code.
V   Value error: operand encountered in expression is improperly formed.

Console Error Messages

NO SOURCE FILE PRESENT. The file specified in the ASM command does not exist on disc.

NO DIRECTORY SPACE. The disc directory is full, erase files which are not needed, and retry.

SOURCE FILE NAME ERROR. Improperly formed ASM File name.

SOURCE FILE READ ERROR. Source file cannot be read properly by the assembler, execute a TYPE to determine the point of error.

OUTPUT FILE WRITE ERROR. Output files cannot be written properly, most likely cause is a full disc, erase and retry.

CANNOT CLOSE FILE. Output file cannot be closed, check to see if disc is write protected.

CP/M ASSEMBLER VERSION 2.2

Invoking The Assembler

The CP/M Assembler is invoked by typing:

ASM filename or ASM filename.parms

where 'filename' is the name of the file 'filename.ASM' to be assembled. In the case of the first command, the following files are created:

filename.HEX —"HEX" file containing machine code in Intel hex format
filename.PRN —listing file

In the case of the second command, these files are created according to the parameters specified:

ASM filename.pqr

where
p : A,B,... —designates the disc name which contains the source.
q : A,B,... —designates the disc name to receive the hex file.
Z   —skips generation of the hex file.
r : A,B,... —designates the disc name which will receive the print file.
X   —outputs the listing to the console.
Z   —skips generation of the print file.

Pseudo-Ops

ORG   Set the program or data origin.
END   End program.
EQU   Numeric equate.
SET   Numeric set.
IF   Begin conditional assembly.
ENDIF   End conditional assembly.
DB   Define data bytes.
DW   Define data words.
DS   Define data storage area.

In-Line Error Messages

D   Data error: element in data statement cannot be placed in the specified data area.

E   Expression error: expression is ill-formed and cannot be computed as assembly line.

L   Label error: label cannot appear in this context (may be duplicate label).

N   Not implemented: features which will appear in future ASM versions.

O   Overflow: expression is too complicated to compute; simplify.

P   Phase error: label does not have the same value on two subsequent passes through the program.

R   Register error: the value specified as a register is not compatible with the operation code.

V   Value error: operand encountered in expression is improperly formed.

Console Error Messages

NO SOURCE FILE PRESENT. The file specified in the ASM command does not exist on disc.

NO DIRECTORY SPACE. The disc directory is full, erase files which are not needed, and retry.

SOURCE FILE NAME ERROR. Improperly formed ASM file name.

SOURCE FILE READ ERROR. Source file cannot be read properly by the assembler, execute a TYPE to determine the point of error.

OUTPUT FILE WRITE ERROR. Output files cannot be written properly, most likely cause is a full disc, erase and retry.

CANNOT CLOSE FILE. Output file cannot be closed, check to see if disc is write protected.

THE BDS C COMPILER

Invoking BDS C Using C.SUB

BDS C may be invoked either by the conventional means or by using the SUBMIT file C.SUB. If the SUBMIT file is used, it is engaged as follows:

SUBMIT C filename

where 'filename' is the name of 'filename.C', the file

to compile. Note that the user is NOT to type filename.C, but is just to type filename. As execution of the two passes of the compiler and the linker proceeds, the user will be given the chance to abort processing at various critical points in the process by the execution of the ABORTSUB program. If an error has occurred during the previous processing, ABORT when this program is executed.

Overview of The BDS C Language System

The main components of C are: 4 executable programs, a standard library file, and one skeleton run-time subroutine file. A description of each follows.

CC1, C COMPILER-PASS 1. Because C loads the entire source file into memory in one shot, the compilation is broken up into two phases (not "passes," strictly; The two phases end up taking about 8 passes to actually implement), maximizing the amount of memory available for the source file.

CC1, the first half of the compiler, accepts a C source file with any filename and extension (say, "foo.c") and writes out a temporary file (with the same filename and extension ".CCI") containing a symbol table and an encoded form of the source code.

The file extension ".C" is NOT assumed for the input file, so saying "FOO" for "FOO.C" would not work.

If the source file name is preceded by a disc designation, then the input is taken from the specified disc and the output is also written to that disc.

If any errors are detected during CC1, the output file will not be written.

In addition to the name of the source file, a few options may also be specified on the command line by preceding the option list with a dash (-):

1. s causes undeclared identifiers to be implicitly declared as integer variables, wherever possible.

2. Hex digit (4-f) sets symbol table size to the specified value (in K bytes); default is 8 (5 for versions x.xT.)

For example, A>cc1 foobar.c−s6, suppresses

errors for undefined variables and sets symbol table size to 6 K bytes;

A>cc1 zot.c −e

sets symbol table size to 14 K bytes. Note that the option list must contain no blanks.

A>cc1 b:td.c

takes the source file from disc B and writes the .CCI file to disc B (regardless of what the currently 'ogged disc is). On an 8080, speed is about 12 lines source/sec.

CC2, C COMPILER-PASS 2. This is the second half of the compiler. CC2 accepts a ".CCI" file as input, and writes out a ".CRL" file if no errors are detected. (CRL is mnemonic for 'C ReLocatable')

If all goes well, writing out of the CRL file is followed by deletion of the "CCI" file, and compilation is complete.

As for CC1, if a disc is specified explicitly as in

A>cc2 c:yahoo

then the .CCI file is loaded from the specified disc and the .CRL file is written to that same disc. On an 8080, execution time = about 35 lines/sec.

CLINK, C LINKER. This program links a "main" function from some CRL file together with C.CCC (for common system subroutines) and any subordinate functions which "main" may require (from perhaps many CRL files).

A successful linkage causes a ".COM" file to be generated. At this point, the 8080 absolute machine code file is ready to be executed (for better or worse) as a transient command by CP/M.

The first argument on the command line must be the name of a CRL file containing a "main" function. If the name is specified with an extension, then that extension is interpreted specially as indicating which discs are to be involved in the operation (this is akin to the mechanism ASM uses to determine source and destination discs).

For example, if the first argument to CLINK were given as:

A*clink foo.bc

then CLINK would interpret the "b" in ".bc" as specifying the disc on which "DEFF.CRL" and "C.CCC" are to be found, and the "c" in ".bc" as specifying which disc the .COM file is to be written to. Both of these values, if omitted, default to the currently logged in disc.

The first argument may also be preceded by a disc designation, to specify where all .CRL files are to be searched for (by default). For example, the command

A>clink b:zot.ac

tells CLINK to get C.CCC and DEFF.CRL from disc A; to write the output file to disc C; and to find ZOT.CRL on disc B.

Any other CRL files to search may also be specified on the command line (WITHOUT their .CRL suffixes), causing those to be searched in the order specified. The default disc to search will be the same disc from which the orignal CRL file was taken; this default can be overridden by specifying an explicit disc designation for any appropriate CRL file name needing it. For example,

A>clink c:foo.bb bar a:zot fraz

causes disc C to be searched for the files FOO. CRL, BAR.CRL and FRAZ.CRL, while disc A would be searched to find ZOT,CRL. disc B is where CLINK would expect DEFF.CRL and C.CCC to reside, and the output would go to disc B also.

When all given CRL files have been searched, CLINK will automatically search DEFF.CRL.

If there are still some unresolved references, then CLINK will ask for input from the keyboard to try resolving them.

There are also several options which may be specified on the command line. Each option must be preceded by a dash (-); the space between options and their argument (if needed) is optional. The presently supported options are:

1. -s prints out load statistics;

2. -t nnnn reserves location nnnn (hex) and above for user; default is to reserve no space. What this really does is to cause the first op in the object file to be 1xi sp,nnnn instead of 1xi sp,bdos.

3. -o name causes the .COM file generated to have the given name. Default is the name of the first .CRL file given (the one with the "main" function.)

4. -e xxxx sets start of data area to address xxxx, to maintain consistency between several separate .COM files when chaining (via the library function "exec") is used.

5. -c specifies that the .COM file is to be chained to from another .COM file. If the resultant .COM file is invoked directly from CP/M instead of via the "exec" function, then ARGC & ARGV processing is suspended, since upon being chained to you wouldn't want ARGC & ARGV processing to take place.

Note that if you use this option, you should also use the -e option to set the data area address equal to that of the chaining .COM file.

Examples

A>clink foo bar gets "main" from the file FOO.CRL, searches for needed functions first in FOO.CRL and then, if needed, in BAR.CRL and DEFF.CRL. All files are assumed to reside on the currently logged in disc.

A>clink b:ihtfp belle -s searches for IHTFP.CRL and BELLE.CRL on disc B; prints a statistics summary when linkage is complete. The files DEFF.CRL and C.CCC are assumed to reside on the currently logged in disc; output also goes to the currently logged in disc.

A>clink b:ihtfp.aa -s belle -o zot is the same as the last example except: the output file is called ZOT.COM, DEFF.CRL and C.CCC are assumed to reside on A, and output goes to A.

A>clink stoned -t7000 -s sets top of memory to 7000h and prints out load statistics. Current disc is used for everything

Note that if the load statistics tell you that the "LAST ADDRESS" is greater than the "TOP OF MEMORY," the program hasn't got the chance of a snowball in hell of running correctly.

C Librarian

CLIB. This program maintains .CRL files, allows transfer of functions from one CRL file to another, etc. To invoke CLIB, just type

A>clib

Clib will print a line such as

FUNCTION BUFFER SIZE = nnnnn

specifying the largest function size that can be handled. Attempting to "transfer" or "extract" a function larger than this size could be destructive. Next CLIB will prompt with a "*". Typing "h" at this point will give you a command summary. Basically, you work CLIB by opening one to six CRL files (which then become associated with "file numbers"), diddling the files to your hearts content, closing all files which you altered, and typing control-C.

The old version of any CRL file you change with CLIB is renamed to name.BRL (for Backup ReLative). A sample session of CLIB to, say, transfer the functions named "FOO", "BAR", and "ZOT" from a .CRL file named "DSSR" to one named "RTS" would go as follows:

A>clib

BD SOFTWARE C LIBRARIAN VERSION x.x FUNCTION BUFFER SIZE = xxxx BYTES

```
* open 0 dssr
* open 1 rts
* t 0 1 foo
* t 0 1 bar
* t 0 1 zot
* c 1
* ^C
A> ...
```

The "open commands" prepare to do work on a .CRL file,. and associate each .CRL file opened with a digit (0-5). The "transfer" commands tell CLIB to transfer the named function from the first file (named by file #) to the second file (also named by number). The "close" command need only be given for files which have been altered; since DSSR wasn't written to in the above example, it didn't need to be closed, but RTS did need to be closed.

DEFF.CRL. This file contains the standard function library... all 60+ functions worth. See the BDS C User's Guide for documentation on these functions.

C Skeleton File

C.CCC. The run-time skeleton file, containing code for processing the command line (generating argc and argv, for you UNIX lovers), room for file I/O buffers, some math subroutines, etc.

The BDS C compiler is not an interpreter. Some hacks, such as BASIC-E, are billed as compilers but actually just do some preprocessing and then interpret the program. BDS C is a true compiler, generating not-too-optimal but nevertheless quick 8080 code.

Variable Types

Variable types supported: int, char, unsigned, struct, union, arrays (of one or two dimensions), pointers, are simple combinations of these. For example,

char *foo[10] [15]

declares foo to be a two dimensional array of pointers to characters;

char (*foo) ( ) ;

declares foo to be a pointer to a function returning a character;

char *mfoo, bar, zot[10];

declares foo to be a pointer to characters, bar to be a single char variable, and zot to be an array of 10 characters.

Braces

If your keyboard doesn't support the '{' and '}' characters (open and close brace, for those of you whose printer doesn't know about ASCII 7B and 7D), the symbols 'begin' and 'end' may be substituted. Don't unless you have to; '{' and '}' take up less memory.

The CONVERT program will perform this conversion, if necessary.

Variable Accessing

Since all functions in C may be used recursively, all variable accessing is done relative to a base-of-stack-frame pointer, kept in the BC register pair during execution. Note that it takes 8 bytes of code to transfer a simple local variable whose address is

(Base of stack pointer) + foo

to the HL register pair; The code appears as:

```
lxi h,foo
dad b
mov a,m
inx hvv
mov h,m
mov m,a .
```

To get an array element or structure element is even more hairy. Facts like this are enough to make me REALLY wish Intel had bothered to implement a double byte indirect load instruction. Oh well.

C Library

The following are the names of the routines available in the C Library DEFF.CRL. They are listed here as a memory convenience. Refer to the manual for further details. Each name is separated by a comma and is not part of the name.

1. General purpose functions.

    csw ( ), exit ( ), bdos (c, de), peek (n), poke (n,b), inp (n), outp (n,b), pause ( ), sleep (n), call (adr, h, a, b, d), abs (n), srand (n), rand ( ), setmem (adr, count, byte), movmem (source, dest, count), qsort (base, nel, width, compar) char *source, *dest; char *base; int (*compar)( );, exec (name), char *name;

2. Character input/output.

getchar ( ), ungetch (c), kbhit ( ), putchar (c), puts (str), char *gets(str), char *star; char *str;, printf (format, arg1, arg2, . . .), scanf (format, arg1, arg2, . . .) char *format; char *format;

3. String and character processing.

isalpha (c), isupper (c), islower (c), isdigit (c), char c;, char c;, char c;, char c;, touppper (c), tolower (c), isspace (c), strcat (s1, S2), char c;, char c;, char c;, char *s1, *s2;, strcmp (s1, s2), strcpy (s1, s2), strlen (str), atoi (str), char *s1, *s2; char *s1,*s2;, char *str;, char *str;, initw(array, string), initb (array,string), int *rray; char *string; char *array, *string; getval (strptr), char **strptr;

4. File I/O.

creat (filename), unlink (filename), char *filename;, char *filename;, open (filename, mode), close (fd), char *filename;, (mode=0 – input, mode=1 – output, mode=2 – input and output) read (fd, buf, nbl), write (fd, buf, nbl), char *buf;, char *buf;, seek (fd, offset, code), tell (fd), fopen (filename, iobuf), fcreat (filename, iobuf), char *filename;, char *filename;, struct buf *iobuf;, struct buf *iobuf;, getc (iobuf), putc (c, iobuf), struct buf *iobuf;, char c; struct buf *iobuf;, getw (iobuf), putw (w, iobuf), struct buf *iobuf;, struct buf *iobuf;, fflush (iobuf), struct buf *iobuf;

5. Plotting functions (for memory-mapped video boards).

setplot (base, xsize, ysize), clrplot ( ), plot (x, y, chr), char chr;, txtplot (string, x, y, ropt), char *string;, line (c, x1, y1, x2, y2)

6. Plotting functions for Hazeltine 1500.

clear ( ), cplot (x, y, chr), char chr;, ctxtplot (x, y, string), char *string;

7. Special I/O - CIO.

cio (fn) or cio (fn, arg)

CIO indexes directly into the BIOS Jump Table. 'fn' is the index offset, and 'arg' is an argument passed (up to 16 bits). The offsets and functions permitted are:

Offset   Function
0   CONST—Console status; Returned value = 0 if no char ready, 255 if char ready.
1   CONIN—Console input; Returned value = char typed.
2   CONOUT—Console output; Input value = char to output.
3   LIST—List output; Input value = char to output.
4   PUNCH—Punch output; Input value = char to output.
5   READER—Reader input; Returned value = char input.

Special I/O Using CIO

CIO is called by:

cio (fn) or cio (fn, arg)

CIO indexes directly into the BIOS Jump Table. 'fn' is the index offset, and 'arg' is an argument passed (up to 16 bits). The offsets and functions permitted are:

Offset   Function
0   CONST - Console status; Returned value = 0 if no char ready, 255 if char ready.
1   CONIN - Console input; Returned value = char typed.
2   CONOUT - Console   output;   Input value = char to output.
3   LIST - List output; Input value = char to output.
4   PUNCH - Punch output; Input value = char to output.
5   READER - Reader input; Returned value = char input.

CATALOG SYSTEM FOR CP/M FILES

This section describes a system for cataloging all of a users CP/M discs. It was written by Ward

Christensen. The master cataloging system consists of the following:

- ☐ MAST.CAT   The catalog itself.
- ☐ FMAP.COM Used to create NAMES. SUB, the "transaction file" for catalog update.
- ☐ CAT.COM   Like DIR, i.e., the lookup program.
- ☐ CAT2.COM   Quick kludge program, lists entire catalog, printing each filename only once, & stringing disc names out after.
- ☐ UCAT.COM   The update program, merges NAMES.SUB into MAST.CAT.
- ☐ UCAT.COM   It now catalogs the "volume serial" (-name.nnn).

Format of MAST.CAT File

The format of MAST.CAT has two parts.

First, a list of names of files not to be cataloged, in parentheses. The list supplied with the sample is:

```
(ASM.COM
DDT.COM
LOAD.COM
PIP.COM
SID.COM
STAT.COM
SUB.COM    <-- I renamed SUBMIT on most
                discs
SUBMIT.COM)
```

Then a list of all cataloged files, in the form:

```
filename.type discname.serial
```

For example: ALLOC.COM SYSRES.802.

Volume Identifiers

A disc must have a special filename on it, which is the volume identifier: -discname.serial, such as "-SYSRES.801". This may be done via:

```
save 0 b:-sysres.801      (FOR CP/M SYSTEMS)
save b:-sysres.801 1      (FOR CDOS SYSTEMS)
```

Note that the SAP (sort and pack directory) program previously distributed by the CP/M U.G. deletes all 0-length file entries, so if you use this utility, do a save 1, not a save 0.

Updating Process

To update the catalog for a disc, use FMAP to create the NAMES.SUB file (which contains a sorted listing of the files on the particular disc). Filename $$$.SUB is automatically skipped, as I recall.

FMAP B: Q will write NAMES.SUB to the logged in disc. Then type UCAT which will merge NAMES.SUB with MAST.CAT, and erase NAMES.SUB.

Note that UCAT is a "belts and suspenders" type program, i.e.. it creates NEW.CAT, and merges NAMES.SUB with MAST.CAT and puts it there. It then does:

```
era mast.bak
ren mast.bak_mast.cat
ren mast.cat_new.cat
```

This means that unless you era mast.bak, there will be 3 copies of the master catalog on the disc during the ucat execution. If you don't have sufficient space for it, era mast.bak first.

Retrieving Data From Catalog

CAT works just like DIR, i.e., "*" and "?" are allowed. However, it takes a second operand (after the filename/type) which is the disc information, in the form NAME.SERIAL - without the dash. Sample queries:

```
CAT              <-- ALL FILES

CAT *.* WORK.* <-- ALL  FILES  ON  ANY
                     "WORK" disc
CAT *.ASM        <-- ALL .ASM FILES

CAT *.* *.8*     <-- ALL FILES ON discS
                     WITH SERIAL NUMBERS 8xx
```

Note that the "discname.serial" file is written to the disc (it wasn't under the earlier UCAT in the CP/M users group). Thus you can get a list of all disc serials via:

CAT —*.*

But other than this one file entry, the "—" characters are eliminated from the directory, i.e., the disc names are stored as 7 characters (or less). :CATALOG:Special Features of FMAP.

FMAP has some additional options:

FMAP displays a sorted listing on the console.

FMAP specs displays a selective listing. Specs mean *.asm, etc., just like DIR.

FMAP specs D writes the names to NAMES.SUB with $1 $2 before the name, and $3 after:

$1 $2FOO.COM $3

Thus $1 may be substituted with a command name, $2 with a disc name, and $3 if the program takes options (only my programs do, as far as I know).

FMAP specs Q writes the sorted names, without any "$", to NAMES.SUB.

FMAP specs M writes the name to NAMES.SUB with $1 $2 $3 before the name, and $4 after:

$1 $2 $3FOO.COM $4

This is specifically for use with the modem program. For example, to send all .ASM files from the B: disc to another person:

```
FMAP B: M          <-- MAKE NAMES.SUB
MODEM SO.600       <-- SEND THEM NAMES.SUB
   NAMES.SUB
SUBMIT NAMES       <-- SUBMIT THE SEND
   MODEM SO.600.B
```

MODEM gets substituted for $1, SO.600 for $2, and B: for $3.

FMAP specs UNN creates CP/M users group catalog volume nn. Not generally useful, but thought you might like to know how it was done. NOTE: the FIND program is very useful when used with MAST.CAT—suppose you have the following in MAST.CAT:

BIOS1.ASM
BVIOS.ASM
CBIOS.ASM
M2BIOS.ASM

It's obvious that CAT cannot find all your BIOS related files: but if you type:

FIND MAST.CAT IOS

Now you will find them all.

CBASIC COMPILER

CBASIC is a compiler BASIC which may be executed on any floppy disc based CP/M system having at least 20 K bytes of memory. In order to make the best use of the power and flexibility of CBASIC, a dual floppy disc system and at least 32 K of memory is recommended. If CBASIC is executed in a system smaller than 20 K, a CP/M LOAD ERROR may occur.

The CBASIC system consists of two programs — CBASIC and CRUN. CBASIC is the compiler, and CRUN is the run-time interpreter. In a typical CBASIC session, the user will write the program using ED, compile it using CBASIC (with the $B option to suppress listing), and run it using CRUN.

Refer to the 84-page CBASIC manual:

C B A S I C
A Commercially Oriented
Compiler/Interpreter BASIC
Language Facility for
CP/M Systems
February 17, 1978

Compile-Time Toggled Options

Compiler toggles are a series of switches that can be set when the compiler is executed. The toggles are set by typing a dollar-sign ($) followed by the letter designations of the desired toggles starting one space or more after the program name on the command line. Toggles may only be set for the compiler.

Examples of compiler toggles and invocation forms are:

```
CBASIC INVENTRY $BGF
B:CBASIC A:COMPARE $GEC
CBASIC PAYROLL $B
CBASIC B:VALIDATE $E
```

Toggle B suppresses the listing of the program on the console during compilation. If an error is detected, the source line with the error and the error message will be printed even if Toggle B is set. Toggle B does not affect listing to the printer (Toggle F) or disc file (Toggle G). Toggle B is initially off.

Toggle C suppresses the generation of an INT file. Engaging this toggle will provide a syntax check without the overhead of writing the inter-mediate file.

Toggle C is initially off.

Toggle D suppresses translation of lower-case letters to upper-case. For example, if Toggle D is on, 'AMT' will not refer to the same variable as 'amt'.

Toggle D is initially off.

Toggle E causes the run-time program (CRUN) to accompany any error messages with the CBASIC line number in which the error occurred. Toggle E must be set in order for the TRACE option (see section 13.4 of the manual) to work.

Toggle E is initially off.

Toggle F causes the compiler output listing to be printed on the LST: device in addition to the system console. Toggle F is initially off.

Toggle G causes the compiler output listing to be written to disc. The file containing the compiler listing has the same name as the .BAS file, but its type is .LST. Toggle G is initially off.

Compiler Error Messages

The error message in this section are of two types: text messages and two letter error codes.

No Source File: <Filename>.BAS. The com-piler could not locate a source file used in either a CBASIC command or an INCLUDE directive.

Program Contains n Unmatched for State-ment(s). There are n FOR statements for which a NEXT could not be found.

Program Contains n Unmatched while State-ment(s). There are n WHILE statements for which a WEND could not be found.

Warning: Invalid Character Ignored. The pre-vious line contains an invalid ASCII character; this character is ignored by the compiler, and a question mark is printed in its place.

CE - Close Error. The intermediate (.INT) file could not be closed.

DE - Disc Error. A disc error occurred while trying to read the .BAS file.

DF - Disc Full. There was no space on the disc or the disc directory was full. The .INT file was not created.

DL - Duplicate Line number. The same line number was used on two different lines. Other compiler errors may cause a DL error message to be printed even if duplicate line numbers do not exist.

DP - Defined Previously. A variable in a DIM statement was previously defined.

EF - Exponential Format. A number in expo-nential format was input with no digits following the E.

FD - Function Definition. A function name that has been previously defined is being redefined in a DEF statement.

FI - FOR Index. An expression which is not an unsubscripted numeric variable is being used as a FOR loop index.

FN - Function parameter Number. A function reference contains an incorrect number of parame-ters.

FP - Function Parameter Type. A function reference parameter type does not match the parameter type used in the function's DEF state-ment.

FU - Function Undefined. A function has been referenced before it has been defined.

IE - IF Expression. An expression used im-mediately following an IF evaluates to type string. Only type numeric is permitted.

IF - In File. A variable used in a FILE state-ment is of type numeric where type string is re-quired.

IP - Input Prompt. An input prompt string is not surrounded by quotes.

IS - Invalid Subscript. A subscripted variable was referenced before it was dimensioned.

IU - Invalid Use. A variable defined as an array is used with no subscripts.

MF - Mixed Format. An expression evaluates to type string when type numeric is required.

MM - Mixed Mode. Variables of type string and type numeric are combined in the same expression.

NI - NEXT Index. A variable referenced by a NEXT statement does not match the variable referenced by the associated FOR statement.

NU - NEXT Unexpected. A NEXT statement occurs without an associated FOR statement.

OO - ON Overflow. More than 25 ON statements were used in the program.

SE - Syntax Error. The source line contains a syntax error.

SN - Subscript Number. A subscripted variable contains an incorrect number of subscripts.

SO - Syntax Overflow. The expression is too complex and should be simplified and placed on more than one line.

TO - Table Overflow. The program is too large for the system. The program must be simplified or the system size increased.

UL - Undefined Line number. A line number that does not exist has been referenced.

US - Undefined String. A string has been terminated by a carriage return rather than quotes.

VO - Variable Overflow. Variable names are too long for one statement. This should not occur.

WE - WHILE Error. The expression immediately following a WHILE statement is not numeric.

WU - WHILE Undefined. A WEND statement occurs without an associated WHILE statement.

Run-Time Error Messages - Warnings

Two textual run-time error messages are presented by CRUN.

No Intermediate File. A file name was not specified with the CRUN command, or no file of type .INT and the specified file name was found on disc.

Improper Input - Reenter. This message occurs when the fields entered from the console do not match the field specified in the INPUT statement. This can occur when field types do not match or the number of fields entered is different from the number of fields specified. All fields specified by the INPUT statement must be reentered.

Two-Letter Warning Codes

DZ - Divide by Zero. A number was divided by zero. The result is set to the largest valid CBASIC number.

FL - Field Length. A field length greater than 255 bytes was encountered during a READ LINE. Only the first 255 characters of the record are retained.

LN - Logarithm error. The argument given in the LOG function was zero or negative. The value of the argument is returned.

NE - NEgative number. A negative number was specified following the raise to a power operator (^). The absolute value is used in the calculation.

OF - OverFlow. A calculation produced a number too large. The result is set of the largest valid CBASIC number.

SQ - SQuare root error. A negative number was specified in the SQR function. The absolute value is used.

Run-Time Error Messages - Error Codes

AC - AsCii error. The string used as the argument in an ASC function evaluated to a null string.

CE - Close Error. An error occurred upon closing a file.

CU - Close Undefined file. A close statement specified a file number that was not active.

DF - Defined File. An OPEN or CREATE was specified with a file number that was already active.

DU - Delete Undefined file. A DELETE statement specified a file number that was not active.

DW - Disc Write error. An error occurred while writing to a file. This occurs when either the directory or the disc is full.

EF - End of File. A read past the end of file occurred on a file for which no IF END statement has been executed.

ER - Error in Record. An attempt was made to write a record of length greater than the maximum record size specified in the associated OPEN, CREATE, or FILE statement.

FR - File Rename. An attempt was made to rename a file to an existing file name.

FU - File Undefined. An attempt was made to read or write to a file that was not active.

IR - Invalid Record number. A record number less than one was specified.

LW - Line Width. A line with less than 1 or greater than 133 was specified in an LPRINTER WIDTH statement.

ME -MAKE Error. An error occurred while creating or extending a file because the disc directory was fill.

MP - MATCH Parameter. The third parameter in a MATCH function was zero or negative.

NF - Number of FILE. The file number specified was less than 1 or greater than 20.

NM - No Memory. There was insufficient memory to load the program.

NN - No Number field. An attempt was made to print a number with a PRINT USING statement but there was not a numeric data field in the USING string.

NS - No String Field. An attempt was made to print a string with a PRINT USING statement but there was not a string field in the USING string.

OD - Overflow Data. A READ statement was executed with no DATA available.

OE - OPEN Error. An attempt was made to OPEN a file that didn't exist and for which no IF END statement had been previously executed.

OI - ON Index. The expression specified in an ON... GOSUB or an ON ... GOTO statement evaluated to a number less than 1 or greater than the number of line numbers contained in the statement.

OM - Overflow Memory. The program ran out of memory during execution.

QE - Quote Error. An attempt was made to PRINT to a file a string containing a quotation mark.

RE - READ Error. An attempt was made to read past the end of a record in a fixed file.

RG - RETURN with no GOSUB. A RETURN occurred for which there was no GOSUB.

RU - Random Undefined. A random read or print was attempted to other than a fixed file.

SB - SuBscript. An array subscript was used which exceeded the boundaries for which the array was defined.

SL - String Length. A concatenation operation resulted in a string of more than 255 bytes.

SS - SubString error. The second parameter of a MID$ function was zero or negative.

TF - Too many Files. An attempt was made to have more than 20 active files simultaneously.

TL - TAB Length. A TAB statement contained a parameter less than 1 or greater than the current line width.

UN - UNdefined edit string. A PRINT USING statement was executed with a null edit string.

WR -WRite error. An attempt was made to write to a file after it had been read, but before it had been read to the end of the file.

CBASIC Reserved Words

ABS	EQ	LEN	POS	STOP
AND	EXP	LET	PRINT	STR$
AS	FEND	LINE	RANDOMIZE	SUB
ASC	FILE	LOG	READ	TAB
ATN	FOR	LPRINTER	RECL	TAN
CALL	FRE	LT	REM	THEN
CHR$	GE	MATCH	REMARK	TO
CLOSE	GO	MID$	RENAME	USING
CONSOLE	GOSUB	NE	RESTORE	VAL
COS	GOTO	NEXT	RETURN	WEND
CREATE	GT	NOT	RIGHT$	WHILE
DATA	IF	ON	RND	WIDTH
DEF	INP	OPEN	SGN	XOR
DELETE	INPUT	OR	SIN	
DIM	INT	OUT	SIZE	
ELSE	LE	PEEK	SQR	
END	LEFT$	POKE	STEP	

CBASIC COMPILER VERSION 2 CBASIC2
CBASIC in General

CBASIC is a compiler BASIC which may be executed on any floppy disc based CP/M system having at least 20 K bytes of memory. In order to make the best use of the power and flexibility of CBASIC, a dual floppy disc system and at least 32 K of memory is recommended. If CBASIC is executed in a system smaller than 20 K, a CP/M LOAD ERROR may occur.

The CBASIC system consists of two programs - CBASIC and CRUN. CBASIC is the compiler, and CRUN is the run-time interpreter. In a typical CBASIC session, the user will write the program using ED, compile it using CBASIC (with the $B option to suppress listing), and run it using CRUN. Refer to the 84-page CBASIC manual:

C B A S I C

A Commercially Oriented
Compiler/Interpreter BASIC
Language Facility for
CP/M Systems
February 17, 1978

CBASIC2 is an upward-compatible (in terms of source code) extension of the original CBASIC. In addition to all of the features of the original CBASIC, CBASIC2 adds the following:

- ☐ Integer variables
- ☐ Chaining with common variables
- ☐ Additional pre-defined functions
- ☐ Cross Reference capability

Note that CBASIC2 is upward-compatible with CBASIC only in terms of the source code files. An INT file created under CBASIC will not execute with the Version 2 Run-Time Monitor (CRUN2). For further information, refer to the 100-page reference manual:

C B A S I C

A Commercially Oriented
Compiler/Interpreter BASIC
Language Facility for
CP/M Systems
Version 2

May 1, 1979

Compile-Time Toggled Options

Compiler toggles are a series of switches that can be set when the compiler is executed. The toggles are set by typing a dollar-sign ($) followed by the letter designations of the desired toggles starting one space or more after the program name on the command line. Toggles may only be set for the compiler.

Examples of compiler toggles and invocation forms are:

CBAS2 INVENTRY $BGF
B:CBAS2 A:COMPARE $GEC
CBAS2 PAYROLL $B
CBAS2 B:VALIDATE $E

Compiler Toggles

Toggle B suppresses the listing of the program on the console during compilation. If an error is detected, the source line with the error and the error message will be printed even if Toggle B is set. Toggle B does not affect listing to the printer (Toggle F) or disc file (Toggle G). Toggle B is initially off.

Toggle C suppresses the generation of an INT file. Engaging this toggle will provide a syntax check without the overhead of writing the inter- mediate file. Toggle C is initially off.

Toggle D suppresses translation of lower-case letters to upper-case. For example, if Toggle D is on, 'AMT' will not refer to the same variable as 'amt'. Toggle D is initially off.

Toggle E causes the run-time program (CRUN2) to accompany any error messages with the CBASIC line number in which the error oc- curred. Toggle E must be set in order for the TRACE option (see section 13.4 of the manual) to work. Toggle E is initially off.

Toggle F causes the compiler output listing to be printed on the LST: device in addition to the system console. Toggle F is initially off.

Toggle G causes the compiler output listing to be written to disc. The file containing the compiler listing has the same name as the .BAS file, but its type is .LST. Normally the disc listing will be placed on the same source drive as the source file. The operator may select another drive by specify- ing the desired drive, enclosed in parens, following the G toggle; for example, CBAS2 B:TAX $G(A:) extracts the source from drive B: and sends the listing to drive A:. Toggle G is initially off.

XREF Cross Reference Facility

The XREF.COM Cross Reference utility program produces a file which contains an alphabetized list of all identifiers used in a CBASIC program. The usage of the identifier (function, parameter, or global) is provided, as well as a list of each line in which that identifier is used. The file created has the same name as the CBASIC source file and is of type XRF. The standard output is 132 columns wide. The following command is used to invoke XREF:

XREF <filename> [disc ref] [$<toggles>] ['title']

If the disc reference is specified, it instructs XREF as to what disc to place the output on. The toggles are described on the next display.

The optional title field must be the last field in the command line. All characters following the first apostrophe on the command line up to the second apostrophe or until the end of the command line become the title. The title is truncated to 30 characters if the listing is 132 columns wide and 20 characters if the D toggle (80 column listing) is specified.

XREF Toggles

Toggle A causes the listing to be output to the list device as well as the disc file.

Toggle B suppresses output to the disc. If only the B toggle is specified, no output is produced.

Toggle C suppresses output to the disc and permits output to the list device; same as A and B combined.

Toggle D causes output to be 80 columns wide instead of 132.

Toggle E produces output with only the identifiers and their usage.

For example, the following command produces a cross reference listing on the list device which is 80 columns wide:

XREF PROG $CD

Compiler Error Messages

Compiler error messages take two forms: text messages and two letter error codes.

No Source File: <Filename>.BAS. The compiler could not locate a source file used in either a CBASIC command or an INCLUDE directive.

Program Contains n Unmatched FOR Statement(s). There are n FOR statements for which a NEXT could not be found.

Program Contains n Unmatched WHILE Statements. There are n WHILE statements for which a WEND could not be found.

Warning: Invalid Character Ignored. The previous line contains an invalid ASCII character; this character is ignored by the compiler, and a question mark is printed in its place.

Out of Disc Space. The compiler has run out of disc space while attempting to write either the INT or LST files.

Out of Directory Space. The compiler has run out of directory entries while attempting to create or extend a file.

Disc Error. A disc error occurred while trying to read or write to a disc file.

INCLUDE NESTING TOO DEEP NEAR LINE n. An include statement near line n in the source program exceeds the maximum level of nesting of source files.

BF - Branch into Function. A branch into a multiple line function from outside was attempted.

BN - Bad Number. An invalid numeric constant was encountered.

CE - Close Error. The intermediate (.INT) file could not be closed.

CI - Close Include. An invalid file name in an %INCLUDE statement.

CS - COMMON Statement error. A COMMON statement which was not the first statement in the program was detected.

CV - COMMON Variable error. An improper reference to a subscripted variable in a COMMON statement.

DE - Disc Error. A disc error occurred while trying to read the .BAS file.

DF - Disc Full. There was no space on the disc or the disc directory was full. The .INT file was not created.

DL - Duplicate Line number. The same line number was used on two different lines. Other compiler errors may cause a DL error message to be printed even if duplicate line numbers do not exist.

DP - Defined Previously. A variable in a DIM statement was previously defined.

EF - Exponential Format. A number in exponential format was input with no digits following the E.

FA - Function Attribute. A function name appears on the left side of an assignment statement but is not within that function.

FD - Function Definition. A function name that has been previously defined is being redefined in a DEF statement.

FE - FOR Error. A mixed mode expression exists in a FOR statement which the compiler cannot correct.

FI - FOR Index. An expression which is not an unsubscripted numeric variable is being used as a FOR loop index.

FN - Function parameter Number. A function reference contains an incorrect number of parameters.

FP - Function Parameter type. A function reference parameter type does not match the parameter type used in the function's DEF statement.

FU - Function Undefined. A function has been referenced before it has been defined.

IE - IF Expression. An expression used immediately following an IF evaluates to type string. Only type numeric is permitted.

IF - In File. A variable used in a FILE statement is of type numeric where type string is required.

IP - Input Prompt. An input prompt string is not surrounded by quotes.

IS - Invalid Subscript. A subscripted variable was referenced before it was dimensioned.

IT - Invalid Toggle. An invalid compiler directive was encountered.

IU - Invalid Use. A variable defined as an array is used with no subscripts.

MF - Mixed Format. An expression evaluates to type string when type numeric is required.

MM - Mixed Mode. Variables of type string and type numeric are combined in the same expression.

MS - Mixed String, A numeric expression was used where a string expression is required.

ND - No DEFFN. A FEND statement was encountered without a corresponding DEF.

NI - NEXT Index. A variable referenced by a NEXT statement does not match the variable referenced by the associated FOR statement.

NU - NEXT Unexpected. A NEXT statement occurs without an associated FOR statement.

OF - Out of Function. A branch out of a multiple line function from inside the function was attempted.

OO - ON Overflow. More than 25 ON statements were used in the program.

PM - ??. A DEF statement appeared within a multiple line function. Functions may not be nested.

SE - Syntax Error. The source line contains a syntax error.

SF - SAVEMEM File. A SAVEMEM statement uses an expression of type numeric to specify the file to be loaded. This expression must be a string. Possibly the quotation marks were left off a string constant.

SN - Subscript Number. A subscripted variable contains an incorrect number of subscripts.

SO - Syntax Overflow. The expression is too complex and should be simplified and placed on more than one line.

TO - Table Overflow. The program is too large for the system. The program must be simplified or the system size increased.

UL - Undefined Line number. A line number that does not exist has been referenced.

US - Undefined String. A string has been terminated by a carriage return rather than quotes.

VO - Variable Overflow. Variable names are too long for one statement. This should not occur.

WE - WHILE Error. The expression immediately following a WHILE statement is not numeric.

WU - WHILE Undefined. A WEND statement occurs without an associated WHILE statement.

Run-Time Error Messages - Warnings

Two textual run-time error messages and a

large number of two-letter warning codes are presented by CRUN.

No Intermediate File. A file name was not specified with the CRUN command, or no file of type .INT and the specified file name was found on disc.

Improper input - Reenter. This message occurs when the fields entered from the console do not match the field specified in the INPUT statement. This can occur when field types do not match or the number of fields entered is different from the number of fields specified. All fields specified by the INPUT statement must be reentered.

DZ - Divide by Zero. A number was divided by zero. The result is set to the largest valid CBASIC number.

FL - Field Length. A field length greater than 255 bytes was encountered during a READ LINE. Only the first 255 characters of the record are retained.

LN - Logarithm error. The argument given in the LOG function was zero or negative. The value of the argument is returned.

NE - NEgative number. A negative number was specified following the raise to a power operator (^). The absolute value is used in the calculation.

OF - Overflow. A calculation produced a number too large. The result is set to the largest valid CBASIC number.

SQ - SQuare root error. A negative number was specified in the SQR function. The absolute value is used.

Run-Time Error Messages - Error Codes

AC - AsCii error. The string used as the argument in an ASC function evaluated to a null string.

BN - BUFF Number. The value following the BUFF option in an OPEN or CREATE statement is less than 1 or greater than 52.

CC - Chain Code. A chained program's code area is larger than the main program's code area.

CD - Chain Data. A chained program's data area is larger than the main program's data area.

CE - Close Error. An error occurred upon closing a file.

CF - Chain Function. A chained program's constant area is larger than the main program's constant area.

CP - Chain Var Storage. A chained program's variable storage area is larger than the main program's variable storage area.

CS - Chain SAVEMEM. A chained program reserved a different amount of memory with a SAVEMEM statement than the main program.

CU - Close Undefined file. A close statement specified a file number that was not active.

DF - Defined File. An OPEN or CREATE was specified with a file number that was already active.

DU - Delete Undefined file. A DELETE statement specified a file number that was not active.

DW - Disc Write error. An error occurred while writing to a file. This occurs when either the directory or the disc is full.

EF - End of File. A read past the end of file occurred on a file for which no IF END statement has been executed.

ER - Error in Record. An attempt was made to write a record of length greater than the maximum record size specified in the associated OPEN, CREATE, or FILE statement.

FR - File Rename. An attempt was made to rename a file to an existing file name.

FT - File Toggle. A FILE statement was executed when 20 files were already active.

FU - File Undefined. An attempt was made to read or write to a file that was not active.

IF - Invalid File name. A file name was invalid.

IR - Invalid Record number. A record number less than one was specified.

IV - Invalid Version. An attempt was made to execute an INT file created by a Version 1 Compiler.

IX - ??. A FEND statement was encountered prior to executing a RETURN statement.

LW - Line Width. A line width less than 1 or greater than 133 was specified in an LPRINTER WIDTH statement.

ME - MAKE Error. An error occurred while creating or extending a file because the disc directory was full.

MP - MATCH Parameter. The third parameter in a MATCH function was zero or negative.

NF - Number of FILE. The file number specified was less than 1 or greater than 20.

NM - No Memory. There was insufficient memory to load the program.

NN - No Number field. An attempt was made to print a number with a PRINT USING statement but there was not a numeric data field in the USING string.

NS - No String field. An attempt was made to print a string with a PRINT USING statement but there was not a string field in the USING string.

OD - Overflow Data. A READ statement was executed with no DATA available.

OE - OPEN Error. An attempt was made to OPEN a file that didn't exist and for which no IF END statement had been previously executed.

OI - ON Index. The expression specified in an ON . . . GOSUB or an ON . . . GOTO statement evaluated to a number less than 1 or greater than the number of line numbers contained in the statement.

OM - Overflow Memory. The program ran out of memory during execution.

QE - Quote Error. An attempt was made to PRINT to a file a string containing a quotation mark.

RB - Random BUFF. Random access was attempted to a file activated with the BUFF option specifying more than 1 buffer.

RE - READ Error. An attempt was made to read past the end of a record in a fixed file.

RG - RETURN with no GOSUB. A RETURN occurred for which there was no GOSUB.

RU - Random Undefined. A random read or print was attempted to other than a fixed file.

SB - SuBscript. An array subscript was used which exceeded the boundaries for which the array was defined.

SL - String Length. A concatenation operation resulted in a string of more than 255 bytes.

SO - SAVEMEM. The file specified in a SAVEMEM statement could not be located on the referenced disc.

SS - SubString error. The second parameter of a MID$ function was zero or negative.

TF - Too many Files. An attempt was made to

have more than 20 active files simultaneously.

TL - TAB Length. A TAB statement contained a parameter less than 1 or greater than the current line width.

UN - UNdefined edit string. A PRINT USING statement was executed with a null edit string.

WR - WRite error. An attempt was made to WRITE to a file after it had been read, but before it had been read to the end of the file.

CBASIC Version 2 Reserved Words

ABS	AND	AS	ASC	ATN
BUFF	CALL	CHAIN	CHR$	CLOSE
COMMAND$	COMMON	CONCHAR%	CONSOLE	CONSTAT%
COS	CREATE	DATA	DEF	DELETE
DIM	ELSE	END	EQ	EXP
FEND	FILE	FOR	FRE	GE
GO	GOSUB	GOTO	GT	IF
INITIALIZE	INP	INPUT	INT	INT%
LE	LEFT$	LEN	LET	LINE
LOG	LPRINTER	LT	MATCH	MID$
NE	NEXT	NOT	ON	OPEN
OR	OUT	PEEK	POKE	POS
PRINT	RANDOMIZE	READ	RECL	RECS
REM	REMARK	RENAME	RESTORE	RETURN
RIGHT$	RND	SADD	SGN	SIN
SIZE	SQR	STEP	STOP	STR$
SUB	TAB	TAN	THEN	TO
UCASE$	USING	VAL	WEND	WHILE
WIDTH	XOR			

Expression Hierarchy

The hierarchy for expression evaluation is as follows:

1. nested parentheses ( )
2. power operator ^
3. * /
4. + − concatenation [+] unary [+ −]
5. relational operators:
   $< <= >= = <>$ LT LE GT GE EQ NE
6. NOT
7. AND
8. OR XOR

Predefined Functions

I/O Functions

CONSTAT% -Returns the console status as an integer. If ready, a logical TRUE is returned.

CONCHAR% - Reads one character from the console device.

Machine-Language Functions

PEEK (<exp>) - Returns the contents of the memory location given by the expression.

POKE <exp>, <exp> - Low-order eight bits of second expression are stored in memory location selected by first expression.

CALL <exp> - CALL a machine language program at address specified.

SAVEMEM <constant>, <exp> - Reserve <constant> number of bytes and load the file specified by the string <exp> into the reserved area.

Numeric Functions

FRE	ABS(x)	INT(x)	INT%(x)
FLOAT(i%)	RND	SGN(x)	ATN(x)
COS(x)	EXP(x)	LOG(x) [e]	SIN(x)
SQR(x)	TAN(x)		

String Functions

ASC(a$)	CHR$(i%)	LEFT$(a$,i%)	LEN(a$)
UCASE$(a$)	MATCH(a$,b$,i%)	MID$(a$,i%,i%)	RIGHT$(a$,i%)
STR$(x)	VAL(a$)	COMMAND$	SADD(a$)

Disc Functions

RENAME(a$,b$)   SIZE(a$)

User-Defined Functions

The general forms are:

[<line number>] DEF <function name>
[<dummy arg list>] = <expression>

and

[<line number>] DEF <function name>
[<dummy arg list>]
.
.
.
[<line number>] FEND

CHANGE DIRECTORY
UTILITY - CHDIR - WORKS WITH ZCPR
Overview

CHDIR (CHange DIRectory) is a program which gives a CP/M or CP/ZM system a new virtual directory structure. Ever since CP/M 2.0 came out, users have been forced to refer to the environ-

ments that their files are located in by user number and disc name. This was an improvement over CP/M 1.4 in that projects and files associated to each other for one reason or another could be logically grouped together into a user area or on a particular disc and could easily be kept separate from other files.

This improvement is desirable and useful, but there are some capabilities lacking in this design that limit its usefulness. One such capability is the need for duplication of a COM file or directory entry for a COM file in order to access this file from more than one user area. Another such capability is the human-interface requirement for a logically-named user area that indicates the purpose of the user area as opposed to simply providing a number for it.

Under CP/M 2.×, unfortunately, if you wanted to issue a command, you had to have a copy of that particular COM file in your current user area in order for the operating system to find the command and load it. User areas were of less use because of this, since several commonly-used commands had to be duplicated into each user area. This took up more disc space and was somewhat awkward.

In answer to this and other desired capabilities, ZCPR was created. Placed on top of the CP/M CCP, ZCPR provides a new command processor for the CP/M user which is upward compatible with the old command processor but adds several new features, including a command-search hierarchy. Now, when a user issues a command, ZCPR will search for it if it is not found in the current user area on the current or specified disc. The user can specify the path to follow; however, ZCPR is initially configured to search the current user area on the current disc, user area 0 on the current disc, and user area 0 of disc A before producing an error message. With ZCPR it is no longer necessary to keep several copies of files on disc in order to use the user areas.

The user areas and discs were still addressed as separate elements of an overall file system, however. The user had to be constantly aware of where he was, and ZCPR also gave him a different prompt which indicated the current disc and user number. If a user wished to employ user area 1 for C program development and user area 2 for C source code storage, he had to note for himself that this is where these things were.

Now, CHDIR is introduced which adds a new outlook to the user environment. The user may now give each user area/disc a logical name (such as C-DEV or C-PGMS) and not worry about where they actually are on disc. Combined wisely with ZCPR or ZMCPR, all utilities may be placed in a commonly-scanned directory (user area/disc) so they will always be found by the CPR, and the user's entire microcomputer disc system now resembles one large disc with several named subdirectories which contain related files.

CHDIR artificially imposes a named directory structure onto CP/M and CP/ZM. Each named directory corresponds to a user area on a particular disc, and the user need never be concerned with what user area he is in if he uses ZCPR or ZMCPR with CHDIR. Each disc/user area is called a directory and may be given a logical name (up to 8 characters long).

The simplest form of using CHDIR is:

CHDIR <directory name>

where <directory name> is a logical name (8 chars max) recognized by CHDIR. This command logs the user into the user area/disc associated with the indicated directory name.

For example, given the following environment:

User	Disc	Directory
10	A	SYS1
11	A	SYS2
8	B	C-DEV
7	A	C-PGMS
7	B	PAS-DEV
6	A	PAS-PGMS

the command:

CHDIR C-DEV

logs the user into user area 8 on Drive B:; also, the command:

CHDIR PAS-PGMS

logs the user into user area 6 on Drive A:.

CHDIR combined with ZCPR or ZMCPR, then, provides a useful named-directory working environment which is completely compatible with CP/M, and almost all CP/M programs can run without modification in this new environment.

CHDIR employed in a hard disc environment is especially useful in that the different logical discs associated with the hard disc may now be grouped into one named directory structure and need no longer be treated as separate discs.

In addition to the named directory structure, CDIR also creates a privileged user environment. This environment, which only becomes effective if the USER command (and other such facilities) are removed from ZCPR and the COM files removed from the disc), defines two classes of users. A normal user only has access to certain user areas (0 to 9 by default), and a privileged user has access to all user areas. In order to move into user areas greater than 9, a password must be known. Once in a privileged user area, no password is necessary to move to any other user area.

This feature gives a certain amount of protection to systems, such as Remote Bulletin Board Systems, against hostile users. Certain privileged commands, such as debuggers and language utilities, may be placed into the protected user areas and employed only by those who know the password. Two different command processors can even be made to come into play (in the case of ZMCPR), where the normal user sees a menu-driven set of commands while a privileged user sees a ZCPR-like command line.

Refer to the documentation on ZCPR and ZMCPR for further details.

Installation

Installation of CHDIR is performed in two parts: Compiling CHDIR and Initializing the Internal Buffers of CHDIR.

Before compiling CHDIR, there are several internal default values that the user may wish to set in the source code of the program. These values and their meanings are:

defname - default name for the COM file of CHDIR; change this if you want CHDIR to be known by some other name after initialization; this name may also be later changed under Setup Mode.

dirmax - maximum number of directory names allowed; a minimum value of 64 is recommended.

syspass - default System Password for CHDIR; this is up to 20 characters long, and case is significant; this may be later changed under the Setup Mode.

sysuser - lowest user number for a privileged user; default value is 10; values should be in the range from 0 to 15.

tryent - number of tries permitted to enter a privileged directory before CHDIR aborts; default value is 1.

tryset - number of tries permitted to enter Setup Mode before CHDIR aborts; default value is 3.

exitcmd - command to be executed if a valid password is not given in the required number of tries; default is no command; this should be the name of a COM file, like "HOSTILE" for HOSTILE.COM, and should be in uppercase.

All of these defined values are located just after the initial comments within the program source code.

Part I - Compiling CHDIR

CHDIR was compiled by the BDS C compiler. No special flags or options are necessary. Once compiled, however, the COM file produced must be modified so that the stack used by this program does not overwrite the CCP or CPR.

To do this, the user may use the NOBOOT program from the BDS C user's group or manually modify the code at the beginning of the COM file. Using the 1.45 version of BDS C, the first few bytes of the COM file load the HL register pair from locations 6 and 7 and then load the SP register from HL. This is followed by several NOPs. To correct the stack problem, replace this sequence with an LXI D,-AOOH, DAD D, and SPHL starting with the SPHL instruction. Example follows:

Original Code	New Code
LHLD 6	LHLD 6
SPHL	LXI D,-AOOH
NOP	
NOP	
NOP	DAD D
NOP	SPHL

Once this has been installed using a debugger like DDT, the COM file may be resaved to disc using the SAVE command, and the user is ready to proceed to Part II of the installation. If the NOBOOT command is available and works for the user's version of BDS C, then this manual procedure may be replaced by the command:

NOBOOT CHDIR.COM

Part II - Initializing CHDIR Buffers

Once CHDIR.COM has been patched so that it's stack does not overwrite the CCP or CPR, then its internal buffers must be initialized. This is done to perform two basic functions:

1) define the password for the privileged user
2) clear the directory name table

To perform this initialization, issue the command:

CHDIR /S

This places the user into SETUP Mode. If the user runs this command from user areas 0 to 9, he will be asked for the System Password, which is initially chdir (no quotes). If the user runs this command from user areas greater than 9, he is declared privileged and is not asked for the password.

Once into SETUP Mode, the user is prompted with:

Setup Command (? for Help)?

He should issue the following commands to perform the initialization:

I or i - clear the directory name table: the user

will be prompted with "Verify Initialization (Y/N)?", to which he should respond with a Y or y.

P or p - set the password; the user will be prompted with "New System Password?" and 20 dots to indicate the size of the allotted password: he may then type the new password, and case is significant ("test" is NOT the same as "TEST")

X or x - Exit and rewrite CHDIR.COM to disc; the user will be prompted with "Write New File (Y/N)?", to which he should respond with Y or y, and then "Name of File (RETURN=CHDIR .COM)?", to which he should strike the RETURN key.

Setup Mode is described in more detail later in this help file. The procedure just outlined is all that is required for initialization, and CHDIR is now ready for use. The first step is to plan and define the named directories. The other sections of this HLP file tell you how to do this.

Basic Definitions

The following symbolic names are defined:

<directory name> <du> <password>

A <directory name> may contain up to 8 characters. The characters "*", "?", ".", and "/" should not be used as part of the directory name since the CCP, CPR, or CHDIR routines perform special processing on them. Lowercase letters are automatically converted to uppercase.

<du> is the disc letter and user number combination which is assigned to the <directory name> given. It is a single letter (lowercase is converted to uppercase) in the range from A to P followed immediately by the digits of the user number (0 to 15).

<password> is the System Password for CHDIR. This is a string of up to 20 characters. Case is significant ("test" is NOT the same as "TEST"), and any printable character may be used as part of the password as a general rule.

Moving Into a Directory

The CHDIR command of the following form is used to move into a directory:

CHDIR <directory name>

A <directory name> may contain up to 8 characters. The characters "*", "?", ".", and "/" should not be used as part of the directory name since the CCP, CPR, or CHDIR routines perform special processing on them. Lowercase letters are automatically converted to uppercase.

If the user is not privileged (residing in user area 10 or greater, by default) and the name of a privileged directory is given, he will be asked for the System Password. In this case, he will be given only one try before the command aborts.

Examples:

CHDIR C—DEV	CHDIR work
chdir cpci81	chdir 1temp

Creation of New Directories on The Fly

The CHDIR command of the following form is used to create new directories at will:

CHDIR <directory name> <du>

A <directory name> is of the same form as described above.

<du> is the disc letter and user number combination which is assigned to the <directory name> given. It is a single letter (lowercase is converted to uppercase) in the range from A to P followed immediately by the digits of the user number (0 to 15).

If the user issues this command and is not privileged (running from user area 10 or greater, by default), then he will be asked for the System Password before the command is executed. If he is previleged, CHDIR will execute the command without prompt.

Examples:

CHDIR C—DEV A5	chdir itemp m0
chdir work b4	chdir sys1 a10

Displaying The Directories

The CHDIR command of the following form is

used to display the names of the existing directories:

CHDIR /DISPLAY

Only the /D is required to complete the command; any characters following the /D are ignored.

If the user is not privileged, only the non-privileged directories are displayed. If he is privileged, all directories are displayed. A privileged user is identified by the user number he is currently residing in (10 and above are privileged by default).

A count of the number of directory names defined and amount of directory space left for more names is given, and, if the user is not privileged, the count of defined names may not match the number of displayed directory names since he is not permitted to see the names of the privileged directories.

Setup Mode

The CHDIR command of the following form places the user into Setup Mode:

CHDIR /SETUP

Only the /S is required to complete the command; any characters following the /S are ignored.

Setup Mode is employed by a privileged user to:

1) initialize the directory names
2) set/change the System Password
3) add/delete directory names
4) display the System Password and directory names
5) sort the directory names by disc/user area
6) save the current name directory structure to disc

If the CHDIR /SETUP command is issued from a non-privileged user area (user areas 0 to 9 by default), then the user will be prompted for the System Password. He is given 3 tries to get it right before CHDIR aborts (by default).

Once in Setup Mode, the user is prompted with

Setup Command (? for Help)?

and Setup is waiting for the user to type a single-character command letter. If he types a ? or any other invalid command letter, he is presented with a summary of the Setup Mode commands. These commands are invoked by striking a single letter and case is not significant. A summary of these commands is:

D - Display System Password and Directory Names
I - Initialize and Clear All Directory Names
N - Create a New Directory Name

P - Set the System Password

Q - Quit without Updating

S - Sort Directory by Disc and User Number
X - Exit and Update CHDIR.COM on Disc

Each command is explained on the following screens.

D - Display System Password and Directory Names. This command prints three groups of information. They are:
1. "System Password is ..."
   - current setting for the System Password
2. "Defined Directory Names -
   du: namel du: name2 du: name 3 du: name4"
   -disc, user area, and name for directories
   4 entries are printed per line
3. "n Directory Names Defined, Space Left for m More Names"
   - number of names defined and space left

I - Initialize and Clear All Directory Names. This command performs the following initializations:

1) the System Password is renamed to the default programmed value of the variable syspass; this name is initially "chdir"
2) all disc names, user areas, and directory name strings are initialized to zero.

The user is prompted with "Verify Initialization (Y/N)?" immediately after he strikes the letter I or i. If he replys with any letter other than Y or y, the message "Initialization Aborted" is printed and he is returned to Setup Command level. If he types a Y or y in response to this prompt, the initialization is performed and the message "All Directory Names Cleared" is printed.

N - Create a New Directory Name. In response to this command, the message

System User Areas start at nn

is printed to remind the user where the privileged user areas begin, and the user is placed into a loop, prompted with

Disc Letter and User
(RETURN=Done or A-P 0-15)?

If the user wishes to create a new directory, he types one letter A-P (case is not significant) followed by a number in the range from 0 to 15. If the user does not wish to create a new directory, he strikes the RETURN key to abort to Setup Command level.

If the user selected a valid disc/user combination, he is prompted with

Directory Name (RETURN = Delete Old Name)?

to which he may strike the RETURN key to delete the directory name previously associated with the disc/user specified or he may type a directory name (case is not significant and all lowercase letters are capitalized) to create a new directory or rename an old one.

If the directory name or RETURN is accepted, the "Disc Letter and User" prompt will reappear to allow the user to continue creating directory names or abort to Setup Command level.

Several error messages are possible while in this part of the Setup Mode. These messages are:

"Invalid Disc Letter" - Disc was not in the range from A to P.
"Invalid User Number" - User Number was not in the range from 0 to 15.
"Directory Name is too long - Reenter" - Entered directory name exceeded 8 characters.
"Error - Directory Name Buffer Full" - No more space is available in the internal buffer.
"Directory Name for ud: Deleted" - (NOT an error message) tells the user that a previously-defined name was deleted.

P - Set the System Password. This command in Setup Mode is immediately followed by the prompt

New System Password?

to which the user is allowed to enter up to 20 characters for his password. The user MUST enter a password; simply typing a RETURN sets the password to null and a simple RETURN is required for the new password when asked.

Q - Quit without Updating. This command is answered with the prompt.

Verify Abort (Y/N)?

to which the user replys with Y or y to abort Setup Mode and return to the operating system or any other character to return to Setup Mode.

S - Sort Directory by Disc and User Number. This command causes the internal directory to be sorted by disc and user area. In response to this command, CHDIR sorts the directory (no informative prompt) and prints

Sort Complete

when done:

This command is provided for the convenience of the user.

X - Exit and Update CHDIR.COM on Disc. This command causes the prompt to appear. If the user responds with anything other than Y or y, Setup Mode and CHDIR are aborted and control is returned to the operating system.

If the user responds with Y or y, he is prompted with

Name of File (RETURN = CHDIR, COM)?

to which he may reply by striking the RETURN key to rewrite the file CHDIR.COM on disc or he may give another file name (the .COM is not necessary) to write a new file. The current directory structure is defined as a part of the written file, and it is used to access this new directory ala CHDIR commands. In entering the file name, case is not significant.

The prompt may vary if CHDIR has been rewritten under a different name. By default, the prompt is

Name of File (RETURN = CHDIR.COM)?

and, if, for instance, CHDIR was rewritten as CDIR.COM, the prompt from CDIR would be

Name of File (RETURN = CDIR.COM)?

Once the file name is specified or RETURN is struck, the following messages appear:

Sorting Directory by Disc and User Number
Writing File CHDIR.COM to Disc . . .

An error message "Error - Can't Create File CHDIR.COM" is possible, indicating that the disc or directory are full.

Other Setup Mode Commands. Striking any key other than those just described causes a built-in Help message to be displayed. Control is then returned to Setup Mode command level.

Planning a Directory Structure

This section outlines a few comments and recommendations on a technique to combine ZCPR or ZMCPR with CHDIR to create a working environment.

The ZCPR and ZMCPR command-search hierarchy frequently take the user down to user 0 on drive A before the invalid command error message is given. This directory is, effectively, the ROOT of the system, and this would be a good place to store the CHDIR.COM file. "ROOT" itself is a good name for A0, and by standardizing on this name, any user can place himself here as he moves between systems and see the standard command set.

Since a command-search hierarchy is used under ZCPR and ZMCPR, this, in conjunction with CHDIR, can be used to create a hierarchial directory structure. The first CHDIR.COM that is encountered during a search is the one that is effective, so by placing a CHDIR.COM in the command-search path before the ROOT is encountered, directory subtrees can be formed. Let me illustrate this concept with the proceeding diagram:

CHDIR Directories   Tree

Disc A:	User	0: CHDIR.COM		(1) ROOT--> WORK
Directories:		A0: ROOT	B0: WORK	
Disc B:	User	0: CHDIR.COM		
Directories:		A0: ROOT		ROOT
		B0: C-ROOT	B1: C-DEV	C-DEV
		B2: C-PGMS	B3: C-DOC	(2) C-ROOT --> C-PGMS
	User	1: No CHDIR.COM		C-DOC
	User	2: No CHDIR.COM		
	User	3: CHDIR.COM		
Directories:		B0: C-ROOT	B3: C-DOC	
		B4: COMPILER	B5: PROGRAM	C-ROOT
	User	4: No CHDIR.COM		(3) C-DOC --> COMPILER
	User	5: No CHDIR.COM		ROGRAM

Using the normal ZCPR command-search hierarchy, which is current user/current disc to user 0/current disc to user 0/disc A, the following can be noted:

A) tree (1) is seen from any user number on A:
B) tree (2) is seen from any user number except e on B:
C) tree (3) is seen from user 3 on B:

As the reader can see, this is a very powerful concept. Let's say that you are logged into A0 and want to read the documentation on the C compiler. You would have to issue "CHDIR WORK" to enter the directory WORK on B:. Issuing "CHDIR /D" from here shows you in directory C-ROOT, and you now issue "CHDIR C-DOC" to enter the documentation branch of the tree. From here, you issue "CHDIR COMPILER" to enter the compiler documentation directory. Expressed as a tree, this is:

Feel free to move back to the previous displays via the L command if this is not clear to you.

```
                ROOT
                 |
           C-ROOT (WORK
          /      |      \
      C-DEV   C-PGMS   C-DOC
                         /\
               COMPILER PROGRAMS
```

This is a simple type of tree structure as implemented above. CHDIR goes beyond this, too, and allows as much as a star or ring structure as well, or any combination desired.

One more step that CHDIR allows the user to take is with privileged users. Now, directories can be hidden from normal users. Privileged directories are set up like normal directories, and CHDIR is the program which enforces the security. Note that the USER command must be removed from the CPR for this to work.

Using ZMCPR adds a capability of logging into a new directory and automatically invoking a new command interpreter. The MENU.CP file can be either a menu display or an executable program, and as an executable program, it is run every time control is returned to the CPR while the user is logged into the current directory. In this way, a whole new command processor can be introduced with each directory, and as the user moves from one directory to another, he may move from menu-driven displays to ZCPR-like command line processors to other processors at will. The capabilities and potential are amazing!

Yet another change may be made to enhance the capabilities of CHDIR. This change involves modifying the command-research hierarchy to a new path. For example:

Old Path: User Current/Disc Current
          User 0/Disc Current
          User 0/Disc A

New Path: User Current/Disc Current
          User Current/Disc A
          User 0/Disc A

This provides a new CHDIR environment in which utilities can be grouped into different directories on A and all the work done on B. When a command is issued, command search falls to a project utility area on A before falling to the ROOT. The differences between these to paths can be illustrated as follows:

Old Path: User Current/Disc Current
          User 0/Disc Current
          User 0/Disc A

New Path: User Current/Disc Current
          User Current/Disc A
          User 0/Disc A

Old Path: Work Area —> Common Root Utilities —> ROOT
New Path: Work Area —> Project Utilities —> ROOT

Under the new path, different user areas on A can contain the utilities, say, associated with a particular language, such as user 1 for C, user 2 for PASCAL, etc. Then, the corresponding work areas on B would be user 1 for C work, user 2 for PASCAL work, etc. Now, when a command is issued, the move from C work to C compiler to ROOT or PASCAL work to PASCAL compiler to ROOT.

As the reader can see, the possibilities are staggering. And this is just the beginning.

THE CPM/M OPERATING SYSTEM - VERSION 1.4

CP/M is a monitor control program for microcomputer system development which uses IBM-compatible flexible discs (floppy discs) for mass storage. Using a microcomputer mainframe based on Intel's 8080 or Zilog's Z80 microprocessor, CP/M provides a general environment for program construction, storage, and editing, along with assembly and program debug facilities. An important feature of CP/M is that it can be easily altered to execute with any computer configuration which uses an Intel 8080 or Zilog Z80 Microprocessor and has at least 16 K bytes of main memory with up to four IBM-compatible disc drives.

The CP/M monitor provides access to programs through a comprehensive file management system. The file subsystem supports a named file structure, allowing dynamic allocation of file space as well as sequential and random file access. Using this file system, up to 64 distinct programs can be stored in both source and machine-executable form.

Digital Research, the designer of CP/M, has provided a set of six manuals which describe the use and operation of CP/M in detail. These manuals are:

1. An Introduction to CP/M Features and Facilities.

2. ED: A Context Editor for the CP/M disc System.

3. ASM: CP/M Assembler User's Manual.

4. DDT: CP/M Dynamic Debugging Tool User's Manual.

5. CP/M Interface Guide.

6. CP/M System Alteration Guide.

As the reader can see, CP/M supports a context editor, an assembler (Intel-compatible), and a debugger system. These are available in the basic CP/M package. There is a large variety of other software available which can run under CP/M with little or no modification. Such software includes several assemblers (both 8080 and Z80), a symbolic debugger, several high-level languages (including FORTRAN IV (compiler), BASIC-E (translator), CBASIC (translator), many interpretive BASICs, ALGOL, FOCAL, and C), and several special-purpose applications programs (such as text formatting systems and accounting systems).

CP/M File References

A file reference identifies a particular file or group of files on a particular disc attached to CP/M. These file references can be either unambiguous (ufn) or ambiguous (afn). An unambiguous file reference uniquely identifies a single file, while an ambiguous file reference may be satisfied by a number of different files.

An unambiguous file reference is an exact name of the specified file. It consists of up to eight characters in the file name and three characters in the file type. An unambiguous file reference is of the form —

$$pppppppp.sss$$

The characters used in specifying an unambiguous file reference may not contain any of —

$$< > . , ; : = ? * [ ]$$

An ambiguous file reference is used for directory search and pattern matching. The form of an ambiguous file reference is similar to an unambiguous reference, except the symbol '?' may be interspersed throughout the file reference. In various commands throughout CP/M, the '?' symbol matches any character of a file name in the '?' position. For example, X?Y.C?M will match XZY.COM and X3Y.CEM. The '*' symbol is used to match all characters of a file name or file type. For example, *.COM will match XZY.COM and HELP.COM, while HELP.* will match HELP.COM and HELP.HLP.

CP/M Line Editing And Output Control

The following are the line editing functions supported by CP/M:

rubout - Delete and echo the last character typed at the console.

Ctrl-U - Delete the entire line typed at the console.

Ctrl-X - Same as Ctrl-U.

Ctrl-R - Retype current command line: types a "clean line" following character deletion with rubouts.

Ctrl-E - Physical end of line: carriage is returned, but line is not sent until the carriage return key is depressed.

Ctrl-C - CP/M system reboot (warm start).

Ctrl-Z - End input from the console (used in PIP and ED).

Other control functions affect console output are:

Ctrl-P - Copy all subsequent console output to the currently-assigned list device (LST:). Output is sent to both the list device and the console device until the next Ctrl-P is typed.

Ctrl-S - Stop the console output temporarily. Program execution and output continue when the next character is typed at the console. Typing Ctrl-C returns control to CP/M. Input lines can generally be up to 255 characters in length. They are not acted upon until the carriage return key is typed.

CP/M Built-in Commands

CP/M supports five built-in commands. They are as follows:

ERA afn - The ERA (erase) command removes files from the currently logged-in disc.

DIR afn - The DIR (directory) command causes the names of all files which satisfy the ambiguous file name afn to be listed on the console device. All files are listed if no afn is given.

REN ufn1=ufn2 - The REN (rename) command allows the user to change the names of files on disc. The file satisfying ufn2 is changed to ufn1.

SAVE n ufn - The SAVE command places n pages (256-byte blocks) onto disc from the TPA and names this file ufn.

TYPE ufn - The TYPE command displays the contents of the ASCII source file ufn on the currently logged-in disc at the console device.

CP/M Transient Commands

The CP/M standard transient commands are as follows:

STAT - list the number of bytes of storage remaining on the currently logged-in disc, provide statistical information about particular files, and display or alter device assignment.

PIP - load the Peripheral Interchange Program for subsequent disc file and peripheral transfer operations.

ED - load and execute the CP/M text editor program.

SUBMIT - submit a file of commands for batch processing.

ASM - load the CP/M assembler and assemble the specified program from disc.

LOAD - load the file in Intel "hex" machine code format and produce a file in machine executable form which can be loaded into the TPA (this loaded program becomes a new command under the CCP).

DDT - load the CP/M debugger into the TPA and execute it.

DUMP - dump the contents of a file in hex.

SYSGEN - create a new CP/M system disc.

MOVCPM - regenerate the CP/M system for a particular memory size.

Physical Device Assignments

Logical Device		Physical Device
CON:	TTY:	Model 43 Teletype
	CRT:	Console CRT
	BAT:	CRT and Modem
	UC1:	In=CRT, Out=CRT and Modem
RDR:	TTY:	Model 43 Teletype
	PTR:	Modem
	UR1:	CRT and Modem w/CRT Output
	UR2:	CRT and Modem
PUN:	TTY:	Model 43 Teletype
	PTP:	Modem
	UP1:	CRT and Modem
	UP2:	CRT and Modem
LST:	TTY:	Model 43 Teletype
	CRT:	Hazeltine 1500 CRT
	LPT:	Modem
	UL1:	CRT and Modem

CP/M Stat Command

The STAT Command takes any of the following forms:

STAT - calculate the storage remaining on all active drives and print a message like:

x: R/W, SPACE: nnnK — if disc is Read/Write
x: R/O, SPACE: nnnK — if disc is Read Only

STAT x: - calculate the storage remaining on the specified drive and print

BYTES REMAINING ON x: nnnk

STAT x:afn - scan the specified files on the specified drive (x: is optional), and list all files which satisfy the unambiguous reference in alphabetical order with storage requirements. A table like the following is generated:

RECS BYTS EX D:FILENAME.TYP
rrrr nnnK ee d:pppppppp.sss

where
rrrr = number of 128-byte records allocated to the file
nnnK = number of bytes (in K, K=1024) allocated to the file nnn = rrrr * 128 / 1024
ee = number of 16 K extensions ee = nnn/ 16
d:pppppppp.sss = drive name (d may be A, B, C, D) and file name
STAT x:=R/O - set the specified drive to Read Only. This is cleared by a warm boot. When a disc is Read Only, the message BDOS ERR ON ×: READ ONLY will appear if there is an attempt to write to it.
STAT VAL: - display the possible logical to physical device assignments. STAT will print the following list:

CON: = TTY: CRT: BAT: UC1:
RDR: = TTY: PTR: UR1: UR2:
PUN: = TTY: PTP: UP1: UP2:
LST: = TTY: CRT: LPT: UL1:

STAT DEV: - display the current logical to physical device mapping. For example, the list may appear as:

CON: = CRT: PUN: = PTP:
RDR: = UR1:   LST: = TTY:

STAT 1d1=pd1, 1d2=pd2, . . . - change the logical to physical device assignments. Logical device 1d1 is assigned to physical device pd1, etc. The valid logical device names are:

CON: The system console device
RDR: The paper tape reader device
PUN: The paper tape punch device
LST: The output list device

The valid physical device names are:

TTY: Slow speed output device (teletype)
CRT: High speed output device (cathode ray tube)
BAT: Batch processing (CON: input is RDR:, CON: output is LST:)
UC1:   User-defined console
PTR: Paper tape reader
PTP: Paper tape punch
UR1:   User-defined reader #1
UR2:   User-defined reader #2
UP1:   User-defined punch #1
UP2:   User-defined punch #2
LPT: Line printer
UL1:   User-defined list device #1

CP/M PIP Command

PIP (Peripheral Interchange Program) is the CP/M transient which implements the basic media conversion operations necessary to load, print, punch, copy, and combine disc files. PIP is initiated by one of the following forms—

PIP - engage PIP, prompt the user with '*", and read command lines directly from the console. PIP used in this way is exited by either typing an empty command line (just a carriage return) or a Ctrl-C as the first character of the line.

PIP cmnd - engage PIP, execute the specified command, and return to CP/M.

The form of each command line in PIP is as follows:

destination = source#1, source#2, source#3, . . ., source#n

The general forms of PIP command lines are:

x: =y:afn - copy all files satisfying afn from drive y to drive x. 'y' may be omitted, and, if so, the currently logged-in drive is selected.

x:ufn=y: - copy the file given by ufn from y to x. 'x' may be omitted, and, if so, the currently logged-in drive is selected.

x:afn=y:afn - like the above, but x and/or y may be omitted; the default drive is selected for the omitted drive(s).

1d=pd - copy from the specified physical device to the specified logical device. Valid logical devices are:

CON:, RDR:, PUN:, LST:

Valid physical devices are:

TTY:, CRT:, UC1:, PTR:, PTP:, UR1:, UR2:, UP1:, UP2:, LPT:, UL1:

Additional device names which may be used in PIP commands are:

NUL: - send 40 Nulls (ASCII 0) to the device.
EOF: - send a CP/M End of File character (ASCII Ctrl-Z).
INP: - special PIP input source to be patched (see manual).
OUT: - special PIP output destination to be patched (see manual).
PRN: - same as LST:, but tabs are expanded at every eighth character position, lines are numbered, and page ejects are inserted every 60 lines with an initial eject.

The user can also specify one or more PIP parameters enclosed in square brackets separated by zero or more blanks. These parameters are:

B - block mode transfer. Data is buffered by PIP until an ASCII X-Off character (Ctrl-S) is received from the source device.

Dn - delete characters which extend past column n in the transfer of data to the destination from the character source.

E - echo all transfer operations to the console.

F - filter (remove) form feeds from the file.

H - hex data transfer. All data is checked for proper Intel hex file format.

I - ignore ':00' records in the transfer of Intel hex format file.

L - translate upper case to lower case alphabetics.

N - add line numbers to each line transferred to the destination.

O - object file (non-ASCII) transfer. Ignore End of File.

Pn - include page ejects at every n lines.

Qs^Z - quit copying from the source device or file when the string s (terminated by Ctrl-Z) is encountered.

Ss^Z - start copying from the source file when the string s is seen.

Tn - expand tabs to every nth column.

U - translate lower case to upper case alphabetics.

V - verify that data has been copied correctly.

Z - zero the parity bit on input for each ASCII character.

CP/M ED Commands

The ED Program is the CP/M system context editor, which allows creation and alteration of ASCII files. Complete details are given in the user's manual.

The following are the error indicators given by ED:

?	Unrecognized Command
>	Memory buffer full
#	Cannot apply command the number of times specified
O	Cannot open LIB file in R command

The following are the control characters recognized by ED:

^	C	System reboot
^	E	Physical \<CR\> \<LF\> (not entered in command)
^	I	Logical tab
^	L	Logical \<CR\> \<LF\> in search and substitute strings
^	U	Line delete
^	Z	String terminator
	Rubout	Character delete
	Break	Discontinue command

The following are the commands recognized by ED:

nA	Append lines
+/– B	Beginning/Bottom of buffer

207

+/− nC	Move character positions
+/− nD	Delete characters
E	Exit
nFs^Z	Find string
H	End edit, close and reopen files
Is^Z	Insert characters
nJ	Place strings in juxtaposition
+/− nK	Kill (delete) lines
+/− nL	Move down/up lines
nM	Macro definition
O	Return to original file
+/− nP	Move and print pages
Q	Quit with no file changes
R	Read library file
nSs1^Zs2^Z	Substitute s2 for s1
+/− nT	Type lines
+/− U	Translate lower to upper case if U; none if −U
+/− V	Engage/disengage line numbers (verify)
OV	Print memory buffer info (free/total usage)
nW	Write lines
nX	Transfer n lines to X$$$$$$$$.LIB
OX	Empty X$$$$$$$$.LIB
nZ	Sleep
+/− n	Move and type (+/− nLT)
n:	Move to absolute line (V engaged)
:n	Process from current line to specified line (V engaged)

CP/M ASM Command

The ASM Command loads and executes the CP/M 8080 assembler. It is of the form:

ASM filename.xyz

where filename is the name of the file 'filename.ASM' to assemble, x designates the disc name which contains the source, y designates the disc name to contain the hex file (y=Z suppresses generation of the hex file), and z designates the disc name to contain the print file (y=X lists on CON:, y=Z suppresses listing).

Refer to the ASM Manual for further details.

CP/M LOAD Command

The LOAD Command reads the file specified, which is assumed to contain Intel hex format machine code and produces a memory image file which can be subsequently executed (converts .HEX to

LOAD filename

where filename is the name of the file 'filename.HEX'.

CP/M DDT Command

The DDT Program allows dynamic interactive testing and debugging of programs generated in the CP/M environment. It is invoked by

DDT
DDT filename.HEX
DDT filename.COM

where 'filename' is the name of the program to be loaded or tested.

DDT responds to the normal CP/M input line editing characters. DDT responds to the following commands:

As - perform inline assembly starting at the specified address s.

D - display memory from the current address for 16 display lines.

Ds - display memory from address s for 16 display lines.

Ds,f - display memory from address s to address f.

Fs,f,c - fill memory from start address s to final address f with byte c.

G - start execution at the current value of the PC.

Gs - start execution at the specified address s.

Gs,b - start execution at the specified address s and set a breakpoint at the address b.

Gs,b,c - same as above with breakpoints at b and c.

G,b - start execution at the current value of the PC with breakpoint b.

G,b,c - same as above with breakpoints at b and c.

If - insert a file name f into the default FCB.

L - list 12 lines of disassembled code from the current address.

Ls - list 12 lines from the specified address s.

Ls,f - list lines of disassembled code from s to f.

Ms,f,d - move block from address s to f to destination at address d.

R - read file in FCB into memory at 100H.

Rb - read file in FCB into memory with offset b from 100H.

Ss - set (examine and alter) memory starting at address s.

T - trace the next instruction.

Tn - trace the next n instructions.

U - untrace — like Trace, but intermediate steps are not displayed.

X - Examine all registers and flags.

Xr - examine specified registers or flag, where r may be --

C   Carry flag
Z   Zero flag
M   Minus (sign) flag
I   Interdigit Carry flag
A   Accumulator
B   BC Reg pair
D   DE Reg pair
H   HL Reg pair
S   Stack pointer
P   PC

CP/M SYSGEN Command

The SYSGEN transient command allows generation of an initialized disc containing the CP/M Operating System.

It is invoked by typing

SYSGEN

Once invoked, the user is prompted through the session. Refer to the CP/M Manual for further details.

CP/M SUBMIT Command

The SUBMIT command allows CP/M commands to be batched together for automatic processing. The form of this command is

SUBMIT ufn parm1 parm2 ... parmn

The ufn given in the SUBMIT command must be the filename (not type) of a file which exists on the currently logged-in disc with an assumed file type of '.SUB'. Refer to the CP/M Manual for further details.

CP/M BDOS -- Basic I/O Operations

Function & Number		Input Parameters	Output Parameters
Read Console	1	None	ASCII Char in A
Write Console	2	ASCII Char in E	None
Read Reader	3	None	ASCII Char in A
Write Punch	4	ASCII Char in E	None
Write List	5	ASCII Char in E	None
Get I/O Status	7	None	I/O Status in A
Put I/O Status	8	I/O Status in E	None
Print Buffer	9	Address of string terminated by $ in DE	None
Read Buffer	10	Address of Read Buffer in DE	Read Buffer is filled
Console Ready	11	None	LSB of A is 1 if char ready

All function numbers are passed in Reg. C.

I/O Status Byte

Value	Bits 6&7	Bits 4&5	Bits 2&3	Bits 0&1
00	CON:=TTY:	RDR:=TTY:	PUN:=TTY:	LST:=TTY:
01	CRT:	PTR:	PTP:	CRT:
10	BAT:	UR1:	UP1:	LPT:
11	UC1:	UR2:	UP2:	UL1:

Read Buffer

Byte	Function
1	Maximum Buffer Length
2	Current Buffer Length (returned value)
3-n	Data (returned values)

CP/M BIOS -- Basic Disc Operations

Function & Number		Input Parameters	Output Parameters
Lift Head	12	None	None
Init BDOS	13	None	None
Log-In disc	14	Value in Reg E A=0, B=1, C=2, D=3	None
Open File	15	Address of FCB in DE	Byte address of FCB if found or OFFH if not
Close File	16	Address of FCB in DE	Byte address of FCB if found or OFFH if not
Search for File	17	Address of FCB in DE	Byte address of first FCB if found or OFFH if not

Function & Number		Input Parameters	Output Parameters
Search for Next	18	Address of FCB in DE	Byte address of next FCB if found or OFFH if not
Delete File	19	Address of FCB in DE	None
Read Next Record	20	Address of FCB in DE	0=successful read 1=read past EOF 2=reading random data
Write Next Rec	21	Address of FCB in DE	0=successful write 1=error in extending 2=end of disc data 255=no more dir space
Make File	22	Address of FCB in DE	Byte address of FCB or 255 if no more dir space
Rename FCB	23	Address of FCB in DE	Byte Address of Dir entry or 255 if no match
Read Drive No	25	None	Number of logged-in drive (A=0, B=1, C=2, D=3)
Set DMA Address	26	Address of 128 byte buffer in DE	None

All function numbers are passed in Reg C.

CP/M File Types

ALG	ALGOL 60 Source File
ASM	Assembler Source File
BAK	Backup File
BAS	BASIC Source File (CBASIC)
C	C Source File
COM	"Command" File (Binary ORGed to 100H)
FOR	FORTRAN IV Source File
HEX	Intel "hex" code file
HLP	HELP File
INT	BASIC Intermediate File
LST	Listing File
MAC	MACRO-80 Source File
PRN	Assembler Listing File
SRC	PASCAL/MT Source File
SUB	SUBMIT File
TC	Tiny-C Source File
TXT	Text File
$$$	Temporary File

CP/M BIOS Jump Vector

The following is a table representing the entry points into the CP/M BIOS of the major routines accessible to the user:

Routine	Relative Offset	Comment
BOOT	00H	Cold Start
WBOOT	03H	Warm Start
CONST	06H	Console Status Reg A = 00 if no char ready Reg A = FF if char ready
CONIN	09H	Console char in (Reg A)
CONOUT	0CH	Console char out (Reg C)
LIST	0FH	List out (Reg C)
PUNCH	12H	Punch out (Reg C)
READER	15H	Reader in (Reg A)
HOME	18H	Move to track 00
SELDSK	1BH	Select disc given by Reg C (A=0, B=1,...)
SETTRK	1EH	Set track address given by Reg C (0...76)
SETSEC	21H	Set sector address given by Reg C (1...26)
SETDMA	24H	Set subsequent DMA address (RP B&C)
READ	27H	Read track/sector (block)
WRITE	2AH	Write track/sector (block)

CP/M - VERSION 2.2

CP/M is a monitor control program for microcomputer software development which uses IBM-compatible flexible discs (floppy discs) for mass storage. Using a microcomputer mainframe based on Intel's 8080 or Zilog's Z80 microprocessor, CP/M provides a general environment for program construction, storage, and editing, along with assembly and program debug facilities. An important feature of CP/M is that it can be easily altered to execute with any computer configuration which uses an Intel 8080 or Zilog Z80 microprocessor and has at least 20 K bytes of main memory with up to eight IBM-compatible disc drives. The CP/M monitor provides access to programs through a comprehensive file management system. The file subsystem supports a named file structure, allowing dynamic allocation of file space as well as sequential and random file access. Using this file system, up to 128 distinct programs can be stored in both source and machine-executable form. Digital

Research, the designer of CP/M, has provided a set of nine manuals which describe the use and operation of CP/M in detail.

These manuals are:

1. An Introduction to CP/M Features and Facilities.
2. ED: A Context Editor for the CP/M disc System.
3. ASM: CP/M Assembler User's Manual.
4. DDT: CP/M Dynamic Debugging Tool User's Manual.
5. CP/M 1.4 Interface Guide.
6. CP/M 1.4 System Alteration Guide.
7. CP/M 2.0 User's Guide.
8. CP/M 2.0 Interface Guide.
9. CP/M 2.0 System Alteration Guide.

As the reader can see, CP/M supports a context editor, an assembler (Intel-compatible), and a debugger system. These are available in the basic CP/M package. There is a large variety of other software available which can run under CP/M with little or no modification. Such software includes several assemblers (both 8080 and Z80), a symbolic debugger, several high-level languages (including Fortran IV {compiler}, BASIC-E {translator}, CBASIC {translator}, many interpretive BASICs, ALGOL, FOCAL, and C), and several special-purpose applications programs (such as text formatting systems and accounting systems). This HELP File addresses itself specifically to the CP/M 2.x Operating Systems.

CP/M File References

A file reference identifies a particular file or group of files on a particular disc attached to CP/M. These file references can be either unambiquous (ufn) or ambiguous (afn). An unambiguous file reference uniquely identifies a single file, while an ambiguous file reference may be satisfied by a number of different files. An unambiguous file reference is an exact name of the specified file. It consists of up to eight characters in the file name and three characters in the file type. An unambiguous file reference is of the form:

pppppppp.sss

The characters used in specifying an unambiguous file reference may not contain any of the following:

$$< > . , ; : = ? * [ ]$$

An ambiguous file reference is used for directory search and pattern matching. The form of an ambiguous file reference is similar to an unambiguous reference, except the symbol '?' may be interspersed throughout the file reference. In various commands throughout CP/M, the '?' symbol matches any character of a file name in the '?' position. For example, X?Y.C?M will match XZY.COM and X3Y.CEM. The '*' symbol is used to match all characters of a file name or file type. For example, *.COM will match XZY.COM and HELP.COM, while HELP.* will match HELP.COM and HELP.HLP.

CP/M Line Editing And Output Control

The following are the line editing functions supported by CP/M:

rubout - delete and echo the last character typed at the console.

Ctrl-H - delete the last character typed; Backspace one character; CRT-oriented

Ctrl-U - delete the entire line typed at the console.

Ctrl-X - delete the entire line typed at the console; Backspace to the beginning of the current line; CRT-oriented.

Ctrl-R - retype current command line: types a "clean line" following character deletion with rubouts.

Ctrl-E - physical end of line: carriage is returned, but line is not sent until the carriage return key is depressed.

Ctrl-M - terminates input (carriage return).

Ctrl-J - terminates current input (line feed); CRT-oriented

Ctrl-C - CP/M system reboot (warm start).

Ctrl-Z - end input from the console (used in PIP and ED).

Other control functions affect console output:

Ctrl-P - copy all subsequent console output to the currently-assigned list device (LST:). Output is sent to both the list device and the console device until the next Ctrl-P is typed.

Ctrl-S - stop the console output temporarily. Program execution and output continue when the next character is typed at the console. Typing Ctrl-C returns control to CP/M.

Input lines can generally be up to 255 characters in length. They are not acted upon until the carriage return key is typed.

CP/M Built-in Commands

ERA afn - The ERA (erase) command removes files from the currently logged-in disc.

DIR afn - The DIR (directory) command causes the names of all files which satisfy the ambiguous file name afn to be listed on the console device. All files are listed if no afn is given.

REN ufn1=ufn2 - The REN (rename) command allows the user to change the names of files on disc. The file satisfying ufn2 is changed to ufn1.

SAVE n ufn - The SAVE command places n pages (256-byte blocks) onto disc from the TPA and names this file ufn.

TYPE ufn - The TYPE command displays the contents of the ASCII source file ufn on the currently logged-in disc at the console device.

USER n - Upon cold boot, the user is automatically logged in to User Area 0, which is compatible with CP/M 1.4 directories. The USER command allows the user to move to another logical area within the same directory; areas are numbered 0-15. The ERA, DIR, REN, SAVE, and TYPE commands apply to the current User Area.

CP/M Transient Commands

The CP/M standard transient commands are:

STAT - list the number of bytes of storage and data on the currently logged-in disc, provide statistical information about particular files, and display or alter device assignment.

PIP - load the Peripheral Interchange Program for subsequent disc file and peripheral transfer operations.

ED - load and execute the CP/M text editor program.

SUBMIT - submit a file of commands for batch processing.

XSUB - used in conjunction with SUBMIT, transfers all buffered console input from CON: to the SUBMIT File.

ASM - load the CP/M assembler and assemble the specified program from disc.

LOAD - load the file in Intel "hex" machine code format and produce a file in machine executable form which can be loaded into the TPA (this loaded program becomes a new command under the CCP).

DDT - load the CP/M debugger into the TPA and execute it.

DUMP - dump the contents of a file in hex.

SYSGEN - create a new CP/M system disc.

MOVCPM - regenerate the CP/M system for a particular memory size.

Physical Device Assignments for CP/M

Logical Device	Physical Device
CON:	TTY: Model 43 Teletype
	CRT: Console CRT
	BAT: CRT and Modem
	UC1: In=CRT, Out=CRT and modem
RDR:	TTY: Model 43 Teletype
	PTR: Modem
	UR1: CRT and Modem w/CRT Output
	UR2: CRT and Modem
PUN:	TTY: Model 43 Teletype
	PTP: Modem
	UP1: CRT and Modem
	UP2: CRT and Modem
LST:	TTY: Model 43 Teletype
	CRT: Console CRT
	LPT: Modem
	UL1: CRT and Modem

CP/M STAT Command

The STAT Command takes any of the following forms:

STAT - calculate the storage remaining on all active drives and print a message like

x: R/W, SPACE: nnnK - if disc is Read/Write
x: R/O, SPACE: nnnK - if disc is Read Only

STAT x: - calculate the storage remaining on the specified drive and print

BYTES REMAINING ON x: nnnk

STAT x:afn [$S] - scan the specified files on the specified drive (x: is optional), and list all files which satisfy the unambiguous reference in alphabetical order with storage requirements. A table like the following is generated:

Size Recs Bytes Ext Acc
sssss rrrr nnnk ee a/b d:pppppppp.sss

where

sssss - number of virtual 128-byte records in file. This field is displayed if the optional $S is given.
rrrr - number of 128-byte records in each extent of the file.
nnnk - number of bytes (in K, K=1024) allocated to the file.
ee - number of 16 K extensions.
a/b - access mode of file; R/O or R/W.
d:pppppppp.sss - drive name (d may be A, B, C, D) and file name.

STAT x:=R/O - set the specified drive to Read Only. This is cleared by a warm boot. When a disc is Read Only, the message BDOS ERR ON x: READ ONLY will appear if there is an attempt to write to it.

STAT VAL: - summarize the status commands. STAT VAL: will print the list:

Temp R/O disc: d:=R/O
Set Indicator: d:filename.typ $R/O $R/W $SYS $DIR
disc Status : DSK: d:DSK:
User Status : USR:
Iobyte Assign:

CON: = TTY: CRT: BAT: UC1:
RDR: = TTY: PTR: UR1: UR2:
PUN: = TTY: PTP: UP1: UP2:
LST: = TTY: CRT: LPT: UL1:

STAT DEV: - display the current logical to physical device mapping. For example, the list may appear as:

CON: =CRT: PUN: =PTP:
RDR: =UR1: LST: = TTY:

STAT d:afn [$R/O or $R/W or $SYS or $DIR] - set the various permanent file indicators. R/O=Read/Only, R/W=Read/Write, SYS=System, DIR=Non-System.

STAT 1d1=pd1, 1d2=pd2, . . . change the logical to physical device assignments. Logical device ld1 is assigned to physical device pd1, etc. The valid logical device names are:

CON: The system console device
RDR: The paper tape reader device
PUN: The paper tape punch device.
LST: The output list device

The valid physical device names are:

TTY: Slow speed output device (teletype)
CRT: High speed output device (cathode ray tube)
BAT: Batch processing (CON: input is RDR:, CON: output is LST:)
UC1:   User-defined console
PTR: Paper tape reader
PTP: Paper tape punch
UR1:   User-defined reader #1
UR2:   User-defined reader #2
UP1:   User-defined punch #1
UP2:   User-defined punch #2
LPT: Line printer
UL1:   User-defined list device #1

STAT d:DSK: list the characteristics of the disc named "d:"; if "d:" is not specified, list the characteristics of all active discs. A sample listing:

213

d: Drive Characteristics
65536: 128 Byte Record Capacity
8192: Kilobyte Drive Capacity
128: 32 Byte Directory Entries
0: Checked Directory Entries
1024: Records/Extent
128: Records/Block
58: Sectors/Track
2: Reserved Tracks

STAT USR: - list the User Number the user is currently in and the User Numbers which have files on the currently addressed disc. A sample listing;

Active User : 0
Active Files: 0 1 3

CP/M PIP Command

PIP (Peripheral Interchange Program) is the CP/M transient which implements the basic media conversion operations necessary to load, print, punch, copy, and combine disc files. PIP is initiated by one of the following forms:

PIP - engage PIP, prompt the user with '*', and read command lines directly from the console. PIP used in this way is exited by either typing an empty command line (just a carriage return) or a Ctrl-C as the first character of the line.

PIP cmnd - engage PIP, execute the specified command, and return to CP/M.

The form of each command line in PIP is:

destination = source#1, source#2, source#3, . . ., source#n

The general forms of PIP command lines are:

x: =y:afn - copy all files satisfying afn from drive y to drive x. 'y' may be omitted, and, if so, the currently logged-in drive is selected.

x:ufn=y: - copy the file given by ufn from y to x. 'x' may be omitted, and, if so, the currently logged-in drive is selected.

x:afn=y:afn - like the above, but x and/or y may be omitted; the default drive is selected for the omitted drive(s).

1d=pd - copy from the specified physical device to the specified logical device. Valid logical devices are:

CON:, RDR:, PUN:, LST:

Valid physical devices are:

TTY:, CRT:, UC1:, PTR:, PTP:, UR1:, UR2:, UP1:, UP2:, LPT:, UL1:

Additional device names which may be used in PIP commands are:

NUL: - send 40 Nulls (ASCII 0) to the device.
EOF: - send a CP/M End of File character (ASCII Ctrl-Z).
INP: - special PIP input source to be patched (see manual).
OUT: - special PIP output destination to be patched (see manual).
PRN: - same as LST:, but tabs are expanded at every eighth character position, lines are numbered, and page ejects are inserted every 60 lines with an initial eject.

The user can also specify one or more PIP parameters enclosed in square brackets separated by zero or more blanks. These parameters are:

B - block mode transfer. Data is buffered by PIP until an ASCII X-Off character (Ctrl-S) is received from the source device.
Dn - delete characters which extend past column n in the transfer of data to the destination from the character source.
E - echo all transfer operations to the console.
F - filter (remove) form feeds from the file.
Gn - get File from User Number n (n in the range 0 - 15)
H - hex data transfer. All data is checked for proper Intel hex file format.
I - ignore ':00' records in the transfer of Intel hex format file.
L - translate uppercase to lowercase alphabetics.

N - add line numbers to each line transferred to the destination.

O - object file (non-ASCII) transfer. Ignore End of File.

Pn - include page ejects at every n lines.

Qs Z - quit copying from the source device or file when the string s (terminated by Ctrl-Z) is encountered.

R - read system files.

Ss Z - start copying from the source file when the string s is seen.

Tn - expand tabs to every nth column.

U - translate lowercase to uppercase alphabetics.

V - verify that data has been copied correctly.

W - write over R/O files without console interrogation.

Z - zero the parity bit on input for each ASCII character.

CP/M ED Command

The ED Program is the CP/M system context editor, which allows creation and alteration of ASCII files. Complete details are given in the user's manual.

The following are the error indicators given by ED:

?	Unrecognized Command
>	Memory buffer full
#	Cannot apply command the number of times specified
O	Cannot open LIB file in R command

The following are the control characters recognized by ED:

^C	System reboot
^E	Physical <CR> <LF> (not entered in command)
^H	Character delete (backspace)
^I	Logical tab
^J	New line (line feed)
^L	Logical <CR> <LF> in search and substitute strings
M	New line (carriage return)
^U	Line delete
^X	Line delete and backspace
^Z	String terminator
Rubout	Character delete
Break	Discontinue command

The following are the commands recognized by ED:

nA	Append lines
+/− B	Beginning/Bottom of buffer
+/− nC	Move character positions
+/− nD	Delete characters
E	Exit
nFs^Z	Find string
H	End edit, close and reopen files
Is ^Z	Insert characters
nJ	Place strings in juxtaposition
+/− nK	Kill (delete) lines
+/− nL	Move down/up lines
nM	Macro definition
O	Return to original file
+/− nP	Move and print pages
Q	Quit with no file changes
R	Read library file
nSs1^Zs2^Z	Substitute s2 for s1
+/− nT	Type lines
+/− U	Translate lower to uppercase if U; none if − U
+/− V	Engage/disengage line numbers (verify)
OV	Print memory buffer into (free/total usage)
nW	Write lines
nX	Transfer n lines to X$$$$$$$.LIB
OX	Empty X$$$$$$$.LIB
nZ	Sleep
+/− n	Move and type (+/− nLT)
n:	Move to absolute line (V engaged)
:n	Process from current line to specified line (V engaged)

CP/M ASM Command

The ASM Command loads and executes the CP/M 8080 assembler. It is of the form:

ASM filename.xyz

where filename is the name of the file 'filename.ASM' to assemble, x designates the disc name which contains the source, y designates the disc name to contain the hex file (y=Z suppresses generation of the hex file), and z designates the disc name to contain the print file (y=X lists on CON:, y=Z suppresses listing).

Refer to the ASM Manual for further details.

CP/M LOAD Command

The LOAD Command reads the file specified, which is assumed to contain Intel hex format machine code and produces a memory image file which can be subsequently executed (converts .HEX to

LOAD filename

where filename is the name of the file 'filename.HEX'.

CP/M DDT Command

The DDT Program allows dynamic interactive testing and debugging of programs generated in the CP/M environment. It is invoked by

DDT
DDT filename.HEX
DDT filename.COM

where 'filename' is the name of the program to be loaded or tested.

DDT responds to the normal CP/M input line editing characters.

DDT responds to the following commands:

As - perform inline assembly starting at the specified address s.

D - display memory from the current address for 16 display lines.

Ds - display memory from address s for 16 display lines.

Ds,f - display memory from address s to address f.

Fs,f,c - fill memory from start address s to final address f with byte C.

G - start execution at the current value of the PC.

Gs - start execution at the specified address s.

Gs,b - start execution at the specified address s and set a breakpoint at the address b.

Gs,b,c - same as above with breakpoints at b and c.

G,b - start execution at the current value of the PC with breakpoint b.

G,b,c - same as above with breakpoints at b and c.

If - insert a file name f into the default FCB.

L - list 12 lines of dissassembled code from the current address.

Ls - list 12 lines from the specified address s.

Ls,f - list lines of disassembled code from s to f.

Ms,f,d - move the block from address s to f to destination at address d.

R - read file in FCB into memory at 100H.

Rb - read file in FCB into memory with offset b from 100H.

Ss - set (examine and alter) memory starting at address s.

T - trace the next instruction.

Tn - trace the next n instructions.

U - untrace - like Trace, but intermediate steps are not displayed.

X - examine all registers and flags.

Xr - examine specified registers or flag, where r may be:

C Carry flag
Z Zero flag
M Minus (sign) flag
I Interdigit Carry flag
A Accumulator
B BC Reg pair
D DE Reg pair
H HL Reg pair
S Stack pointer
P PC

CP/M BDOS - Basic I/O Operations

Function & Number		Input Parameters	Output Parameters
System Reset	0	None	None
Read Console	1	None	ASCII Char in A
Write Console	2	ASCII Char in E	None
Read Reader	3	None	ASCII Char in A
Write Punch	4	ASCII Char in E	None
Write List	5	ASCII Char in E	None
Direct Con I/O	6	ASCII Char in E	I/O Status in A if E=OFFH
Get I/O Status	7	None	I/O Status in A
Put I/O Status	8	I/O Status in E	None
Print Buffer	9	Address of string terminated by $ in DE	None
Read Buffer	10	Address of Read Buffer in DE	Read Buffer is filled
Console Ready	11	None	LSB of A is 1 if char. ready

*All function numbers are passed in Reg C.

I/O Status Byte

Value	Bits 6&7	Bits 4&5	Bits 2&3	Bits 0&1
00	CON:=TTY:	RDR:=TTY:	PUN:=TTY:	LST:=TTY:
01	CRT:	PTR:	PTP:	CRT:
10	BAT:	UR1:	UP1:	LPT:
11	UC1:	UR2:	UP2:	UL1:

Read Buffer

Byte	Function
1	Maximum Buffer Length
2	Current Buffer Length (returned value)
3-n	Data (returned values)

CP/M BIOS - Basic Disc Operations

Function & Number		Input Parameters	Output Parameters
Return Version #	12	None	Version Info in HL H=0 CP/M, H=1 MP/M L=00 CP/M 1.x, 2x 2.x
Init BDOS	13	None	None
Log-In disc	14	Value in Reg E A=0, B=1, C=2, D=3	None
Open File	15	Address of FCB in DE	Byte address of FCB if found or OFFH if not
Close File	16	Address of FCB in DE	Byte address of FCB if found or OFFH if not
Search for File	17	Address of FCB in DE	Byte address of FCB (0-3) if found or OFFH if not
Search for Next	18	Address of FCB in DE	Byte address of next FCB if found or OFFH if not
Delete File	19	Address of FCB in DE	Byte address of FCB (0-3) if found or OFFH if not
Read Next Record	20	Address of FCB in DE	0=successful read 1=read past EOF 2=reading random data
Write Next Rec	21	Address of FCB in DE	0=successful write 1=error in extending 2=end of disc data 255=no more dir space
Make File	22	Address of FCB in DE	Byte address of FCB or 255 if no more dir space
Rename FCB	23	Address of FCB in DE	Byte Address of Dir entry or 255 if no match

Function & Number		Input Parameters	Output Parameters
Return Log Code	24	None	Login vector in HL
Read Drive No	25	None	Number of logged-in drive (A=0, B=1, C=2, D=3)
Set DMA Address	26	Address of 128 byte buffer in DE	None
Get Alloc Vect	27	None	Allocation Vect Addr in HL
Write Prot disc	28	None	None
Get R/O Vect	29	None	HL=R/O Vect Val
Set File Attrib	30	Ptr to FCB in DE	Dir code in A
Get disc Parms	31	None	HL=DPB Address
Set/Get Usr Code	32	E=OFFH (get)/Code no	A=Current Code (get)/no value (set)
Read Random	33	DE=FCB addr	A=return code 1=reading unwritten data 2=(not used) 3=can't close curr ext 4=seek to unwritten ext 5=(not used) 6=seek past end of disc
Write Random	34	DE=FCB addr	A=return code 1=reading unwritten data 2=(not used) 3=can't close curr ext 4=seek to unwritten ext 5=dir overflow 6=seek past end of disc
Compute File Siz	35	DE=FCB	Random Rec Field set to file size
Set Random Rec	36	DE=FCB addr	Random Rec Field set addr

All function numbers are passed in Reg C.

CP/M File Types

AIN	ALGOL 60 Intermed-iate	ALG	ALGOL 60 Source File
ASM	Assembler Source File	BAK	Backup File

217

BAS	BASIC Source File	C	C Source File
COB	COBOL Source File	COM	"Command" File
FOR	FORTRAN IV Source File	HEX	Intel "hex" code file
HLP	HELP File	INT	BASIC Intermediate File
LST	Listing File	MAC	MACRO-80 Source File
PAS	PASCAL Source File	PRN	Assembler Listing File
REL	Relocatable Module	SRC	PASCAL/MT Source File
SUB	SUBMIT File	SYM	Symbol File
TC	Tiny-C Source File	TFS	TFS Source File
TXT	Text File	$$$	Temporary File

CP/M BIOS Jump Vector

The following is a table representing the entry points into the CP/M BIOS of the major routines accessable to the user:

Routine	Relative Offset	Comment
BOOT	00H	Cold Start
WBOOT	03H	Warm Start
CONST	06H	Console Status
		Reg A = 00 if no char ready
		Reg A = FF if char ready
CONIN	09H	Console char in (Reg A)
CONOUT	0CH	Console char out (Reg C)
LIST	0FH	List out (Reg C)
PUNCH	12H	Punch out (Reg C)
READER	15H	Reader in (Reg A)
HOME	18H	Move to track 00
SELDSK	1BH	Select disc given by Reg C (A=0, B=1,...)
SETTRK	1EH	Set track address given by Reg C (0...76)
SETSEC	21H	Set sector address given by Reg C (1...26)
SETDMA	24H	Set subsequent DMA address (RP B&C)
READ	27H	Read track/sector (block)
WRITE	2AH	Write track-sector (block)
LISTST	2DH	Lost Device Status
		Reg A = 00 if no char ready
		Reg A = FF if char ready
SECTRAN	30H	Translate sector number in Reg C using table pointed to by DE; physical sector number returned in Reg L

EBASIC

EBASIC is invoked by typing the following:

EBASIC filename $o

where 'filename' is the name of the source file 'filename.BAS' to be compiled and 'o' is one or more of the following options:

A List Productions (for compiler debugging); normally OFF

B List only source statements with errors; normally OFF

C Check syntax only; don't create .INT file; normally OFF

D Convert lowercase to uppercase; normally ON

E Generate line number code; normally OFF

After compilation, the program may then be executed by:

ERUN filename

where 'filename' is the name of the intermediate code file 'filename.INT'.

EBASIC Statements

The following statements are valid in EBASIC:

FOR	NEXT	FILE	GOTO	LET
CLOSE	GOSUB	INPUT	ON	PRINT
READ	RESTORE	RETURN	OUT	RANDOMIZE
STOP	DATA	DEF	DIM	END
IF	REM	ELSE	THEN	

EBASIC Functions

The following built-in functions are valid in EBASIC:

ABS	ASC	ATN	CHR$	COS
COSH	FRE	INP	INT	LEFT$
LEN	LOG	MID$	POS	RIGHT$
RND	SGN	SIN	SINH	STR$
SQR	TAB	TAN	VAL	EXP

Differences Between EBASIC and CBASIC

The following features are not available in EBASIC, but they are available in CBASIC:

1. PEEK or POKE
2. PRINT USING
3. CALL to machine code programs
4. LPRINT

EBASIC Error Messages

Sicne EBASIC is a "subset" of CBASIC, refer to the CBASIC SUMMARY for assistance and information on the EBASIC error messages. Most EBASIC error messages are covered in the CBASIC SUMMARY.

FORTRAN-80

The FORTRAN-80 compiler and the MACRO-80 assembler, named F80 and M80 respectively, are invoked in a similar fashion. In both cases, the name of the program is given followed by an argument list. This argument list is of the general form:

obj-dev:
filename.ext,list-devG
filename.ext
= source-dev:filename.ext

These symbols are defined as follows:

obj-dev: The device on which the object program is to be written.

list-dev: The device on which the program listing is written.

source-dev: The device from which the source program input to FORTRAN-80 or MACRO-80 is obtained.

filename.ext: The filename and filename extension of the object program file, the listing file, and the source program file.

The default extensions are:

FOR FORTRAN-80 Source File
MAC MACRO-80 Source File
PRN Print (Listing) File
REL Relocatable Object File
COM Absolute Object File ORGed to 100H

The specifications for either the object file, the listing file, or both may be omitted. If neither a listing file nor an object file is desired, place only a comma to the left of the equal sign. If the names of the object file and the listing file are omitted, the default is the name of the source file. Logical CP/M devices may be specified as follows:

A:, B:	Disc Drives (Only A: or B:)
HSR:	High Speed Reader
LST:	Line Printer
TTY:	Teletype or CRT

Examples:

A>F80
*=TEST

Compile the program TEST.FOR and place the object in TEST.REL.

*,TTY:=TEST

Compile the program TEST.FOR and list the program on the terminal. No object is generated.

*TESTOBJ=TEST.FOR

Compile the program TEST.FOR and put object in TESTOBJ.REL.

*TEST,TEST=TEST

Compile the program TEST.FOR, put the object in TEST.REL and listing in TEST.PRN.

*,=TEST.FOR

Compile TEST.FOR but produce no object or listing file. Useful for checking for errors.

In all cases, the * is the prompt from FORTRAN-80. The indicated operations may also be performed by typing 'F80' followed by the option, like 'F80 = TEST'. Refer to the 'FORTRAN-80 User's Manual', Copyright 1977, by Microsoft.

FORTRAN-80 Compilation Switches

A number of different switches may be given in the command string that will affect the format of the listing file. Each switch should be preceded by a slash (/):

Switch Function

O - print all listing addresses in octal

H - print all listing addresses in hexadecimal (default)

N - do not list generated code

R - force generation of an object file

L - force generation of a listing file

P - each /P allocates an extra 100 bytes of runtime stack space

M - specifies to the compiler that the generated code should be in a form which can be loaded into ROM.

FORTRAN-80 Library Subroutines

The standard library (FORLIB.REL) includes the following subroutines and functions:

ABS	IABS	DABS	AINT	INT	IDINT
AMOD	MOD	AMAXO	AMAX1	MAXO	MAX1
DMAX1	AMINO	AMIN1	MINO	MIN1	DMIN1
FLOAT	IFIX	SIGN	ISIGN	DSIGN	DIM
IDIM	SNGL	DBLE	EXP	DEXP	ALOG
DLOG	ALOG10	DLOG10	SIN	DSIN	COS
DCOS	TANH	SQRT	DSQRT	ATAN	DATAN
ATAN2	DATAN2	DMOD	PEEK	POKE	INP
OUT					

FORTRAN-80 Logical Device Assignments

LUN*	Device
1,3,4,5	Preassigned to CON:
2	Preassigned to LST:
6-10	Preassigned to Disc Files (Reassignable)
11-255	User-Assignable

* LUN = Logical Unit Number

Invoking LINK-80

Each command to LINK-80 consists of a number of filenames and switches separated by commas:

obj-dev1:filename.ext/sw1,obj-dev2:filename.ext,...

If the input device for a file is omitted, the default is the currently lodged disc. If the extension of a file is omitted, the default is .REL. After each line is typed, LINK-80 will load or search the specified files, and, when finished, it will list all symbols that remain undefined followed by an asterisk. LINK-80 is invoked by the program name 'L80'.

LINK-80 can be used to generate a .COM file of a FORTRAN-80 program. This can be done by typing:

L80 program/E

LINK-80 will respond with a string of the form:

[aaaa bbbb nn]

The user may then create the .COM file by typing:

SAVE nn program.COM

LINK-80 Switches

The following are the switches for LINK-80. As for FORTRAN-80, these switches are preceeded by a slash (/).

Switch	Function
R	Reset. Initialize loader

E,E:name Exit LINK-80. FORLIB.REL will be searched to satisfy existing undefined references. If 'name' is specified, the value of this symbol is used as the start address of the program.

G,G:name Go. Start execution of program. FORLIB.REL will be searched to satisfy any existing undefined references.

U - List all undefined references.

M - Map. List all defined references and their values; all undefined references are followed by an asterisk.

S - Search. Search the file specified before this switch to satisfy references.

N - If a filename/N is specified, the program will be saved on disc under the selected name with a default extension of .COM.

P and D - See Addenda to Section 2 of documentation.

Three numbers are specified after the /E and /G switches are executed. They are given in the form:

[aaaa bbbb nn]

aaaa - start address of program
bbbb - address of next available byte
nn - number of 256-byte pages used

Creating a FORTRAN-80 .COM File

There are two basic ways to create a .COM file of a FORTRAN-80 program. For example, to generate PROG.COM from PROG.FOR, proceed in one of the following ways:

1. Using SAVE
   F80 =PROG
   L80 PROG/E
   [aaaa bbbb nn] - response from LINK-80 (necessary data)
   SAVE nn PROG.COM
2. Using /N LINK-80 Switch
   F80 =PROG
   L80 PROG/E,PROG/N

LINK-THE LINKER FOR MICROSOFT PRODUCTS

The linker is used to link assembled, compiled program modules together, load them into memory, and begin execution if desired. The program modules can come from different sources. Some of the sources are:

BASCOM
COBOL
FORTRAN
ASSEMBLER
RPG

Invoking Link

The format for the invoke of Linker is:

LINK <filename1.ext/s,filename2.ext/s,....>

where filename stands for disc drive letter followed by a colon followed by the absolute file name. ext is used if the module extension is different than .rel. /s stands for switch options.
EXAMPLE of a link:

LINK MAIN,FORLIB/S,MAIN/N/G/E

The first MAIN is the name of the module from the Fortran compiler. The FORLIB/S is the library of standard Fortran routines that will be selected. The MAIN/N/G/E means to name the .COM file MAIN and to save it on current disc then execute MAIN automatically.

Switch Options

Each switch option is preceded by a /.

E . . . Exit to operating system.
G . . . Go start execution
Start execution of the program as soon as the current command line has been interpreted.
M . . . Map al symbols
List both all the defined globals and their values and all undefined globals followed by an asterisk.
R . . . Reset the linker
Puts the linker back to its initial state. The /R is used to restart LINK if the wrong file was loaded by mistake.
S . . . Search file
Search the disc file having the filename immediately preceding the /S in the command string, to satisfy any undefined globals. This is convenient for having the linker searh a library file of much-used routines.
U . . . List all undefined globals
List all undefined globals as soon as the current command line has been interpreted and executed. Link defaults to this switch; therefore it is generally not needed.

Errors

No start address. - A /G is issued but no main program module has been loaded.
Loading error. The file given is not a properly formatted link object file.
Fatal Table Collision. There is not enough memory.

Command error. Unrecognizable link command.

File not found. Specified file not on specified disc.

Mult def global. More than one definition of the global name (possibly wrong modules combined).

MAC ASSEMBLER - INTRODUCTION

MAC is the CP/M Standard Macro Assembler; it is upward-compatible with ASM, the CP/M Standard Assembler. The facilities of MAC include assembly of Intel 8080 microcomputer mnemonics, along with assembly-time expressions, conditional assembly, page formatting features, and a macro processor which is compatible with the standard Intel definition (MAC implements the mid-1977 revision of Intel's definition).

MAC requires approximately 12 K of machine code and table space, along with an additional 2.5 K of I/O buffer space.

Executing MAC

MAC is invoked by the following command:

MAC d:filename $parms

Only 'filename' is required, and it represents a file named 'filename.ASM'. MAC may then generate up to 3 other files: filename.HEX (the Intel Hex Format File), filename.PRN (the Print or Listing file), and filename.SYM containing a sorted list of the symbols used in the program).

MACRO Library files may be referenced by the program; these files are named 'filename.LIB'. $parms represents the optional assembly control parameters which are discussed in the next section.

MAC may be executed by employing the SUBMIT file MAC.SUB.MAC.SUB assembles the specified MAC .ASM file, converts it into a .COM file via LOAD, and erases the .HEX file. MAC.SUB is invoked by:

SUBMIT MAC filename

where 'filename' is the name of the MAC file 'filename.ASM'.

XMAC Version

XMAC is a version of MAC which does NOT recognize the intrinsic Intel 8080 assembler language mnemonics. XMAC is intended to be used for Cross-Assembly using .LIB files which contain the assembler mnemonics for the target machine. XMAC is invoked in exactly the same way MAC is (except that no SUBMIT file is available), and it recognizes the same pseudo-ops and control parameters. The patch file XMAC.ASM contains the patches used to convert MAC into XMAC. The library files MAC40.LIB and XMAC40.LIB contain the macros necessary to assemble code for the Intel 4040 microprocessor, for example. MAC40.LIB renames the 4040 mnemonics for ADD, SUB, etc., to ADD4, SUB4, etc., so that it will not conflict with MAC. XMAC40.LIB does not rename these, since XMAC does not recognize these in the first place.

Assembly Control Parameters

The control parameter list is preceded by a $, and may contain any of the following in any order:

A - controls the source disc for the .ASM file.

H - controls the destination of the .HEX machine code file.

L - controls the source disc for the .LIB files.

M - controls MACRO listing in the .PRN file.

P - controls the destination of the .PRN listing file.

Q - controls the listing of LOCAL symbols.

S - controls the generation and destination of the .SYM file.

1 - controls pass 1 listing.

In the case of the A, H, L, P, and S parameters, they may be followed by the drive name from which to obtain or to which to send data, where:

A,B,C,D	— designates that particular drive
P	— designates the LST: device
X	— designates the user console (CON:)
Z	— designates a null file (no output)

For example,

$PB AA HB SX

sends the .PRN file to drive B:, gets the .ASM file from drive A:, sends the .HEX file to drive B:, and sends the .SYM file to CON:.

The parameters L, S, M, Q, and 1 may be preceded by either + or − to enable or disable their respective functions:

+L - list the input lines read from the MACRO library.

−L - suppress listing of the MACRO library (default).

+S - append the .SYM output to the end of the .PRN file (default).

−S - suppress the generation of the sorted symbol table.

+M - list all MACRO lines as they are processed (default).

−M - suppress all MACRO lines as they are processed.

*M - list only HEX code generated by macro expansions in listing.

+Q - list all LOCAL symbols in the symbol list.

−Q - suppress all LOCAL symbols in the symbol list (default).

+1 - produce a listing file on the first pass (for MACRO debugging).

−1 - suppress listing on pass 1 (default).

The programmer can intersperse controls throughout the assembly language source or library files. Interspersed controls are denoted by a "$" in the first column of the input line followed immediately by a parameter.

Assembler Pseudo-Ops

The following Pseudo-Ops are supported:

DB	defines data bytes or strings of data
DS	reserves storage areas
DW	defines words of storage
ELSE	alternate to IF
END	terminates the physical program
ENDIF	marks the end of conditional assembly
ENDM	marks the end of a MACRO
EQU	performs a numeric "equate"
EXITM	abort expansion of the current MACRO level
IF	begins conditional assembly
IRP	INLINE MACRO with string substitution
IRPC	INLINE MACRO with character substitution
LOCAL	define LOCAL variables unique to each MACRO repetition
MACLIB	specify MACRO Library to load
MACRO	defines beginning of a MACRO
ORG	sets the program or data origin
PAGE	defines the listing page size for output
REPT	defines the beginning of a INLINE MACRO
SET	performs a numeric "set" or assignment
TITLE	enables page titles and options

In-Line Error Messages

B - Balance error: MACRO doesn't terminate properly or conditional assembly is ill-formed.

C - Comma error: expression was encountered but not delimited properly from the next item by a comma.

D - Date error: element in a data statement (DB,DW) cannot be placed in the specified data area.

E - Expression error: expression is ill-formed and cannot be computed.

I - Invalid character: a non-graphic character has been found.

L - Label error: label cannot appear in this context.

M - MACRO overflow error: internal MACRO expansion table overflow.

N - Not implemented error: unimplemented feature used.

O - Overflow error: expression is too complicated or the number of LOCAL labels has exceeded 9999.

P - Phase error: labels do not have same value on both passes (multiple label).

R - Register error: value specified for a register is not compatible with op code.

S - Statement/Syntax error: statement is ill-formed.

V - Value error: operand is improperly formed or out of range.

Console Error Messages

NO SOURCE FILE PRESENT. .ASM file not found.

NO DIRECTORY SPACE. Directory is full.

SOURCE FILE NAME ERROR. The form of the source file name is invalid; note that MAC is invoked by 'MAC filename', and the .ASM file type is NOT specified.

SOURCE FILE READ ERROR. Error in reading source file.

OUTPUT FILE WRITE ERROR. Error in writing output file.

CANNOT CLOSE FILE. An output file cannot be closed.

UNBALANCED MACRO LIBRARY. No ENDM encountered for a MACRO definition.

INVALID PARAMETER. Invalid assembly parameter was found in the input line.

MACRO-80

MACRO-80 is invoked by the following command:

M80 obj:fn1.ext,1st:fn2.ext=src:fn3.ext

where

obj:fn1.ext is the device/filename for the object program.

1st:fn2.ext is the device/filename for the listing.

src:fn3.ext is the device/filename for the source.

MACRO-80 Switches

The following switches may be specified in the command line:

O - print all listing addresses in octal.
H - print all listing addresses in hexadecimal.
R - force generation of an object file.
L - force generation of a listing file.
C - force generation of a cross reference file.
Z - assemble Zilog (Z80) mnemonics.
I - assemble Intel (8080) mnemonics.
P - each /P allocates an extra 256 bytes of stack space for use during assembly. Use /P if stack overflow errors occur during assembly.

MACRO-80 Pseudo-Ops

The following are the pseudo-ops recognized by MACRO-80:

ASEG	COMMON	CSEG	DB	DC
DS	DSEG	DW	END	ENTRY
PUBLIC	EQU	EXT	EXTRN	NAME
ORG	PAGE	SET	SUBTTL	TITLE
COMMENT	PRINTX	RADIX	REQUEST	Z80
8080	IF	IFT	IFE	IFF
IF1	IF2	IFDEF	IFNDEF	IFB
IFNB	ENDIF	LIST	XLIST	CREF
XCREF	REPT	ENDM	MACRO	IRP
IRPC	EXITM	LOCAL	COND	ENDC
*EJECT	DEFB	DEFS	DEFW	DEFM
DEFL	GLOBAL	EXTERNAL	INCLUDE	MACLIB
ELSE	.LALL	.SALL	.XALL	

In-Line Error Messages

A Argument Error
C Conditional nesting err
D Double Defined Symbol
E External error
M Multiply Defined Symbol
N Number error
O Bad opcode or syntax
P Phase error
Q Questionable
R Relocation
U Undefined symbol
V Value error

Console Error Messages

No end statement encountered in input file-no END statement.

Unterminated conditional-at least one conditional is unterminated.

Unterminated REPT/IRP/IRPC/MACRO-at least one block is unterminated.

[xx] [No] Fatal error () [,xx warnings]-the number of fatal errors and warnings.

Invoking Link-80

LINK-80 is invoked by typing

L80 obj1:filename.ext/sw1,obj2:filename,ext/sw2,...

where objn:filename.ext denotes a .REL file to be linked and swn denotes switches which control the linking process.

LINK—80 Switches

/R - reset - put loader back in initial state.

/E or /E:Name - exit LINK-80 and return to CP/M. Search the system library for any undefined references. /E:Name uses Name for the start address of the program.

/G or /G:Name - start execution of the program. Again, if /G:Name is specified, Name defines the start address of execution.

<filename>/N - save the binary on disc under the name 'filename.COM'.

/P:adr and /D:adr - set the Program and Data area origins for the next program to be loaded.

/U - list the origin and end of the program and data area as well as all undefined globals.

/M - list the origin and end of the program and data area, all defined globals and their values, and all undefined globals followed by an asterisk.

<filename>/S - search 'filename.REL' to satisfy references.

/X - if a filename/N was specified, /X will cause the file to be saved in Intel HEX format with an extension of .HEX.

/Y - if a filename/N was specified, /Y will create a filename.SYM file when /E is entered. This file contains the names and addresses of all globals for use with SID or ZSID.

Invoking LIB-80

To invoke LIB-80, type - LIB

Commands to LIB-80 consist of an optional destination filename which sets the name of the library being created, followed by an equal sign, followed by module names separated by commas or filenames with module names enclosed in angle brackets separated by commas.

To select a given module from a file, use the name of the file followed by the module(s) specified enclosed in angle brackets and separated by commas. If no modules are selected from a file, then all modules are selected.

LIB-80 Switches

/O Set listing radix to Octal
/H Set listing radix to Hexadecimal
/U List undefineds
/L List cross reference

/C Create - start LIB over
/E Exit - rename .LIB to .REL and exit
/R Rename - rename .LIB to .REL

Invoking CREF-80

CREF-80 is invoked by typing:

CREF80 listing=source

where 'listing' is the name of the file 'listing.LST' generated and 'source' s the name of the file 'source.CRF' generated by MACRO-80. 'listing' is optional, and, if omitted, the listing file generated is named 'source.LST'.

Using DEBUG.MAC

DEBUG.MAC is a package of MACROs which the user may employ to aid himself in debugging MACRO—80 programs. This package contains two print MACROs, one register display MACRO, and one exit MACRO. In all cases, these MACROs have no net affect on any register.

DEBUG.MAC is used by first specifying it as a MACRO Library within the user's program. This is accomplished by the statement

MACLIB DEBUG.MAC

as an assembly-language instruction at the beginning of his program. This statement loads the library DEBUG.MAC and makes its MACROs available for use. These MACROs are:

Name	# Args	Size (Bytes)	Function	Example
EXIT	0/1	275 or 263+	Print an exit message, print the contents of all registers, and warm boot CP/M	EXIT EXIT <CONDITION 1>
PRINT	1	19+	Print a message on CON:	PRINT <MESSAGE>
PRINTC	1	17+	Print a char string on CON:	PRINTC <'M1',0DH>
REGS	0	241	Print the contents of all registers on CON:	REGS

Note: The + after a size indicates that one must add to the indicated size the number of characters specified in the parameter.

Note: Messages specified for EXIT and

PRINT should not contain restricted MACRO-80 symbols (such as !) or an error message will result.

An example of the use of these MACROs follows:

```
MACLIB    DEBUG.MAC
- code -
REGS                          ; print all register values at this
- code -                        POINT
PRINT     <Ck Pt 1>           ; got to check point 1
- code -
EXIT      <Exit error 1>      ; should not have taken this
- code -                        path
PRINT     <Ck Pt 2>           ; got to check point 2
- code -
EXIT                          ; normal exit
- code -
```

MICROSOFT BASIC

This HELP File is derived from the "Microsoft BASIC Reference Book," and it is divided into two parts—one covering the Interpreter and the other covering the Compiler. These programs process programs written in almost exactly the same language—Microsoft BASIC; there are minor differences between the two, however, and these are discussed in the file under the Compiler.

Interpreter

The MBASIC (Microsoft BASIC) Interpreter is invoked as follows:

MBASIC [<filename>] [/F:<# files>]
[/M:<memory loc>]

If <filename> is present, MBASIC proceeds as if a RUN <filename> command were typed after initialization is complete. A default extension of .BAS is assumed. If /F:<# files> is present, it sets the number of disc data files that may be open at any one time during the execution of a program. The default here is 3. The /M:<memory loc> sets the highest memory locations that will be used by MBASIC. All memory to the start of CP/M is used by default.

Special Characters

^A - enters Edit Mode on line being typed or last line typed.

^C - interrupts program execution and returns to MBASIC.

^G - rings <BELL> at terminal.

^H - deletes last char typed

^I - tab (every 8).

^O - halts/resumes program output.

^R - retypes the line currently being typed.

^S - suspends program execution.

^Q - resumes execution after ^S.

^U, X - deletes line being typed.

<CR> - ends every line being typed in.

<LF> - breaks a logical line into physical lines.

<DEL> - deletes last char typed.

<ESC> - escapes Edit Mode Subcommands.

Special Commands

&O, & - prefix for Octal Constant.

&H - prefix for HEX Constant.

: - separates statements typed on the same line.

? - equivalent to PRINT statement.

Variable Type Declaration Characters

$	String	0 to 255 chars
%	Integer	−32768 to 32767
!	Single precision	7.1 digit floating point
#	Double Precision	17.8 digit floating point

Commands

Command Syntax	Function
AUTO [line[, inc]	Generate line numbers
CLEAR [,[exp1][,exp2]]	Clear program variables; Exp1 sets end of memory and Exp2 sets amount of stack space
CONT	Continue program execution
DELETE [[start][-[end]]]	Delete program lines
EDIT line	Edit a program line
FILES [filename]	Directory
LIST [line[-[line]]]	List program line(s)
LLIST [line[-[line]]]	List program line(s) on printer
LOAD filename[,R]	Load program; ,R means RUN
MERGE filename	Merge prog on disc with that in mem

NAME old AS new	Change the name of a disc file
NEW	Delete current prog and vars
NULL exp	Set num of <NULL>s after each line
RENUM [[new][,[old][,inc]]]	Renumber program lines
RESET	Init CP/M; use after disc change
RUN [line number]	Run a prog (from a particular line)
RUN filename[,R]	Run a prog on disc
SAVE filename[,A or ,P]	Save prog onto disc; ,A saves prog in ASCII and ,P protects file
SYSTEM	Return to CP/M
TROFF	Turn trace off
TRON	Turn trace on
WIDTH [LPRINT] exp	Set term or printer carriage width; default is 80 (term) and 132 (prin)

Edit Mode Sub-Commands

A	Abort - restore original line and re-start Edit.
nCc	Change n characters.
nD	Delete n characters.
E	End edit and save changes; don't type rest of line.
Hstr<ESC>	Delete rest of line and insert string.
Istr<ESC>	Insert string at current pos.
nKc	Kill all chars up to the nth occurrence of c.
L	Print the rest of the line and go to the start of the line.
Q	Quit edit and restore original line.
nSc	Search for nth occurrence of c.
Xstr<ESC>	Go to the end of the line and insert string.
<DEL>	Backspace over chars; in insert mode, delete chars.
<CR>	End edit and save changes.

Program Statements (except I/O)

Statement Syntax Function	
CALL variable [(arg list)]	Call assembly or FORTRAN routine
CHAIN [MERGE] filename [,[line exp][,ALL][,DELETE range]]	Call a program and pass variables to it; MERGE with ASCII files allows overlays; start at line exp if given; ALL means all variables will be passed (otherwise COMMON only); DELETE allows deletion of an overlay before CHAIN is executed.

COMMON list of vars	Pass vars to a CHAINed prog
DEF FNx[(arg list)]=exp	Arith or String Function
DEF USRn=address	Define adr for nth assembly routine
DEFINT range(s) of letters	Define default var type INTeger
DEFSNG range(s) of letters	Define default var type Single
DEFDBL range(s) of letters	Define default var type Double
DEFSTR range (s) of letters	Define defaults var type String
DIM list of subscripted vars	Allocate arrays
END	Stop prog and close files
ERASE var [, var . . .]	Release space and var names
ERROR code	Generate error code/message
FOR var=exp TO exp [STEP exp] FOR loop	
GOSUB line number	Call BASIC subroutine
GOTO line number	Branch to specified line
IF exp GOTO line [ELSE stmt . . .]	
	IF exp <> 0 then GOTO
IF exp THEN stmt[:stmt] [ELSE stmt . . .]	
	IF exp < > 0 then . . . else . . .
[LET] var=exp	Assignment
MID$(string,n[,m])=string2	Replace a portion of string with string2; start at pos n for m chars
NEXT var[,var . . .]	End FOR
ON ERROR GOTO line	Error trap subroutine
ON exp GOSUB line[,line]	Computed GOSUB
ON exp GOTO line[,line]	Computed GOTO
OPTION BASE n	Min val for subscripts (n=0,1)
OUT port,byte	Output byte to port
POKE address,byte	Memory put
RANDOMIZE [exp]	Reseed random number generator
REM any text	Remark - comment
RESTORE [line]	Reset DATA pointer

RESUME or RESUME 0	Return from ON ERROR GOTO	
RESUME NEXT	Return to stmt after error line	
RESUME line	Return to specified line	
RETURN	Return from subroutine	
STOP	Stop prog and print BREAK msg	
WAIT prot,mask[,select]	Pause until input port [XOR select] AND mask <> 0	
WHILE exp stmts . . . WEND	Execute stmts as long as exp is T	

PRINT USING Format Field Specifiers

Numeric Specifiers

Specifier	Digits	Chars	Definition
%	1	1	Numeric field
.	0	1	Decimal point
+	0	1	Print leading or trailing sign
−	0	1	Trailing sign (− if neg, <sp> otherwise)
**	2	2	Leading asterisk
$$	1	2	Floating dollar sign; placed in front of leading digit
**$	2	3	Asterisk fill and floating dollar sign
,	1	1	Use comma every three digits
^^^^	0	4	Exponential format
-	0	1	Next character is literal

String Specifiers

Specifier	Definition
!	Single character
/<spaces>/	Character field; width=2+number of <spaces>
&	Variable length field

Input/Output Statements

CLOSE [[#]f[,[#]f . . .]]
Close disc files; if no arg, close all
DATA constant list
List data for READ statement
FIELD [#]f,n AS string var [,n AS string var . . .]
Define fields in random file buffer
GET [#]f[, record number]

Read a record from a random disc file
INPUT [;] [prompt string;] var [,var . . .]
INPUT [;] [prompt string,] var [,var . . .]
Read data from the terminal; leading semicolon suppresses echo of <CR>/<LF> and semicolon after prompt string causes question mark after prompt while comma after prompt suppresses question mark
KILL filename
Delete a disc file
LINE INPUT [;] [prompt string;] string var
Read an entire line from terminal; leading semicolon suppresses echo of <CR>/<LF>
LINE INPUT #f,string var
Read an entire line from a disc file
LSET field var=string exp
Store data in random file buffer left-justified or left-justify a non-disc string in a given field
OPEN mode,[#] f,filename
Open a disc file; mode must be one of:

    I = sequential input file
    O = sequential output file
    R = random input/output file

PRINT [USING format string;] exp [,exp . . .]
Print data at the terminal using the format specified
PRINT #f, [USING format string;] exp [,exp . . .]
Write data to a disc file
LPRINT [USING format string;] var [,var . . .]
Write data to a line printer
PUT [#] f [,record number]
Write data from a random buffer to a data file
READ var [,var . . .]
Read data from a DATA statement into the specified vars
RSET field var = string exp
Store data in a random file buffer right justified or right justify a non-disc string in a given field
WRITE [list of exps]
Output data to the terminal
WRITE #f, list of exps Output data to a sequential file or a random field buffer

Operators

Symbol	Function
=	Assignment or equality test

Symbol	Function
–	Negation or subtraction
+	Addition or string concatenation
*	Multiplication
/	Division (floating point result)
^	Exponentiation
/	Integer division (integer result)
MOD	Integer modulus (integer result)
NOT	One's complement (integer)
AND	Bitwise AND (integer)
OR	Bitwise OR (integer)
XOR	Bitwise exclusive OR (integer)
EQV	Bitwise equivalence (integer)
IMP	Bitwise implication (integer)
=, >, <, <=, =< >=, =>, <>	Relational tests (TRUE=–1, FALSE=0)

The precedence of operators is:

1. Expressions in parentheses
2. Exponentiation
3. Negation (Unary –)
4. *,/
5. /
6. MOD
7. +,–
8. Relational Operators
9. NOT
10. AND
11. OR
12. XOR
13. IMP
14. EQV

Arithmetic Functions

Function	Action
ABS(exp)	Absolute value of expression
ATN(exp)	Arc tangent of expression (in radians)
CDBL(exp)	Convert the expression to a double precision number
CINT(exp)	Convert the expression to an integer
COS(exp)	Cosine of the expression (in radians)
CSNG(exp)	Convert the expression to a single precision number
EXP(exp)	Raises the constant E to the power of the expression
FIX(exp)	Returns truncated integer of expression
FRE(exp)	Gives memory free space not used by MBASIC

Function	Action
INT(exp)	Evaluates the expression for the largest integer
LOG(exp)	Gives the natural log of the expression
RND[(exp)]	Generates a random number
	exp <0 seeds new sequence
	exp =0 returns previous number
	exp >0 or omitted returns new random number
SGN(exp)	1 if exp >0
	0 if exp =0
	–1 if exp <0
SIN(exp)	Sine of the expression (in radians)
SQR(exp)	Square root of expression
TAN(exp)	Tangent of the expression (in radians)

String Functions

Function	Action
ASC(str)	Returns ASCII value of first char in string
CHR$(exp)	Returns a 1-char string whose char has ASCII code of exp
FRE(str)	Returns remaining memory free space
HEX$(exp)	Converts a number to a hexadecimal string
INPUT$(length [,[#]f])	Returns a string of length chars read from console or from a disc file; characters are not echoed
INSTR([exp,]str1,str2)	Returns the first position of the first occurrence of str2 in str1 starting at position exp
LEFT$(str,len)	Returns leftmost length chars of the string expression
LEN(str)	Returns the length of a string
MID$(string,start[,length])	Returns chars from the middle of the string starting at the position specified to the end of the string or for length characters
OCT$(exp)	Converts an expression to an Octal string
RIGHT$(str,len)	Returns rightmost length chars of the string expression
SPACE$(exp)	Returns a string of exp spaces

Function	Action
STR$(exp)	Converts a numeric expression to a string
STRING$(length, str)	Returns a string length long containing the first char of the star
STRING$(length, exp)	Returns a string length long containing chars with numeric value exp
VAL(str)	Converts the string representation of a number to its numeric value

I/O And Special Functions

Function	Action
CVI(str)	Converts a 2-char string to an integer
CVS(str)	Converts a 4-char string to a single precision number
CVD(str)	Converts an 8-char string to a double precision number
EOF(f)	Returns TRUE (−1) if file is positioned at its end
ERL	Error Line Number
ERR	Error Code Number
INP(port)	Inputs a byte from an input port
LOC(f)	Returns next record number to read or write (random file) or number of sectors read or written (sequential file)
LPOS(n)	Returns carriage position of line printer (n is dummy)
MKI$(value)	Converts an integer to a 2-char string
MKS$(value)	Converts a single precision value to a 4-char string
MKD$(value)	Converts a double precision value to an 8-char string
PEEK(exp)	Reads a byte from memory location specified by exp
POS(n)	Returns carriage position of terminal (n is dummy)
SPC(exp)	Used in PRINT statements to print spaces
TAB(exp)	Used in PRINT statements to tab to specified position
USR[n](arg)	Calls the user's machine-language subroutine with the arg
VARPTR(var)	Returns address of var in memory or zero if var has not been assigned a value
VARPTR(#f)	Returns the address of the disc I/O buffer assigned to file number

Interpreter Error Codes

Code	Error		Code	Error
1	NEXT without FOR		14	Out of string space
2	Syntax error		15	String too long

Code	Error		Code	Error
3	RETURN without GOSUB		16	String formula too complex
4	Out of data		17	Can't continue
5	Illegal function call		18	Undefined user function
6	Overflow		19	No RESUME
7	Out of memory		20	RESUME without error
8	Undefined line		21	Unprintable error
9	Subscript out of range		22	Missing operand
10	Redimensioned array		23	Line buffer overflow
11	Division by zero		26	FOR without NEXT
12	Illegal direct		29	WHILE without WEND
13	Type mismatch		30	WEND without WHILE

Disc Errors:

Code	Error		Code	Error
50	Field overflow		58	File already exists
51	Internal error		61	disc full
52	Bad file number		62	Input past end
53	File not found		63	Bad record number
54	Bad file mode		64	Bad file name
55	File already open		66	Direct statement in file
57	Disc I/O error		67	Too many files

Compiler

The following direct mode commands are NOT implemented on the compiler and will generate an error message:

AUTO	CLEAR	CLOAD
CSAVE	CONT	DELETE
EDIT	LIST	LLIST
RENUM	COMMON	SAVE
LOAD	MERGE	NEW
ERASE		

The following statements are used differently with the compiler than with the interpreter (refer to the manual for details):

CALL	DEFINT	DEFSNG
DEFDBL	DEFSTR	DIM
ERASE	END	ON ERROR GOTO
RESUME	STOP	TRON
TROFF	USRn	

Basic Compiler Commands And Switches

The compiler is invoked by the BASCOM command; it may be called by:

BASCOM or
BASCOM command line

where "command line" is:
[dev:][obj
file][,dev:][1st file]]=[dev:]source file[/switch
. . .]

If just BASCOM is used, the user will be prompted with an asterisk, after which he should enter the command line.

Switches

/E Use this switch if ON ERROR GOTO with RESUME <line number> is used.

/X Use this switch if ON ERROR GOTO with RESUME, RESUME 0, or RESUME NEXT is used.

/N Do not list generated object code.

/D Generate debug/checking code at run-time.

/S Write quoted strings of more than 4 chars as they are encountered.

/4 Recognize Microsoft 4.51 BASIC Interpreter conventions.

/C Relax line numbering constraints; lines need not be numbered sequentially; /4 and /C may not be used together.

/Z Use Z80 opcodes.

Basic Compiler Error Messages

Compile-Time Fatal Errors:

SN	Syntax error	OM	Out of memory
SQ	Sequence error	TM	Type mismatch
TC	Too complex	BS	Bad subscript
LL	Line too long	UC	Unrecognizable command
OV	Math overflow	/O	Division by zero
DD	Array already dim'ed	FN	FOR/NEXT error
FD	Function already def	UF	Function not defined
WE	WHILE/WEND error	/E	Missing /E switch
		/X	Missing /X switch

Compile-Time Warning Errors:

ND Array not dimensioned	SI Statement ignored

Run-Time Error Messages:

2 Syntax error	5 Illegal function call
3 RETURN without GOSUB	6 Floating/Integer ovfl
4 Out of data	9 Subscript out of range

11	Division by zero	55	File already open
14	Out of string space	57	disc I/O error
20	RESUME without error	58	File already exists
21	Unprintable error	61	disc full
50	Field overflow	62	Input past end
51	Internal error	63	Bad record number
52	Bad file number	64	Bad filename
53	File not found	67	Too many files
54	Bad file mode		

INTRODUCTION TO PASCAL/MT

The Pascal/MT compiler exists in two versions, each consisting of two 8080 object code files: FLTCOMP.COM and P2/FLT.OVL for the version in which REAL numbers are implemented as floating point values internally and BCDCOMP. COM and P2/BCD.OVL for the version in which REAL numbers are implemented as BCD values internally. These files are Pass 1 and Pass 2 of the Pascal/MT compiler, respectively. Also required by the compiler are the following files:

P1ERRORS.TXT	—Pass 1 Error Messages
P2ERRORS.TXT	—Pass 2 Error Messages
PASCAL/F.RTP	—Run-time Package (including debugger) for FLT
PASCAL/B.RTP	—Run-time Package (including debugger) for BCD

The input files to the Pacal/MT compiler must have the extension '.SRC' or '.PAS' indicating that it is a source program file. There must be a carriage return/line feed sequence at the end of each input line and an input line may not be longer than 80 characters.

Invoking Pascal

The Pascal/MT compiler is invoked by using the following command:

PASCAL filename.DL

where 'filename' is the name of the file with the extension '.SRC' or '.PAS' containing the Pascal/MT source statements to be compiled, D is Y or N to indicate whether to include the debugger in the resultant .COM file, and L is Y or N to indicate whether to produce a .PRN file (listing).

PASCAL defaults to no debugger and no listing. The four invocation options are:

PASCAL filename	— no debugger, no listing
PASCAL filename.Y	— debugger, no listing
PASCAL filename.NY	— no debugger, listing
PASCAL filename.YY	— debugger, listing

For usage with the BCD version of the compiler, the commands are similar except that 'PASCAL' is replaced by 'BCDCOMP'.

Compile Switches

Compile-time options may be specified to the compiler from within the source file. Such options take the form of special comments. The form of these comments is:

(*$o info*) or {$o info}

where 'o' is the letter of the option and 'info' is information particular to that option. These options are:

$I<filename>	Include <filename>.SRC into source stream.
$L+ or $L−	Turn listing on (default) or off.
$P	Insert form feed into .PRN file.
$D+ or $D−	Turn debug code on (default) or off.
$C+	Use CALL instructions for real operations.
$Cn	Use RST n for real operations (n=0 . . . 7).
$O $aaaa	ORG program $aaaa (default 100H).
$R $bbbb	ORG RAM data at $bbbb.
$Z $cc00	Set run-time size to $cc 256-byte pages.
$X $dddd	Set run-time stack space to $dddd. (default $200)
$S+ or $S−	Turn recursion or or off (default).
$Q+ or $Q−	Enable verbose output (default) or. Disable verbose.

File Input/Output

The standard Pascal READ, READLN, WRITE, and WRITELN statements are implemented for the CP/M console device. WRITE or WRITELN to a built-in file called PRINTER is allowed to directly access the CP/M list device (like, WRITE(PRINTER,'Hello')).

The following extensions are implemented to handle files:

OPEN(fcbname,title,result{,extent_number});

(extent_numher defaults to 0)
CLOSE(fcbname,result);
CREATE(fcbname,title,result);
DELETE(fcbname);
BLOCKREAD?fcbname,buffer,result {,relativeblock});
BLOCKWRITE(fcbname,buffer,result {,relativeblock});

where fcbname: a variable of type TEXT (array 0..32 of CHAR)

title: ARRAY [0..11] of CHAR with title[0]=disc select byte (0=logged-in disc, 1=A,...) title[1..8]=filename and title[9..11]=filetype
result: integer to contain returned value
buffer: ARRAY [0..127] of CHAR
relative block: optional integer 0..255

Special Functions And Procedures

Pascal/MT supports the following special routines:

PROC MOVE(source,dest,length-in-bytes);
PROC EXIT;
FUNC TSTBIT(16-bit-var,bit#):BOOLEAN;
PROC SETBIT(VAR 16-bit-var,bit#);
PROC CLRBIT(VAR 16-bit-var,bit#);
FUNC SHR(16-bit-var,#bits):16-bit-result; {Shift Right}
FUNC SHL(16-bit-var,#bits):16-bit-result; {Shift Left}
FUNC LO(16-bit-var):16-bit-result:
FUNC HI(16-bit-var):16-bit-result;
FUNC SWAP(16-bit-var):16-bit-result;
FUNC ADDR(variable reference):16-bit result;
PROC WAIT(portnum:constant;mask:constant;polarity:boolean);
FUNC SIZEOF(variable or type name):integer;

Please refer to pp 32-33 of "Pascal/MT 3.0 Guide" for further info.

Symbolic Debugger

The debugging facilities available to the user

when using the debugger fall into two categories—program flow control and variable display. If the user wishes to see the commands during the execution of the debugger, type a'?' followed by a return.

The program flow commands provided in the symbolic debugger allow the user to debug the Pascal/MT program at the Pascal source statement level. Included are go/continue (with optional breakpoint), trace, set/clear/display permanent breakpoint and a mode which will display the name of each procedure/function on the console as the procedure or function is entered. These commands are discussed briefly on the following displays:

Debugger Command: G - Go with optional breakpoint

Syntax: G{,<linenumber>}
        G{,<proc/func name>}
Go resumes execution where the program last stopped.
Breakpoint may be optionally set at a specific line or function/procedure.

Debugger Command: T - Trace

Syntax: T {<integer>}
Execute one or more lines of the program.

Debugger Command: E - Procedure/Function Display Toggle

Syntax: {-}E
E engages display of the names of procedures/functions entered; —E disengages it.

Debugger Command: S - Set/Clear Slow Execution Mode

Syntax: {-}S
S allows the user to select Fast, Medium, or Slow execution
speed; -S causes the program to run at full speed.

Debugger Command: P - Set/Clear Permanent Breakpoint

Syntax: -P (* Clears breakpoint *)
        P<linenumber>
        P<proc/func name>
P sets the permanent breakpoint; -P clears it.

Debugger Command: B - Display Permanent Breakpoint

Syntax: B
Displays line the permanent breakpoint is set for.

Debugger Command: D - Variable Display

Syntax: D <global var>
        D <proc/func name>:<local var>
        D <func name>
        D <pointer name>
The D command is used as indicated.

Debugger Commands: +,−,* - Variable Display

Syntax: * - display last value requested (using D or some other)
        +n - display variable n bytes forward from last
        − - display variable n bytes backward from last

Reserved Words

ABS	DO	LO	READ	TSTBIT
ADDR	DOWNTO	MAXINT	READLN	TYPE
AND	ELSE	MOD	REAL	UNTIL
ARRAY	ENABLE	MOVE	RECORD	VAR
BEGIN	END	NIL	REPEAT	WAIT
BLOCKREAD	EXIT	NOT	RIM85	WHILE
BLOCKWRITE	EXTERNAL	ODD	ROUND	WRITE
BOOLEAN	FALSE	OF	SETBIT	WRITELN
CASE	FILE	OPEN	SHL	
CHAIN	FOR	OR	SHR	
CHAR	FUNCTION	ORD	SIM85	
CHR	GOTO	OUTPUT	SIZEOF	
CLOSE	HI	PACKED	SQR	
CLRBIT	IF	PRED	SQRT	
CONST	INLINE	PRINTER	SUCC	
CREATE	INPUT	PROCEDURE	SWAP	
DELETE	INTEGER	PROGRAM	THEN	
DISABLE	INTERRUPT	RANDOMREAD	TO	
DIV	LABEL	RANDOMWRITE	TRUE	

Notes

1. Hexadecimal values may be specified as $hhhh, like $1A = 1AH.

2. All standard Pascal type definitions except ARRAY are supported. The standard form ARRAY . . . OF ARRAY . . . must be specified as ARRAY[. . ., . . ., . . .], and a maximum of three dimensions may be used.

3. Type TEXT is ARRAY [0..35] OF CHAR.

4. Interrupt Procedures, declared as "PROCEDURE INTERRUPT[i] proc;", are supported, where i is the restart vector number (0..7).

5. CP/M V2 random file access is supported by RANDOMREAD and RANDOMWRITE.

6. Machine code, constant data, and assembly language code may be inserted using INLINE (see pp. 37-39 of "Pascal/MT 3.0 User Guide").

7. Chaining is supported by CHAIN, whose usage is "CHAIN(filename)".

8. Redirected I/O is supported (see pp. 42-43).

RESOURCE

RESOURCE commands are inconsistent at best. RESOURCE is a kludge based on years of disassembler experience and hacking, and was never "planned"—just coded sitting at a tube, and modified over 2 years before being contributed to the CP/M UG (1/80). For example, to kill a symbol: k.label but to kill a control value: caddr,k and to kill a comment: ;addr, but RESOURCE does the job like no other I have seen.

Note: pardon the editorial, but I feel hardware without good software is useless to 99% of us. Most good software has to be paid for. I strongly support the legitimate purchase of licensed software. I do not regularly use any programs which I have not purchased. (Yes, I do occasionally "try" one, but then buy it if I plan on using it). I have been asked by software businesses to not distribute RE-SOURCE—because of it's ability to produce good .asm source quickly. But, there are so many disassemblers out, why not a good, conversational one? Please use it in the spirit in which it was contributed: to enlarge your understanding of the microcomputer world around you, and to allow you to customize programs which you legitimately own, for your own use.

Structure of Resource

It is a .COM file which runs at 100H. It goes through 1700 or so, then the stack. At 1800 is a 512 entry table for control commands. Each is 3 bytes long, and controls the format of the resourced list, i.e., is it DB, DS, DW, instructions, etc. At 1E00 is the start of the symbol table. It has no defined length as such. If it is not used, it occupies only 2 bytes. If you want to resource something which is in memory, such as a PROM, a program previously loaded in high memory, CP/M itself, or whatever, you can just do so. However, typically you want to disassemble a program which runs at 100H, which is where RESOURCE runs. Bob Van Valzah would have solved that by making resource relocatable and moving itself up under BDOS. I wasn't that industrious. Instead, RESOURCE uses the concept of an "invisible" OFFSET. After all, what do you care where it is as long as it LOOKS like it's at 100h?

So, you set an offset. 02F00 sets it to 2F00 Hex. Reading a .COM file (RF00.COM) causes it to come ino 3000 on. If you say D100 or L100 it dumps or lists what LOOKS like your program. Internally, RESOURCE is adding the offset to the D and L addresses. What should you set the offset to? Well, that depends upon how many symbols you will use. 01F00 will load the program at 2000, thus allowing only 00-1FFF for symbols, i.e., 512 bytes or about 50-60 labels. If you didn't leave enough space, then use B to build a default symbol table. The table could run into and clobber your .com file! (easy recovery, however: just change the offset to being higher, and read in the .COM file again). Each entry takes 3 bytes + the symbol length, and if you like 7 byte labels like I do, that means 10 bytes/label. An offset of 2F00 should be adequate. If you want to put comments into the disassembled program, you will have to designate an area to Use for the comments. The U command (e.g., U4000) specifies what area is to be used. Before issuing the O (offset) command, do: L5 7 which will show the JMP to BDOS, which is the highest memory you may use. (Note if you have, for example, an empty 4 K memory board in high memory, you can Use THAT for comments). Let's take an example: You have an 8 K file, FOO.COM which you want to disassemble. It will have about 300 labels. 300 × 10 is 3000, or call it 4 K (what's a K unless your tight). The symbol table starts at 1E00. 4 K more is 2E00. Let's load the 2D00. 02D00 is the command. We then RF00.COM to read it in. It says 4E00 2100 which means it came into actual memory to 4E00, but 2100 if we are talking with respect to loading at 100. Thus, we could set our comments table up after the .COM program—say at 5000: U5000

The ? command shows the memory utilization for control, symbol, and comments entries. (no, I never put in anything to keep track of the .COM—you'll just have to do that yourself).

If you ever want to dump real memory, you'll have to reset the offset to 0: O0 but then set it back. If you are not sure what it is, typing O will tell the current offset.

Resource Usage

Given: a COM file (lets say test.com) which runs at 100 (as any good COM file should), and goes through 2FF. Lines preceded with ---> are typed by you.

---> RESOURCE

---> o2200	Set the offset to 2200, which means the program will read into 2200 + 100 = 2300.
---> rtest.com	Reads the com file into memory. system says: 2500 0300 which is the actual hi load addr, (2500) and the original hi load addr (300). REMEMBER this address (300) because you might want to put a "E" (and of assembly) control entry there.

Note that all 'L' (disassembly list) and 'D' (dump) commands work with the offset added. Thus, you should learn to forget that the disassembler is in memory, and think of it as if your program were actually at 100. D100 will dump your program.

Also note: if the program being "RE-SOURCEd" will have a fairly large symbol table, then you will have to set the offset higher: o2f00 or some such. (The ? command will show symbol table usage: if your symbol table is nearing the .com file, then just set a new offset (higher) and reload the .com).

If you want to dump real memory, you would have to reset the offset to 0: o0 (but don't forget to reset it to 1f00 before continuing with your program.) If you are disassembling something which is in memory at it's correct address (such as looking at ccp) then don't set the offset. It defaults to 0 when dis is first loaded.

---> 1100	list your program - lists "about" 10 lines.
---> d100	do a dump of your program.

Disassembly

Use the dump command to find the ASCII DB areas. Note that the 'a' command may be used to automatically find the db's, but you must then check them to insure that they don't extend too far. All printable characters, 0dh, 0ah, and 00h are considered candidates for ASCII db's. At least 8 characters in a row must be found to make sure that long sequences of mov instructions won't be taken as db's. Use this cnnnn,k command to kill erroneous entries put in the right address, such as via cnnnn,i. If you wanted to scan the program for ASCII db's yourself, use the 'c' (control) command to set the beginning and end of ASCII areas. For example, a program which starts out:

0100	jmp start
0103	db 'copyright . . . . .'
0117 start	

would show up in the dump as:

```
0100 c3170144 4f50xxxx xxxxxxxx xxxxxxxx *...copyr ight.*
0110 xxxxxxxx xxxxxxxx xxxxxxxx xxxxxxxx *xxxxxxxx......*
```

thus you would want to instruct the disassembler to switch to db mode at 103, and back to instruction mode at 117, thus:

c103,b
c117,i

Continue doing this, bracketing every ASCII db which is in the middle of instructions, by a b control instruction and an i control instruction. Note that multiple db's in a row need not have separate cnnnn,b instructions, but that these do cause a 'line break', i.e., if you have a table of ASCII commands, for example:

```
02e5    db    'load'
02e9    db    'save'
```

the disassembler would disassemble these as:

```
02e4    db    'loadsave'
```

you could put in an additional control entry: c2e9,b, which would cause the disassembler to generate:

```
02e4    db    'load'
02e8    db    'save'
```

which is much more readable and realistic. Note that before generating each byte of a db, a symbol table lookup is done to determine if there is a label at that location, and if so, a new line is started. Thus if 'loadlit' and'savelit' were in the symbol table, as the labels on the 'load' and 'save' above, no separate 'b' control instruction would be required as the label would cause the break.

Note: at this time the automatic label checking is not done for ds instructions. Make sure that each ds instruction references only up to the next label. This means that multiple ds's in a row must each be explicitly entered into the control table. Presence of a label is not sufficient.

After building the control entries with cnnnn,b and cnnnn,i put in a control entry cnnnn,e which defines the address of the end of your program. The 1 command will then automatically stop there, and in addition, if you are in 'save xxx.asm' mode, the output .asm file will be closed. If you do not define a control 'e' entry, then you will have to use the break facility to stop the 1 command (don't use control-c as that will reboot cp/m). If you were writing an asm. file, you would have to use the z command to close the file.

Next, you would list your program to determine how it looks. When you recognize a routine by it's function, insert a label. For example, if you saw that location 7ef was a character out routine (type) then enter a label into the symbol table:

E7EF,.TYPE

Note that all symbols start with a '.', so as to be distinguished from hex data.

Note that if you want the disassembler to make default labels for you, use b (for build labels) instead of 1 (for list program). The b commands causes lnnnn default labels to be inserted in the symbol table for every 2 byte operand encountered (LXI, SHLD, JMP, etc). It will undoubtedly make some you don't want, such as L0000. You will have to:

K.L0000   kill label L0000 from the table.

When you encounter data reference instructions, try to determine what type of area the instruction points to. Typically,, LXI instructions may point to a work area which should be defined as a DS, or to an ASCII string, in which case we will have already made it a 'b' control instruction. Operands of LHLD and SHLD instructions should be made DW instructions. For example if you encounter LHLD 0534H, then issue a control instruction:

C534,W

Note that whatever mode you are last in will remain in effect. Therefore if 534,w is the last entry in the control table, all data from there on will be taken to be DW's.

Suppose that you determine that address 7cf is a 128 byte buffer for disc I/O. You want it to disassemble to:

```
DKBUF              ;07CF
DS      80H
```

You do this as follows:

```
C7CF,S        to start the DS
C84F,B        to define it's end, and
E7CF,.DKBUF   to put the symbol in the table
```

Continue, iteratively using the 'l' command and the 'c' and 'e' commands until you have the listing in a nice format. You will then probably want to save the control symbol, and comments tables. Or, you could have been saving them at checkpoint times (so if you make a major mistake you could go

```
```

back to a previous one). To save a control file: sfilename.CTL (any filename, may include a: or b:)

To save a symbol file: sfilename.sym
To save a comments file: sfilename.doc
(not ".com" of course)

Note that the filetypes must be used as shown, but that any legal filename (or disc:filename such as b:xxxx.CTL) may be used.

You could now control-c to return to CP/M, and come back later to resume your disassembly:

RESOURCE
o2200
rtemp.com
rtemp.sym
rtemp.ctl
uxxxx   (such as u4000)
rtemp.doc

This will take you back exactly where you left off. If you want to save a .asm file out to disc, do the following: Make sure that there is a control entry defining the end of the program (such as c200,e) or else you will have to specify the ending address and manually type a z command to close the file.

sfilename.asm

A message will indicate that the file is opened. Any subsequent a, b, or l command will have whatever is listed written to disc. Encountering a 'e' control, or typing a z command will then close the .asm file. The listing may be interrupted, and continued. Since the l command types only 10 lines, use laddr,ffff to list thru the end of the assembly. If this is the 'final' save of the .asm file, you will probably want to put an 'org' at the beginning of the output file, as well as generate equ instructions for any references outside of the program. For example, a typical CP/M program will have references to:

bdos   at 5
fcb   at 5ch
tbuff   at 80h

The 'p' (for prologue) command generates the org, then scans the symbol table and generates equates:

BDOS   EQU   05H
FCB   EQU   05CH (etc.)

If you have a "e" control entry in your file, you can list as follows: laddr,ffff—the listing will continue until the "e" control entry is found.

Commands

RESOURCE types an "*" prompt when it is loaded. You may then enter any of the following commands. Each command is a single letter, followed by operands. Commas are shown. Note: any command taking a hex address (Dnnnn, etc.) may take a value in the form .label but arithmetic may not be performed (i.e., d.start is ok, but d.start+8 is not).

A semicolon: puts comments into the program (must execute "u" command first, to assign area for comments to be placed).

;addr,comment	enter a comment
;addr	lists existing comment
;	list entire comments table
;addr,	deletes existing comment

Note that '/' is treated as a new line, i.e., /test/ will be formatted:

;
;TEST
;

A, Attempt to find DB's while listing the program. This command works just like "L", but attempts to find DB's of 8 chars or longer (see "L" command for operand formats).

B, Build default sym tbl (LXXXX) labels for each 2 byte operand encountered. Note "B" is identical to "L" except labels are built. (see "L" command for operand formats) C Control table usage:

237

c	dump ctl tbl
cnnnn	dump from starting
cnnnn,x	define format from nnnn
	to next entry. values of x:
	B = DB (attempts ASCII
	printable, 0DH, 0AH, 0)
	W = DW (attempts label)
	S = DW to next ctl entry
	I = instructions
	K = kill this ctl entry
	E = end of disassembly

Note every control entry causes a control break (NO, RESOURCE was NOT written in RPG) which means a new line will be started. Thus if you have a string in memory which disassembles as:

```
DB      'Invalid operand',0DH
DB      0AH
```

You might want to change it putting the 0DH, 0AH together on the second line—just enter a "B" control entry for the address of the 0DH. The same technique could be used to make

```
DB      'TYPESAVEDIR ERA REN'
```

appear as

```
DB      'TYPE'
DB      'SAVE'
DB      'DIR'
DB      'ERA'
DB      'REN'
```

D, Dump:

dxxxx	Dumps 80H from xxxx on
daaaa,bbbb	Dumps from aaaa thru bbbb
d,bbbb	Continues, thru bbbb
d	Continues, 80H more

Note: 80H is the default dump length. If you have a larger display, you can change the default via:

d=nn	nn is the HEX new default.

For example, a 24 line tube could display 100H:

d=100	or..
d=100,200	Defaults to 100, dumps 200-2ff

Other dumps:

ds	dumps the symbol table. Interrupt it by typing any key.
ds.symbol	starts dumping at the specified symbol, or the nearest symbol. thus "ds.f" starts the dump at the first label starting with the letter 'f'.

E, Enter symbol:

ennnn,.symbol	symbol may be of any length, and contain any char A-Z or 0-9, or "+" or "−". This allows: E5D,.FCB+1. Note the "+" is not checked, i.e., E5D,.FCB+2 would be wrong (assuming FCB is at 5C) but would be allowed to be entered.

Note that if you enter two symbols for the same address, whichever one is first alphabetically will show up on the disassembled listing. If you have a label which has the wrong address, you need not explicitly kill the old one before entering the new. A label which is spelled exactly the same as an existing one will replace the existing one even if the addresses are different.

F, Find occurrence of address or label. Note this function runs until interrupted (press any key).

fnnnn,ssss	find address nnnn in memory. Start the search at ssss. Runs forever. Press any key to stop.
f	continue previous find command
fnnnn	find nnnn starting at address you last stopped at in the f command

K, Kill symbol from table:

k.symbol

Note that to rename a symbol, such as when you had a system assigned lnnnn label but now want to make it meaningful:

k.10334
e334,.type

You could even:

e.10334,.type
k.10334

but that takes more typing.

L, List (disassemble). This command is used to list the file, or to list it to disc after enabling the .ASM file save via 'SFILENAME. ASM' command

l	lists 10 lines from prev pc
lssss,eeee	lists from ssss to eeee
l,eeee	lists from current pc to eeee
lssss	lists 10 lines at ssss

Note that if you have a control 'e' entry, then the list will stop when that address is found. This allows you to 'lstart,ffff'.

The 10 line default may be changed via:

| L=nn | where nn is a HEX line count, e.g. |
| L=14 | set to 20 lines/screen |

You can change the default and list, e.g.

L=9,100   Dflt to 9 lines, list at 100.

Note that when using L to list the .ASM program to disc, you should either list the entire program at once using: Lssss,eeee or, you can list small pieces at a time. As long as you list again without specifying a starting address, (L or L,nnnn) then the output file will continue uninterrupted.

You may do dump commands, and others, without affecting what is being written to disc.

O, Offset for disassembly.

| o | print current offset |
| onnnn | establish new offset |

(note the offset is always added to any address specified in an a, b, d, or l command. To dump real memory, the offset must be reset to 0 (Do) before the dump.)

P, Prolog generation generates an ORG instruction, and equates for any label outside of a given low-hi address pair. (the start and end addresses of your program). e.g., if disassembling from 100 to 3ff, it will generate 'fcb equ 5ch' if FCB is in the symbol table. In typical use, you would 'sfilename.asm' then use the P command to write the prolog, then the L command to write the program itself.

Pstart addr,end addr

Q, Quiet command: any command which is preceded by a q will be done 'quietly'. For example, to save a .asm program, you could just do:

ql100,3ff   or   ql100,ffff

if you have set the 'e' control in the control table. Another use is to build a default symbol table by taking a pass thru the program:

QB100,xxxx

R, Read .com, .ctl, .sym, or .doc file.

rfilename.com	reads in at offset+100h
rfilename.ctl	loads the ctl table
rfilename.sym	loads the sym file
rfilename.doc	loads comments table (note 'u' must have been issued)

S, Save .asm, .ctl, .sym, or .doc file.

sfilename.asm	use '1' command to write, z to end
sfilename.CTL	saves the CTL table
stablename.sym	saves the sym file
sfilename.doc	saves the comments table

U, Use area of memory for comments table.

unnnn such as ud000 if you had an open board at 0d000h

X, purge sym tbl and CTL tbl.

Z, close .asm file (note that a preferred way to close the .asm file is to have specified a control entry for the end address (e.g., cliff,e)).

A ? prints statistics on symbol and control table usage, etc.

Watch For

Hoo, boy! Hope this kludge of documentation is enough to get you going. Hmmm, better give you some of the gotcha's I've discovered.

☐ Symbols overflowing into the .COM (Use ? command to see how full symbol table is).

☐ Control entries overflowing into .SYM (although I can't believe anyone will have a program with more than 512 control entries!!!).

☐ Comments overflowing into BDOS (ug!!).

☐ Using an offset which is not in free memory and overlaying BDOS or whatever.

☐ The B(uild) command gobbling up too much when building a DB: "B" will take a DB 'GOB-BELDY GOOK' followed by LXI, H, FOO and take the LXI as a '!' (21H) so you'll have to manually stick a new "I" control entry in at the address of the LXI. You might also delete the incorrect "I" entry which RESOURCE stuck in (typically at the second byte of the LXI)

☐ Trying to dump real memory without setting the offset back to 0. (then forgetting to set it back to its proper value)

☐ Forgetting how big the .COM file you are disassembling was.

☐ Using RESOURCE to rip off software (yes, I know, you heard that before, but only 3 in 100 needed to be told, and 2 in 100 need to be told again, and 1 in 100 doesn't give a rat's fuzzy behind anyway!!)

☐ Forgetting to take checkpoints when disassembling large files. You may even want to rotate the names under which things are saved:

STEMP1.SYM

STEMP1.CTL
STEMP1.DOC

☐ Missing a label: Suppose you have a control entry for a DW, resulting in:

```
DFLT:                    ;172C
            DW           100H
```

but somewhere in the program, the following exists:

```
            LDA          172DH
```

Even if you did a B and have a label L172D, it won't show up since it's in the middle of a DW. Instead, do this:

```
K.l172d          kill the old label
e172d,.dflt+1    put in the new label as a dis-
                 placement off the beginning.
```

☐ Improperly disassembling DW's (see previous item). You might be tempted to make DFLT a DB so that

```
DFLT:                    ;172C
            DB   0
L172D:                   ;172D
            DB   1
```

Note that while this disassembles and reassembles properly, it is not "as correct" as the technique used in the previous item.

☐ Having the "B" command overlay your "E" control entry. What? Well, "B"uild is pretty dumb. If he finds 8 DB type characters in a row, he fires off a DB from then on until he runs out of those characters. Suppose your program was 200 long (ended at 3FF), and you had zeroed (aha! Nice DB candidates) memory there (there meaning at your offset address + whatever). Then you QB100,400 and viola! RESOURCE overlaid your "E" control with a "B".

☐ Targets of LHLD, SHLD should automatically be flagged as type DW in the control table. Ditto LDA and STA as DB or as second half of DW. Ditto targets of LXI as DB (?).

□ E5C,.FCB followed by E6C,.FCB+ should automatically calculate the appropriate displacement, and put it in the symbol table.

□ The comments facility should be enhanced to allow total SUBSTITUTION of entire line(s) of the code, i.e., at address such-and-such, replace the next 3 bytes with the following arbitrary line. This would help those "how do I explain what was being done" cases such as: LXI H,BUFFER AND OFFOOH.

□ Add the ability to, in one instruction, rename a default (LXXXX) label to a meaningful name.

Command Summary

Any address may be replaced by .symbol i.e., D.START

;addr,comment	Enter a comment
;addr	Lists existing comment
;	Lists entire comments table
;addr,	Deletes existing comment
A (see "L" for operands)	Attempt to find DB's
B (see "L" for operands)	Build default sym tbl (Lxxxx)
C	Dump ctl tbl
Cnnnn	Dump ctl starting at nnnn
Cnnnn,x	Define format from nnnn (B,E,I,S,W)
Dxxxx	Dumps 80H from xxxx on
Daaaa,bbbb	Dumps from aaaa thru bbbb
D,bbbb	Dump thru bbbb
D	Dump 80H more
D=nn	nn= Hex dump size default.
Ds	Dumps the symbol table.
Ds.symbol	Sym dump starting at .symbol
Ennnn,.symbol	Enter symbol into table
Fnnnn,ssss	Find address nnnn starting at ssss
F	Continue previous find command
Fnnnn	Find nnnn
K.symbol	Kill symbol from symbol table
L	Lists 10 lines from prev pc
Lssss,eeee	Lists from ssss to eeee
L,eeee	Lists from current pc to eeee
Lssss	Lists 10 lines at ssss
L=nn	nn is hex list default # of lines
O	Print current offset
Onnnn	Establish new offset
Pstart addr,end addr	Generate program prolog
Q	Before any command suppresses console output: QB100,200
Rfilename.COM	Reads in at offset+100h
Rfilename.CTL	Loads the ctl table
Rfilename.SYM	Loads the sym file
Rfilename.DOC	Loads the comments table (note
Sfilename.ASM	Save .ASM file. Write w/L, Z to end
Sfilename.CTL	Saves the CTL table
Sfilename.SYM	Saves the sym file
Sfilename.DOS	Saves the comments table
Unnnn	Use nnnn for comments table
X	Purge all symbols and control
Z	Write eof to .ASM file (
?	Prints statistics (sym,ctl, comments)

ZSOURCE Disassembler

This disassembler for Z-80 programs ZESOURCE is a modification to the original RESOURCE to give the capability of disassembling Z80 object into TDL mnemonic source files. A file called Z80TEST.COM was used to test ZSOURCE. When Z80TEST.COM is disassembled it will result in what would be an alphabetic listing of all of the Z-80 opcodes if the mnemonics were Zilog's instead of TDL's. This object file should agree exactly with the listings that Zilog has in their 'Z-80 CPU Programming Reference Card' and in the back of 'Z-80 Assembly Language Programming Manual'.

It should be pointed out that ZSOURCE will generate TDL opcode mnemonics but not TDL pseudo-op mnemonics. The pseudo-op mnemonics are the same as those generated by RESOURCE (ORG,DB,DW,DS, and EQU). If one is using a TDL type of assembler it is a simple matter to use .OPSYN to equate ORG with .LOC, DB with .BYTE, etc.

The primary documentation for ZESOURCE is found under RESOURCE. Listed below is a description of the enhancements added to ZESOURCE.COM:

1. Disassembly to TDL mnemonics

2. Typing 'Rfilename.ALL' will cause the .DOC, .SYM, and .CTL files to all be read in for 'filename'. If one of the files is missing from the disc the read operation will abort. Note also that the 'Uxxxx' command must still be used prior to using 'R'.

3. Typing 'Sfilename.ALL' will cause all three of the files mentioned above to be saved.

4. When the 'E' command is used to create a new symbol the existing symbol at that address (if there is one) will be automatically killed with a message sent to the console so stating. If there is

more than one symbol at that address (impossible if the .SYM file was created under ZESOURCE) only the first in the table will be killed.

5. Use of 'L' command in the format 'L=-xx,addr' causes the new default length, xx, to take effect immediately.

ZCPR

ZCPR (Z80 Command Processor Replacement) is a replacement of the CP/M CCP which is designed to run as part of CP/M on Z80-based microcomputers. In most cases it is upward-compatible to the original CP/M Version 2.2 CCP.

ZCPR, however, provides many extensions over the CP/M CCP. Included in these extensions are:

☐ The TYPE function can be made to page or not page its output at the user's discretion.

☐ A LIST function is available which sends its output to the CP/M LST: Device and does NOT page.

☐ The DIR command has been extended to allow the display of the system files or all files.

☐ The ERA command now prints out the names of the files it is erasing.

☐ The current user number may be included as part of the command prompt; if the user is under a number other than 0, the prompt is of the form 'du>' (like 'A2>' or 'B10>'), and, if the user is under 0, the prompt may be 'd>' or 'd0>' as per his choice.

☐ The SUBMIT facility has been changed in two basic ways. The prompt changes to 'du$' or 'd$' when the SUBMIT command is printed. The $$$.SUB is executed from drive A: only (note that the original SUBMIT problem now exists, but the new SUB.COM facility corrects it); Indirect Command Files now perform according to the basic philosophy that any command sequence that can be input from the console may be used in an Indirect Command File as well; the ZCPR.DOC file also gives details as to how to patch SUBMIT.COM if SUB.COM is not available.

☐ A command-search hierarchy is now implemented which is executed as follows:

1. The user's command is checked against the CPR-resident commands and executed immediately if a match is found.

2. Failing that, the current user number on the current disc is scanned for the COM file; the COM file is loaded and executing if found.

3. Failing that, a default user number (initially 0 but can be reset with the DFU CPR-resident command) on the current disc is scanned for the COM file; the COM file is loaded and executed if found.

4. Finally, failing that, the default user number on disc A: is scanned for the COM file; the COM file is loaded and executed if found or an error message (COMMAND?, when COMMAND was the user's command name) is printed.

☐ The numeric argument for the SAVE CPR-resident command (viz the number of 256-byte pages to save) can be input in HEX rather than decimal.

☐ A GET command which loads a file at a specified memory address and a JUMP command which "calls" the subroutine at a specified memory address have been added; a GO command which "calls" the subroutine starting at 100H is also added (this is redundant with JUMP 100H).

The ZCPR Command Hierarchy Search

The first, and most basic thing, to learn about ZCPR is the order in which it searches for a COM file for execution or a file specified by the GET command. Under the CP/M 2.2 CCP, if the specified COM file command was not found on the current drive in the current user area, the CCP aborted with an error message. ZCPR, however, continues searching from this point a maximum of two more levels. This command hierarchy search was outlined above and is described here in further detail.

1. If the command is of the form 'COMMAND' and NOT 'd:COMMAND', the CPR-resident command list is searched for a match. If the match is found, the CPR-resident command is immediately

processed. If the match is not found or the command is of the form 'd:COMMAND', the next step is taken. Note that the 'd:COMMAND' form is good for executing a COM file which has the same name as a CPR-resident command (such as SAVE or DIR).

2. If the command is of the form 'd:COMMAND', disc drive 'd:' is temporarily logged in for the purpose of the command search. Otherwise, the currently logged-in drive is used.

3. Now the file named COMMAND.COM is searched for. If found, it is loaded into memory starting at 100H and executed. If not, proceed to step 4.

4. Now that the first search for COMMAND.COM has failed, the CPR checks to see if the user is under the current Default User Number. The Default User Number may be that set by the DEFUSR equate in the CPR or that set by the user via the DFU command. DEFUSR is in effect if DFU has not been issued since the last Warm or Cold Boot, and DFU is in effect if it was issued since the last Warm or Cold Boot. If the user is NOT under the current Default User Number, ZCPR temporarily logs him into it and searches the directory. If COMMAND.COM is found, it is loaded as described above and executed. If not, ZCPR proceeds to the next step.

5. The user is now in the Default User Number, and at this point, ZCPR checks to see if the user is on disc drive A:. If not, it temporarily logs into A: and searches the default user number of A: for COMMAND.COM. If found, it is loaded as described above and executed. If not, ZCPR prints the command name as an error message and returns to command input mode, aborting the SUBMIT file if COMMAND came from it.

In all cases of the previous search, if COMMAND.COM is found, after it is loaded into memory, ZCPR resets the user to his original disc drive and user number. Hence, the files referenced by the user by default are obtained from this environment.

To illustrate this command hierarchy search, consider the following examples:

Example 1: DEFUSR equ 0 {default user number is 0}

B10>   <--User is on Drive B:, User Number 10
B10>ASM TEST.BBZ <--User wishes to assemble TEST.ASM in
            Drive B:, User 10
    <--At this point, ZCPR looks on B:/10 for ASM.COM, fails, looks on B:/O, fails, and finally looks on A:/O; it finds ASM.COM here and goes back to B:/10 for the file

Example 2: DEFUSR equ 0 and DFU issued

B10>   < -- User is on Drive B:, User Number 10
B10>DFU 5   < -- User Selects User 5 as default
B10>ASM TEST.BBZ <—— As above
    <--At this point, ZCPR looks on B:/10 for ASM.COM, fails, look on B:/5, fails, and finally looks on A:/5; it fails here also and prints ASM? as an error message

Example 3: DEFUSR equ 0
B>   < -- User is on Drive B:, User Number 0
B>ASM TEST.BBZ   <-- As above
    <--At this point, ZCPR looks on B:/0 for ASM.COM, fails, looks on A:/0, fails, and prints error message

Example 4: DEFUSR equ 0
A10>   < -- User is on Drive A:, User Number 10
A10>ASM TEST.AAZ   <-- As above, but file on A:
    <--At this point, ZCPR looks on A:/10 for ASM.COM, fails, looks on A:/0, fails, and prints error message

Resident Command DIR

Command: DIR

Function: To Display a listing of the names of the files on disc.
Forms:

DIR <afn>	<--Displays $DIR files
DIR <afn> S	<-- Displays $SYS files
DIR <afn> A	<-- Displays both $DIR and $SYS files

Examples:

DIR *.ASM	<-- All $DIR .ASM files

```
DIR *.COM S      <-- All $SYS .COM files
DIR *.COM A      <-- All .COM files
```

Notes:

If a file is scanned for and no such name exists on disc, the 'No Files' message will appear. However, if a file is scanned for and the name exists as a $SYS file and $DIR files are being scanned for, no file name is displayed but the 'No Files' message does NOT appear. For example, if TEST.COM is a $SYS file and 'DIR TEST.COM' is issued, no message appears. If 'DIR TEXT.COM' is issued and TEXT.COM does not exist on disc, the 'No Files' message is displayed.

Resident Command ERA

Command: ERA
Function: To Erase the specified $R/W files from disc.
Forms:
```
ERA <afn>        <-- Erase both $DIR and
                     $SYS files
```
Examples:
```
ERA *.ASM        < Erase all .ASM files
ERA *.*          <-- Erase all files
```
Notes:

If a $R/O file is encountered, a BDOS error message will be displayed and the procedure is stopped. The user is unsure at this time as to which files have been erased and which have not and should check. Sorry for this problem! The ERASE command (to be given to SIG/M by RLC in the near future) is a solution to this problem.

Resident Command LIST

Command: LIST
Function: To Print the specified file on the CP/M LST: device.
Forms:
```
LIST <ufn>       <-- Print the file (no paging)
```
Examples:
```
LIST TEST.TXT    <-- Print TEST.TXT on LST:
```
Notes:

If the file has a $SYS attribute, it will be found as well as those with $DIR attributes.

Resident Command TYPE

Command: TYPE

Function: To Print the specified file on the CP/M CON: device.
Forms:
```
TYPE <ufn>       <-- Print the file with the
                     paging deflt
TYPE <ufn> P     <-- Print the file with the
                     paging deflt negated
```
Examples:
```
TYPE TEST.TXT
TYPE TEST.TXT P
```
Note:

When the display pauses during paging, type any char to continue or ^C to abort.^S also works.

Resident Command SAVE

Command: SAVE
Function: To Copy the TPA starting at 100H to disc.
Forms:
```
SAVE <Number of Pages> <ufn>   <-- <Number of
Pages> in DEC
SAVE <Number of Pages>H <ufn>  <-- <Number of
Pages> in HEX
SAVE <Number of Sectors> <ufn> S <-- <Number of
Sectors> in DEC
SAVE <Number of Sectors>H <ufn> S <-- <Number of
Sectors> in HEX
```
Examples:
```
SAVE FH  MYFILE.TXT    <-- 15 pages saved
SAVE 15  MYFILE.TXT    <-- 15 pages saved
SAVE 10H MYFILE.TXT S  <-- 16 sectors (8 pages)
                           saved
```
Notes:

The error message 'Delete File?' is printed if <ufn> already exists. To go ahead and SAVE, type Y or y to erase the file and proceed with the SAVE.

Resident Command REN

Command: REN
Function: To Change the name of a disc file.

Forms:
```
REN <ufn new>=<ufn old>
```
Examples:
```
REN NEWFILE.TXT=OLDFILE.TXT
```
Notes:

The error message 'Delete File?' is printed if the <ufn new> already exists. To go ahead and complete the REN, type Y or y to erase the current

<ufn new> file and then <ufn old> will be re-named to <ufn new>.

Resident Command User

Command: USER
Function: To Change the current user number.
Forms:

USER <User Number >	<-- <User Number> in DEC
USER <User Number >H	<-- <User Number> in HEX

Examples:

```
USER 15
USER FH
USER 0
USER          <--Same as USER 0
```

Resident Command DFU

Command: DFU
Function: To temporarily change the default user number for the command hierarchy search.
Forms:

DFU <User Number >	<-- <User Number> in DEC
DFU <User Number >H	<-- <User Number> in HEX

Examples:

```
DFU 15
DFU 0
DFU FH
DFU          <--Same as DFU 0
```

Resident Command JUMP

Command: JUMP
Function: To "call" the subroutine at the specified page address
Forms:

JUMP <Address> <Cmd Parms>   <-- <Address> in HEX

Examples:

```
JUMP E000       <-- Jump to E000H
  or JUMP E00H
JUMP 100        <-- Jump to 100H
JUMP 0          <-- Jump to 000H
JUMP            <-- Same as JUMP 0
```

Notes:

JUMP performs a subroutine "call", so the called routine may return to the ZCPR by either a RET or a Warm Boot.

Resident Command GO

Command: GO
Function: To "call" the subroutine at address 100H.
Forms:

Go <Cmd Parms>   <-- Routine at 100H

Examples:

GO *.ASM   <—— Execute TPA-resident prog with *.ASM passed

Notes:

This is identical in function to JUMP 100H.

Resident Command GET

Command: GET
Function: To load a file from disc into memory starting at the specified page.
Forms:

Get <Address> <ufn>   <-- <Address> in HEX

Examples:

```
Get 8000 TEST.80       <-- Load TEST.80
                          starting at 8000H
Get 100 TEST.80 or GET 100H TEST.80  < -- Load
                 TEST.80 starting at 100H
Get 0 TEST.80          <-- Load TEST.80
                          starting at 000H
```

Notes:

GET searches for the specified file according to the same command hierarchy search employed by the ZCPR command scanner. Hence, if the user is on B:/10 and the file is on A:/0 with the current default user number at 0, GET will search from B:/10 to B:/0 to A:/0 in looking for the file.

Error Messages

The following are the error messages issued by ZCPR and their meanings.

Message	Meaning
?	Printed after a command or an argument means that such was invalid
No File	From DIR, this means that DIR did not locate any files Also from ERA with the same meaning
All?	Issued in response ERA *.*, asks the user if he really wants to erase all the files. Unlike under

Full	the original CP/M 2.2 CCP, single character input is required (Y or y for yes and anything else for no) with NO <CR> to end the line From SAVE, means that there is not enough space on disc From GET or command load by CPR, means	Delete File?	that there is not enough space in memory From REN or SAVE, means that the file specified already exists on disc and the user may type Y or y to erase it and continue with the procedure or any other character to abort

Index

All page numbers in *italics* reference figures.

Edited by Brint Rutherford